We The People
Have Been Deceived
Time to Join as One to Overcome
Let Love Be Your Guide
The United States and
the Evolution of Oneness

By Michael B. Allison

Dedication

To my earthly Mother and Father. Whose deep devotion to being loving and kind instilled in me an understanding and a knowing that we are here on purpose. Opening up to the energy emanating from our Hearts will enable us to figure out the reason for our excursion to Earth. Thank you for the latitude to be my own person. It allowed me to become who I am today. For that, I am truly grateful.

Also, thank you for taking me to that meditation class when I was fourteen. It changed everything.

I love you Both so much! Thank you!

Preface

Feels like I always knew that a part of my Soul Mission was to write a book. Ever since my late 30s, I just knew that I had a book to write, and I would ruminate about many different topics... but when I would sit down to write, nothing would come out. It was actually quite frustrating!

During the last moment I spent looking at a blank page, my frustration turned to indignation, and I shouted, "Why is this so hard!" The answer I received was, "Nobody wants to hear you complain! Pick an issue, detail the problems, and find resolutions. People will want to read that kind of book." That answer changed everything. No longer would I spend countless hours on a possible book subject if I had no solution to present. So, I would let each topic go that had no solution or resolution, knowing that an issue would come to me that included a resolution and the words would finally flow; in the meantime…

I was married to a charming and beautiful woman. She was a wonderful, patient, and kind person who loved to laugh and have fun! I was a proud member of an amazing family that enjoyed being together. I owned and operated a residential construction company; everything was good! I was enjoying my life.

And then, my wife was diagnosed with ALS (Amyotrophic Lateral Sclerosis – also known as Lou Gehrig's disease). We were devastated! Simply undone by the verdict of the diagnosis. Undeterred, my courageous wife, Elizabeth, decided to try and get well despite the odds of recovery. We tried everything – special diets, energy healing, and experimental medical procedures. She was so patient, going through all this extra effort just to get well. It brought out the best in our family, everyone pitching in to help, especially near the end when we had to do almost everything for her. She was incredibly patient with me as she talked me through how to do her make-up and curl her hair. I would not have been able to manage if it weren't for her two wonderful daughters. They were always right there for us, helping and looking after us.

Caring for Elizabeth was a special type of intimacy I had never known before or probably ever will again. It really changed me. It broke my heart wide open. The sadness was unbearable. I don't know how I got through all of the despair. I was so lost! Now, all I know is that I am so thankful for the opportunity to have been her husband. She was an amazing person and the love of my life!

Three years later, in the 60th year of my life, I am again preparing to write a book, still unaware of the topic. Late one afternoon, swinging in the hammock, listening to the river, I could feel a topic bubbling to the surface. The words splashing into my awareness... "I want you to write a political book." I thought, "Why would I want to do that!" I don't listen to the news, refuse to engage in political conversations, and have voted for Ross Perot every election cycle since he ran as a protest. I even purchased a website called "noneoftheabove. com," claiming that an additional box should be included in every presidential ballot called "None of the above" and that if enough people voted for this option, then the two nominees would be tossed. The voting would have to start over, and maybe we get candidates worthy of our respect and vote this time.

I struggled with the idea of a political book for quite a while... The impulse toward a politically themed book was insistent! Such a big topic; what could I possibly write about? Then it came to me... The current predicament or plight of the middle class in the United States is such a big problem; easy to detail all of the issues, and I noticed that there even was a solution.

The purpose of writing this book is to clear away the noise of the already polluted waters of American politics. Everyone is talking, and there is no communication – just a lot of angry and annoyed people and a crazy amount of cross-talk that goes nowhere. We can all agree there is something wrong with no clear path to fixing the problems.

Nobody is willing to compromise, listen to each other, or respect the power of the majority. Special interest groups spend a lot of time and money getting everyone to believe what they believe, with damning sound bites and rhetoric full of lies intending to sway the majority to their way of thinking. This 'politics as usual' is not democratic, nor does it serve the people.

Governing 329.5 million people is involved, complex, and easily overwhelming. The majority complain, no one listens, while the minority pays for a captive government audience. This same minority composes the bills that are introduced into Congress. It is simple to see who is running the government.

The amount of information and false information that the regular Joe and Jane must wade through makes their task of being involved citizens daunting. It is, frankly, undoable for most people who work 50 hours a week and have children; they are too busy!

This book intends to simplify the process and deconstruct it so it is easy to understand and everyone can participate. Every citizen will feel like they are a part of the whole and can be proud once again of what this country is doing and know that they had a hand in reshaping a country that believes in its government – a government that actually protects and provides for the people it represents.

For "We the People" to be served, they need to know what they want! Right now, they are being told what they should want, focusing squarely on what is wrong and who is to blame, not what is right and how we fix what is wrong. And the level of public discontent is mounting.

Anarchy is not the answer, but without an outlet for their frustration, the people will end up in the streets…

I have a way for people to channel this frustration into something positive. I have a solution for the frustrations of a middle class whose lifestyle and joy in life have diminished. I am so excited to write this book for you! I have prepared for 60 years to write this book.

Who is the target audience for this book? Short answer: If you are a citizen of the United States or thinking about being one… This book is for you. It is an extraordinary journey asking you to discover yourself and the Truth of your Ultimate Reality. It will enlighten your entrenched beliefs and expand your ideology in ways you would never have thought possible. It will draw you into a dynamic experiment spanning over 400 years. Enjoy the ride!

Sincerely,

Michael B. Allison

Website URL: https://wethepeoplearenowone.com

Email address: Jointogether@wethepeoplearenowone.com

Introduction

The United States of America is a very proud nation, and I understand why. They have amassed amazing accomplishments. At the same time, there lives a darkness among the human species that brings pain and suffering. This darkness forces itself upon us, and some fall prey to its influence. I want to bring Light to this darkness, freeing us from that which flows from ignorance. Ignorance lives in the dark; Ignorance is a bully. Full of fear trampling upon the innocent because it doesn't know any better.

By grasping an understanding of what allows this ignorance to thrive so as to shine a Light so bright that we all evolve past these uninformed inclinations, we can begin to collectively shine the Light on anything that oppresses any member of our society.

"There is no coming to consciousness without pain. One does not become enlightened by imagining figures of light, but by making the darkness conscious." – C.G. Jung

---

I want to fully understand how partnering with this Light has facilitated some of the greatest achievements in human history.

How do we partner with the Light?

What do I mean when I say the Light?

The Light is the loving guiding force that animates every single human being. The Light is the reason for every religion there ever was. The Light is known by many different names. Divine Energy wants the same thing for all human beings. To eventually understand the Truth of their Reality, which is that even though we all present as separate individual beings, at our core we are all made from the same animating Life Force. As we evolve to that understanding, our world becomes more peaceful, benevolent, loving, kind, compassionate, and sustainable.

Can religions be sustainable? Not as long as they are competing for adherents, followers, devotees, and believers. Do you think Divine Energy cares how one of its creations discovers the Light? We all come here to re-discover the Light. Only when the focus of religions becomes the sharing of the Light with anyone interested while respecting all other religions, does religion become sustainable.

The Truth is that we are all One and that Oneness, as it has been utilized during the birth and development of the United States, is the reason for all the good that has ever happened to her.

The only subject in this book I feel qualified to write about is the Evolution of Oneness, and that book has already been written many times by many different authors. I was asked to discuss the Evolution of Oneness against the backdrop of the United States and their experiment of Constitutional democracy with their unique founding documents called the Charters of Freedom, blazing the trail.

Subsequently, my desire for an academic-level book guided my decision to include many passages quoted verbatim on subjects that fall outside the range of my studied knowledge. Some questioned this decision, stating its unorthodox manner; be that as it may...

The passages have been carefully selected and work to elevate the breadth and depth of the desired subject matter. Thereby augmenting and providing examples within a framework that most citizens of the United States are familiar with—creating the opportunity for the Evolution of Oneness to be put on full display for a level of understanding that would encompass all people with a desire to evolve into their best self. Which, by the way, is encoded into the nuclei of our collective DNA.

Please allow the quoted subject matter, without judgment, into the delivery of this book; without it, there would be no book nor the sweeping changes that may occur as a result of this book.

To the authors of these articles, I am honored to present your work as the backbone of a subject that rarely gets center stage. Your work helped to make this book a more developed and believable body of words. We have done our best to cite all of your work correctly. Thank you for your contribution.

Opening up to this Divine Source Energy of Light will bring many changes. The joy and sweetness of life will increase and provide the way, making everything you do an opportunity to share the light, love, and joy you have found. Some will discover they have a more prominent role to play once they invite in the Light and let it live life through them. A role they would have never discovered had it not been for the Light.

Anybody interested in becoming their Best Self?

Anyone interested in living in a world where the majority of people are on a path to becoming their Best Self, where peace, compassion, benevolent behavior, trustworthy people, and sustainable caretaking systems for all people are locked into place? Would you like to gift that kind of world to your children and grandchildren? It is all possible and within your reach. Read on and share the news with all you know.

"The intuitive mind is a sacred gift and the rational mind is a faithful servant. We have created a society that honors the servant and has forgotten the gift," – Albert Einstein

---

This book and author assumes that nothing needs to happen to please God, for everything is unfolding perfectly.

God loves to create, and this book was developed to meet every separate being right where they are, presenting the option for further evolution front and center, making it easier for anyone to choose it if they so desire.

We can all be the change we all desire. There is a way. A plan has been put into place. Do you want to be a part of this plan? You may already know you are part of this plan—a joyous and hearty welcome to All.

Get ready! For your Light and Love is about to ascend farther and faster than ever before.

Table of Contents

Chapter One:
A Short History

The existence of the modern middle class has always ridden on a razor's edge, usually short-lived and fashionably new for its time. Exhilarating and life-affirming by the lower classes, derided by the upper class as unnatural for humans. Virtually unheard of in contemporary history and easily crushed by the weight of the upper class. Definitely worthy of protection and is steadily under attack on many different fronts. What made this middle class, in the post-Pilgrim era, different? Before we can answer that question, there needs to be an understanding of how it came to be. To that end, I would like to share a short history of the birth of the United States of America without the whitewash.

Who were the first people to live in the Americas?

Source: http://gorhistory.com/hist110/na.html (Olson-Raymer, G., n.d.)

The Original Inhabitants – What They Lost and What They Retained

By the time European explorers landed in North America, the inhabitants of the native communities comprised somewhere between 5 and 10 million people who belonged to between 500-600 different tribal societies.

Myth. In order to ensure the survival and progress of the civilized, European, Christian settlers, it was inevitable that the Indians be defeated.

Reality. European progress was impeded not because the indigenous peoples were uncivilized and incapable of living harmoniously with the settlers, but because Europeans were unwilling and incapable of accepting the American Indians' political, social, economic, and spiritual traditions as civilized. The real obstacles that got in the way of European acceptance of Indian peoples were that they were not Christians and had no visible forms of worshipping God; they made no effort to subdue the land and make it profitable; they had no understanding of the importance of private property; and they were not willing to give up their land and submit to English rule.

So what are the facts?

- Many first-hand accounts describe the Indians of the North continent and of the West Indies as friendly, peaceful, and welcoming.
- Juan Rodiquez Cabrillo, when writing about his voyage along the Southern California coast in 1542, observed, "very fine valleys [with] maize and abundant food ... many savannahs and groves" that were "densely populated" and "thickly settled" when Indians who often greeted the Spanish ships in friendship and traded with them of peaceful ceremonies. (Stanndard, 1992:23.)
- If such communities were not comprised of uncivilized savages who threatened European settlement and white progress, why has the myth persisted? Several historians have flatly stated that the image of native barbarism and savagery serves to rationalize European conquest. (Francis Jennings, *The Invasion of America: Indians, Colonialism, and the Cost of Conquest.* Chapel Hill: Univ. of No. Carolina Press, 1975; Robert F. Berkhofer, Jr., *The White Man's Indian: Images of the American Indian from Columbus to the Present.* NY: Alfred A. Knopf, 1978; and David Stannard, *American Holocaust.* NY: Oxford Univ. Press, 1992.)

The history of the relationship between the American Indian and European invaders is very troubling. I do not pretend to know how to fix or repair that history. Hopefully, the ideas presented here will be embraced and bring relief to the American Indian, the people from the African nations, and all disenfranchised people displaced by the vast land and money grab ushered in by our very own Christopher Columbus.

I am also not here to damn Columbus or argue his culpability. Damning Columbus doesn't really change anything. If you read Columbus's personal journal he kept while sailing the ocean blue, you can hear in his own words what he was doing. He was basically a pirate funded by the Spanish government. Like any other significant player in history, he had flaws, just like we all do. The more one knows and understands the Truth of our Reality, the more benevolent our behavior can become. So until we are all perfect, let's just agree not to judge one another and do the best we can.

Moving forward, we now had European countries that could cross the Atlantic, and the migration of European people to the New World had begun. And with these new people came their culture, religion, and government. The religion that came across the Atlantic was believed to be the one true and correct religion, which became a sticking point for relations between the established peoples and the newcomers and one that was used to justify the appropriation of land and the genocide of whole nations of people.

The Catholic Church and several European monarchies further developed this belief and concept. That became known as the "Doctrine of Discovery." Many First Nation People have recently petitioned the Catholic Church and government entities to rescind this Doctrine to no avail. I bring it up because it is an essential piece of history that exposes a fundamental flaw in the thinking of humans. (The thought that some of us are better than others.)

Most would like to see this history buried and forgotten, so uncomfortable it is to examine history with the benefit of now being able to see both sides. I am sure that while the history was being made, the reasons for the savagery seemed completely normal, coupled with a very sound rationale for all of the atrocities committed. Almost all of us are guilty of this type of behavior in big and small ways. As you can see, we are all separate, individual human beings. Some of us naturally have to be better than others, giving rise to the belief in the concept of haves and have-nots, peasants and the nobility, original inhabitants, and the explorer/discoverer. Are we really all separate beings? Are some of us really better than others?

The Doctrine of Discovery may seem cruel and unusual to a 21st-century person. But, this behavior had become normalized in the feudal governing system in Europe since the 9th century. People who owned all the land and hoarded all the money were already treating the common folks as indentured servants, forcing them to work the land while only providing subsistence-level wages. People born into these peasant families rarely ever changed their station in life. This became the breeding ground for the birth of "The American Dream," but we will get to that later.

The peasants were downtrodden people, used and abused by the cultural elite, not entirely slaves, but also unable to free themselves from the tyranny they faced. The victims became the victimizers, and the European transplants pushed the American Indians off their land and out of the way of their expansion. I am not making excuses for their behavior. I want to understand how and why this happens so that we can avoid making the same mistakes again.

3

It was disappointing that the European transplants could not treat other human beings as they would have liked to have been treated when they were at the bottom of the social and economic ladder. Indeed, as Christians, you'd think they would have had access to the "Golden Rule!" (Do unto others what you would have them do to you.) But the problem was that the version of Christianity these people were taught was used to subjugate them. They used it the same way with the First Nation People in North America.

Sad to say, but I guess it is true… We are all capable of savagery, and to condemn it in another compels us to do the same… Fascinating and strange, this dynamic of the polarization of opposites drawing us into the very thing we despise. Maybe one day soon, as a species of human beings, we will see through the fallacy of this type of thinking and relinquish our need to judge others as wrong or bad, which is then used as justification for behavior that is just as savage.

So what was happening between 1492 and 1776? This era saw many exploratory expeditions intent on enriching the countries that sponsored each trip. After 1600, the New World saw the arrival of the first wave of European refugees. These people no longer enjoyed living in Europe or were no longer welcome there. The opportunity presented to these newcomers was to learn a new way of life aligned with nature, working with the seasons, respecting the land, and living peaceably among one another without a class system consisting of haves and have-nots. While the newcomers did appreciate the help the indigenous people offered, they ultimately opted to keep their old way of life – ostracizing dissimilar humans, domesticating livestock animals, subjugating the land for their needs, and making land private with contracts on paper deeming it so. This was foreign to the indigenous people, who had no domesticated livestock animals, nor did they own property, and killing animals for sport was appalling.

I have often wondered what it would be like, to have been born in an American Indian tribe? I guess I would never have to worry about foreclosure proceedings on my teepee. There is no need for health insurance because there is free medical, and I would never go hungry as long as my tribe had food. Pretty simplistic, but they had the essential bases covered.

So, we have a whole continent and its surrounding areas of many different types of indigenous people unaware of the takeover that is about to happen and the hordes of marauding invaders from Europe ready to cash in on the booty they have discovered. Now add into the mix, people no longer welcome in Europe, people persecuted so severely that

4

they were willing to take a chance on a 66-day boat ride, huddled in the belly of a boat, amidst their stink and refuse, to a place they have never been to before to see how it goes. The early 1600s sees the beginning of the European refugees' flight into the Americas, Australia and New Zealand, and to some extent, Africa.

Although the opportunity to adopt the ways of the original inhabitants existed, the European refugees were so thoroughly indoctrinated with the feudal system and their established religious beliefs that change was nearly impossible. They set up shop the same as before, but there were key differences they could not ignore and were soon celebrated.

In the beginning, it was tough for Europeans moving to the Americas. There was no infrastructure, roads, houses, markets to buy food, farms that grew food, Door Dash, Grub Hub, or hot and ready pepperoni pizza, and only raw building materials. They had to do everything on their own. That first winter, the original local inhabitants saved them from starving to death. Years later, those same Europeans went to war with the very tribe that saved them during their first winter. Despite their trials, they persevered, and more Europeans continued to arrive on the New World shores.

As more and more Europeans arrived, infrastructure was slowly developed, and it was easy for people to find work and open businesses. It soon became evident that there was no monarchy or nobility to subjugate them. The only enemy was the original inhabitants.

The absence of monarchies and noblemen allowed the European transplants to govern themselves, create businesses that contributed to the whole, and live without a monarchy siphoning off any opportunities they had to improve their lives. Unknowingly, the absence of a monarchy had allowed for the birth of a middle class.

Interestingly, since the beginning of time, most hunter-gathering societies have lived much the same way, with no class distinctions. Since there was no upper or lower class, they were essentially all middle class because they treated each other equally with care, dignity, and respect. Since they only had themselves to rely on, unity became one of their strengths; together, they were stronger! To these indigenous cultures, it was evident that they would all experience childhood, old age, sickness, and death, so all able-bodied members assumed this responsibility for care, knowing that when they needed help, it would be there too.

When did it become okay to abandon frail members of our society?

When did we veer away from classless societies?

How did we end up with an upper class?

Seems to me that the existence of an upper class creates a lower class?

The story of the birth of the upper class:

On an energetic or spiritual level, one day, one person, listening to their lower nature, picks up on the message from their ego that they are different, separate, and more special than the rest of the humans around them. They are not subject to the same rules and social codes. As they begin to believe this erroneous, new story about themselves, it becomes easier and easier to devalue all others. With this belief system, performing jobs that take advantage of other humans becomes effortless. What better reason to take advantage of other humans than to profit from them? And there you have it, the birth of the upper class and the beginning of the lower class. You can't have one without the other!

Hunter gathering and early agricultural societies were all middle-class people who believed in the strength of unity, and this solidarity was always there to help their sisters and brothers in need. Solidarity was encouraged and enforced. When one group member begins to think that they are separate and better than the others, the only option these groups have is to exile these individuals. The offending individual, no longer welcome in the group, has to fend for themselves, which, way back then, was usually a death sentence.

Some believe this "Better than" mythology was one of the consequences of "The Fall from Heaven." The knowledge of good and evil was a false belief in their separation from God. As more and more humans were infected with this thinking, their exile was no longer a death sentence. Wandering hordes of men, certain that they were better than everyone else, would band together for support, just like their tribe of origin, but it was not a true union. They were just using the other exiled men for support, With the more cunning becoming the upper class, oppressing the rest, which became the lower class; for there was no middle class in this type of society.

Once an upper class is established, it is relatively easy to maintain. All they have to do is oppress the lower class by inventing ways to extract time and money from them, leaving them tired and poor at the end of each day and too demoralized, frustrated, and exhausted to stand up for themselves.

In the absence of oppression by an upper class, these once lower-class people rose up in the New World. They assumed the

6

responsibility for their own prosperity. Still, the real miracle that occurred for these European transplants in this new land was the opportunity to experience the Power of Oneness with all others in their new unified community; which was the opposite of their experience from where they had come; everybody only looked out for themselves.

The newcomers in this new land saw the lifestyle modeled by the American Indians. They realized they were all in this together and would prosper if they stuck together. For the first time in Europe's recorded history, people could work together and make a better life for themselves and each other. That is just what they did for the next 150 years. The concept of the "American Dream" grew and solidified during this time frame.

This one-hundred-and-fifty-year time frame is the most crucial period to developing what was to become the United States of America. During this time, the American colonists began to understand a democratic way of working together, learned the value of working together for the benefit of everyone, and that there was no need for a strong-arm leader.

Freed from that oppression, the colonists could now try their hand at whatever endeavor appealed to them, make it their life, passion, and livelihood; and why not? People are not born unto this earth to be slaves, literally or figuratively. So the concept of the American Dream grew, which was good and could be good for everyone. However, these European newcomers were unwilling to share their good fortune with everyone. You had to be similar to them to participate. Such a petty and small ideology to insist upon for inclusion! Are we not all human beings?

Anyway, this seed of equality for all was planted, but would it ever take root and grow? With this faulty thinking firmly entrenched in the minds of the new people, in the new world, destiny was on course with trauma, tragedy, and death, and thus began the eradication of dissimilar groups of people.

The American Indians were subjugated with a fierce ferocity that was shockingly similar to what the monarchies and nobility of Europe did to the peasants of Europe. Not long after the newcomers had established themselves, they searched for people to perform strenuous manual labor for them. The African slave trade was exported to the New World, decimating another group of people half a world away.

Soon, the American colonists would face an enemy they were familiar with but thought they had been freed from, but were mistaken. The sponsoring European countries had poured money into the new world, hoping to cash in, and the results were mixed. The Europeans who populated the new world no longer felt much allegiance to their place of birth. The sponsoring countries felt as if they owned all that was accomplished and tried to assert their authority by selling the fledgling new world people, goods, and services and overcharging them (basic oppression).

It was an agitated situation for a long time until the transplanted people from Europe had had enough. The "Declaration of Independence" was written and presented to everyone living in the new world. The speeches spreading the news of the Declaration were met with mixed reviews. Of course, the growing annoyance of soldiers now everywhere monitoring life in the new world was undoubtedly an issue. Still, most newcomers just wanted to focus on their life and career and do their best until they could take it no more. The Declaration of Independence was soon accepted by a majority of the people and put into action.

Here is the actual document called the Declaration of Independence. I have not included the representatives that signed the Declaration from the different colonies for brevity:

Source: https://www.archives.gov/founding-docs/declaration-transcript
(National Archives, n.d.)

The Declaration of Independence (the thirteen United States of America)

When in the Course of human events, it becomes necessary for one people to dissolve the political bands which have connected them with another, and to assume among the powers of the earth, the separate and equal station to which the Laws of Nature and of Nature's God entitle them, a decent respect to the opinions of mankind requires that they should declare the causes which impel them to the separation.

We hold these truths to be self-evident, that all men are created equal, that they are endowed by their Creator with certain unalienable Rights, that among these are Life, Liberty and the pursuit of Happiness.--That to secure these rights, Governments are instituted among Men, deriving their just powers from the consent of the governed, —That whenever any Form of Government becomes destructive of these ends, it is the Right of the People to alter or to abolish it, and to institute new Government, laying its foundation on such principles and organizing its powers in such form, as to them shall seem most likely to affect their Safety and

Happiness. Prudence, indeed, will dictate that Governments long established should not be changed for light and transient causes; and accordingly all experience hath shewn, that mankind are more disposed to suffer, while evils are sufferable, than to right themselves by abolishing the forms to which they are accustomed. But when a long train of abuses and usurpations, pursuing invariably the same Object evinces a design to reduce them under absolute Despotism, it is their right, it is their duty, to throw off such Government, and to provide new Guards for their future security.—Such has been the patient sufferance of these Colonies; and such is now the necessity which constrains them to alter their former Systems of Government. The history of the present King of Great Britain is a history of repeated injuries and usurpations, all having in direct object the establishment of an absolute Tyranny over these States. To prove this, let Facts be submitted to a candid world.

He has refused his Assent to Laws, the most wholesome and necessary for the public good.

He has forbidden his Governors to pass Laws of immediate and pressing importance, unless suspended in their operation till his Assent should be obtained; and when so suspended, he has utterly neglected to attend to them.

He has refused to pass other Laws for the accommodation of large districts of people, unless those people would relinquish the right of Representation in the Legislature, a right inestimable to them and formidable to tyrants only.

He has called together legislative bodies at places unusual, uncomfortable, and distant from the depository of their public Records, for the sole purpose of fatiguing them into compliance with his measures.

He has dissolved Representative Houses repeatedly, for opposing with manly firmness his invasions on the rights of the people.

He has refused for a long time, after such dissolutions, to cause others to be elected; whereby the Legislative powers, incapable of Annihilation, have returned to the People at large for their exercise; the State remaining in the meantime exposed to all the dangers of invasion from without, and convulsions within.

He has endeavored to prevent the population of these States; for that purpose obstructing the Laws for Naturalization of Foreigners; refusing to pass others to encourage their migrations hither, and raising the conditions of new Appropriations of Lands.

He has obstructed the Administration of Justice, by refusing his Assent to Laws for establishing Judiciary powers.

He has made Judges dependent on his Will alone, for the tenure of their offices, and the amount and payment of their salaries.

He has erected a multitude of New Offices, and sent hither swarms of Officers to harrass our people, and eat out their substance.

He has kept among us, in times of peace, Standing Armies without the Consent of our legislatures.

He has affected to render the Military independent of and superior to the Civil power.

He has combined with others to subject us to a jurisdiction foreign to our constitution, and unacknowledged by our laws; giving his Assent to their Acts of pretended Legislation:

For Quartering large bodies of armed troops among us:

For protecting them, by a mock Trial, from punishment for any Murders which they should commit on the Inhabitants of these States:
For cutting off our Trade with all parts of the world:

For imposing Taxes on us without our Consent:

For depriving us in many cases, of the benefits of Trial by Jury:

For transporting us beyond Seas to be tried for pretended offences

For abolishing the free System of English Laws in a neighboring Province, establishing therein an Arbitrary government, and enlarging its Boundaries so as to render it at once an example and fit instrument for introducing the same absolute rule into these Colonies:

For taking away our Charters, abolishing our most valuable Laws, and altering fundamentally the Forms of our Governments:

For suspending our own Legislatures, and declaring themselves invested with power to legislate for us in all cases whatsoever.

He has abdicated Government here, by declaring us out of his Protection and waging War against us.

He has plundered our seas, ravaged our Coasts, burnt our towns, and destroyed the lives of our people.

He is at this time transporting large Armies of foreign Mercenaries to compleat the works of death, desolation and tyranny, already begun with circumstances of Cruelty & perfidy scarcely paralleled in the most barbarous ages, and totally unworthy the Head of a civilized nation.

He has constrained our fellow Citizens taken Captive on the high Seas to bear Arms against their Country, to become the executioners of their friends and Brethren, or to fall themselves by their Hands.

He has excited domestic insurrections amongst us, and has endeavored to bring on the inhabitants of our frontiers, the merciless Indian Savages, whose known rule of warfare, is an undistinguished destruction of all ages, sexes and conditions.

In every stage of these Oppressions We have Petitioned for Redress in the most humble terms: Our repeated Petitions have been answered only by repeated injury. A Prince whose character is thus marked by every act which may define a Tyrant, is unfit to be the ruler of a free people.

Nor have We been wanting in attentions to our British brethren. We have warned them from time to time of attempts by their legislature to extend an unwarrantable jurisdiction over us. We have reminded them of the circumstances of our emigration and settlement here. We have appealed to their native justice and magnanimity, and we have conjured them by the ties of our common kindred to disavow these usurpations, which, would inevitably interrupt our connections and correspondence. They too have been deaf to the voice of justice and of consanguinity. We must, therefore, acquiesce in the necessity, which denounces our Separation, and hold them, as we hold the rest of mankind, Enemies in War, in Peace Friends.

We, therefore, the Representatives of the united States of America, in General Congress, Assembled, appealing to the Supreme Judge of the world for the rectitude of our intentions, do, in the Name, and by Authority of the good People of these Colonies, solemnly publish and declare, That these United Colonies are, and of Right ought to be Free and Independent States; that they are Absolved from all Allegiance to the British Crown, and that all political connection between them and the State of Great Britain, is and ought to be totally dissolved; and that as Free and Independent States, they have full Power to levy War, conclude Peace, contract Alliances, establish

Commerce, and to do all other Acts and Things which Independent States may of right do. And for the support of this Declaration, with a firm reliance on the protection of divine Providence, we mutually plodge to oaoh othor our Livos, our Fortunes and our sacred Honor

---

I hope you see that the European transplants were not perfect people. They had many flaws, as we all do. They came across another group of people with a totally different organizational, spiritual, and economic style; not right or wrong, just different. I am sure they also had flaws of their own. However, the unique feature about their system was that they were all middle class, which was unusual for the transplants, for they had recently escaped from a society where they were constantly oppressed and from the lowest rung of their community.

This new world was beginning to treat European refugees very well. As they settled in and established themselves, they noticed the lack of upper-class oppression and were delighted. Their experience with the original inhabitants allowed their beliefs to be expanded and revised. All the colonists operating as a middle class worked well and built their collective esteem. For the emerging colonist, every community member mattered, and everyone was important.

This concept is easy to visualize and understand in communities with smaller populations. For example, if the town baker gets sick, the community has no bread. If the blacksmith gets sick, there are no shoes for the horses. In a more populace community, it is harder to see this relationship, but just as important to remember; that everyone has value.

In a corporatocracy (what we have now), people only matter if they can add to the bottom line. Once they are no longer able to add profit, they lose value. Some members of our society are cast out to live the rest of their days on the street, begging for food and shelter. Our government sees this problem and pretends it can't help. Our middle-class brothers and sisters see this and are ashamed, but what can they do all alone? Nothing will change this blight until we all come together and act as one, demanding change. Self-interest brings me to this realization. I don't want to end up on the streets, and I do not wish it on anyone else!

What is a corporatocracy? A society that is dominated politically and economically by the profit-driven needs of large corporations, often to the detriment and neglect of its citizens. This is a common problem with a purely capitalist society. When the drive for profit becomes all-important, everything else is pushed to the side, like an addict stealing from their mom to get a fix; nothing matters anymore with this mindset.

Historian Howard Zinn argues that during the Gilded Age (1877-1900) in the United States, the U.S. government was acting exactly as Karl Marx described capitalist states: "pretending neutrality to maintain order, but serving the interests of the rich" (as quoted in Wikipedia).

I think you can see where this is going... Corporations are the new oppressive monarchy, creating levels of upper classes, and destroying the concept of equality and a middle class that includes everyone and leaves no one behind.

We will elaborate on this idea further, but for now, we will continue with the history of the American colonist and their development of a middle-class society that consisted solely of white males and their property.

This new concept of everyone being in the middle class or created equal brought everyone together with a renewed sense of trust and goodwill. The newfound camaraderie grew unabated for over 150 years, definitely enough time to become accustomed to it and appreciate it enough to want to fight to protect it. When the monarchy oppression returned and they could take it no more, they fought back! This Declaration is their first attempt to protect their new unoppressed, unified way of life.

Let's discuss what the Declaration was trying to protect for the colonists. Protections that shall be for all future U. S. Citizens and the impact it had on the rest of the world governments.

The first paragraph basically states that they are not satisfied with how they are being governed, and it is their duty to declare the reasons for their dissatisfaction. Here they reference the "Laws of Nature" and "Nature's God," declaring their allegiance to a "higher power" with a more universal authority than man or governments of men.

So for this Declaration to make sense and protect all of the people participating, they must understand Natural Law and practice its concepts. So first things first, everyone needs to know what the concept of Natural Law is and why it is essential.

Secondly, the government needs to practice and promote these concepts! For if a government is maligning any minority group of people, these same people will have no compunction to reciprocate the golden rule. Chaos, insurrection, injustice, and mayhem will rule. The abused become the abusers; the victims become the victimizers... and along comes the inevitable – anarchy; a friend to everyone who feels maligned and is inclined to malign all they engage.

So what is Natural Law?

The following article from the National Center for Constitutional Studies provides the answers.

Source: https://nccs.net/blogs/our-ageless-constitution/natural-law-the-ulti-mate-source-of-constitutional-law?_pos=2&_psq=natural+law&_ss=e&_v=1.0 (National Center for Constitutional Studies, n.d.)

Natural Law: The Ultimate Source of Constitutional Law

"Man ... must necessarily be subject to the laws of his Creator. This will of his Maker is called the law of nature.... This law of nature...is of course superior to any other.... No human laws are of any validity, if contrary to this: and such of them as are valid derive all their force... from this original." – Sir William Blackstone (Eminent English Jurist)

The Founders DID NOT establish the Constitution for the purpose of **granting** rights. Rather, they established this government of laws (not a government of men) in order to **secure** each person's Creator-endowed rights to life, liberty, and property. Only in America, did a nation's founders recognize that rights, though endowed by the Creator as unalienable prerogatives, would not be sustained in society unless they were protected under a code of law which was itself in harmony with a higher law. They called it "natural law," or "Nature's law." Such law is the ultimate source and established limit for all of man's laws and is intended to protect each of these natural rights for all of mankind. The Declaration of Independence of 1776 established the premise that in America a people might assume the station "to which the laws of Nature and Nature's God entitle them…" Herein lay the security for men's individual rights – an immuable code of law, sanctioned by the Creator of man's rights, and designed to promote, preserve, and protect him and his fellows in the enjoyment of their rights. They believed that such natural law, revealed to man through his reason, was capable of being understood by both the plowman and the professor. Sir William Blackstone, whose writings trained American's lawyers for its first century, capsulized such reasoning:

"For as God, when he created matter, and endued it with a principle of mobility, established certain rules for the...direction of that motion; so, when he created man, and endued him with freewill to conduct himself in all parts of life, he laid down certain immutable laws of

14

human nature, whereby that freewill is in some degree regulated and restrained, and gave him also the faculty of reason to discover the purport of those laws."

What are those natural laws? Blackstone continued:

"Such among others are these principles: that we should live honestly, should hurt nobody, and should render to every one his due…"

The Founders saw these as moral duties between individuals. Thomas Jefferson wrote:

"Man has been subjected by his Creator to the moral law, of which his feelings, or conscience as it is sometimes called, are the evidence with which his Creator has furnished him .... The moral duties which exist between individual and individual in a state of nature, accompany them into a state of society. their Maker not having released them from those duties on their forming themselves into a nation."

America's leaders of 1787 had studied Cicero, Polybius, Coke, Locke, Montesquieu, and Blackstone, among others, as well as the history of the rise and fall of governments, and they recognized these underlying principles of law as those of the Decalogue, the Golden Rule, and the deepest thought of the ages. An example of the harmony of natural law and natural rights is Blackstone's "that we should live honestly" – otherwise known as "thou shalt not steal" – whose corresponding natural right is that of individual freedom to acquire and own, through honest initiative, private property. In the Founders' view, this law and this right were unalterable and of a higher order than any written law of man. Thus, the Constitution confirmed the law and secured the right and bound both individuals and their representatives in government to a moral code which did not permit either to take the earnings of another without his consent. Under this code, individuals could not band together and do, through government's coercive power, that which was not lawful between individuals.

America's Constitution is the culmination of the best reasoning of men of all time and is based on the most profound and beneficial values mankind has been able to fathom. It is, as William E. Gladstone observed, **"<u>The Most Wonderful Work Ever Struck Off At A Given Time By the Brain And Purpose Of Man.</u>"**

We should dedicate ourselves to rediscovering and preserving an understanding of our Constitution's basis in natural law for the protection of natural rights - principles which have provided American citizens with more protection for individual rights, while guaranteeing more freedom, than any people on earth.

"The end of law is not to abolish or restrain, but to preserve and enlarge freedom." –John Locke

---

Footnote: Our Ageless Constitution, W. David Stedman & La Vaughn G. Lewis, Editors (Asheboro, NC, W. David Stedman Associates, 1987) Part III: ISBN 0-937047-01-5

Natural Law describes a profound evolutionary path that every individual must tread; the reconciliation between themselves and their concept of a Creator. How did they come into being, and for what purpose? Natural Law asks us to understand that while we may present as many different individuals, in actuality, we are all One. We all come from the same place and are all returning to the same place. And while we draw breath on this physical plane of existence, we will do well to remember our true origins and not give in to the fear and illusion that permeates and undermines the best efforts of the human species. When we work together for the common good, the unifying nature of the cosmos will be at our side to assist. When we push that energy aside to alleviate personal prejudices or fears, we will be left standing alone. So let us come together, join as One, and be enabled to move the mountains that stand in our way to freedom with liberty and justice for all!

Embarking on this evolutionary path does not come naturally. The way to this path and the road to enlightenment is fraught with pain and suffering. Veering off course brings pain. Persevering down a dead end causes suffering. While pain and suffering are an effective teacher, must we all endure the pain and suffering for tried and true lessons already learned by humankind throughout history? If we are indeed all One, then helping everyone understand their True nature will not only help each individual experience a more harmonious life but will benefit us all and elevate our state of being to that of living in Eden. Lofty ideals for sure, but who would take up this path were it not for the beauty, and promise of Unity. I have suffered enough! I am prepared to take up this fidelity toward Enlightenment, and it all starts with the sharing of what works to bring us all together. Are you ready to drop your fears and learn to live as One?

Historically, we have not been kind to one another! How do we forgive these transgressions? No amount of restitution would serve justice. How do we move forward from this stalemate of trauma, pain, and injustice? Our honest admission of allowing ourselves to be dissuaded by illusory fears and a willingness to open up to a new way of being in the world. A world where kindness is the rule and a shared dedication by all people to walk the path towards Enlightenment. Which is the True knowing that we are all One and that there is room for all of us to inhabit this planet, sharing life, love, and the bounty that is ours to share with one another. So let us all come together to share the best of what we know to elevate us All!

Pretty powerful stuff coming from the Declaration!

To help explain this path of Enlightenment that we are all on and how to feel Light and Love while we walk this path is an article by Gina Lake.

Source: Gina Lake, from the book, *In the World but not of it: New teachings from Jesus on Embodying the Divine*. A channeled book from Jesus. (Lake, G., 2016)

Perfect Imperfection

You are both human and divine. You are divine perfection expressing as human imperfection, which itself is perfect. You were perfectly designed to be imperfect! Human imperfections are an intentional part of your design and will always be with you to some extent.

Human imperfections stem largely from the ego, which is an essential aspect of being human that never completely disappears. The ego is not a mistake. It is meant to be part of the human experience. However, it is also intended that you evolve from expressing the ego to expressing your divine nature, while retaining some remnant of ego.

These imperfections are the things you might judge about yourself and others. These are also things that cause suffering, such as the tendency to judge, to be unkind, to gossip, to be jealous or envious, to want to be right, to want attention, to try to control others, to compulsively think, to be addicted, to pretend to know, to be selfish or greedy, to blame, to be unaware of or insensitive to other people's needs and feelings, to be prejudiced, to be ignorant, to argue and compete with others—all the things you might be acknowledging when you shrug your shoulders and say, "I'm only human."

Because these human tendencies cause problems and pain, most people would prefer they didn't have them. And although your natural evolution is towards greater kindness, empathy, peace, love, wisdom, and other qualities of your true nature, which is perfect, as a human being, you will never reach such perfection—and you aren't meant to. To express the perfection of your divine self, the human self doesn't have to be perfect.

One of the most important messages I have to offer you is that it's okay for you to be imperfect. It's okay for you to be human, and it's impossible for you to be other than the way you are right now, although you will most certainly continue to evolve and become more Christ-like.

You may imagine that I was perfect and hold this up as a model, but you shouldn't be surprised if you or others don't live up to this imagined ideal. I was not perfect either. To some, this must sound like blasphemy. But it is hurtful to you and misleading for you to believe that you or anyone else can become a perfect human being. You can and will become a vehicle for expressing Christ Consciousness in the world, but you will still have some human imperfections.

As long as you are human, there will be some degree of pull from your programming into fear, anger, judgment, blame, hatred, self-doubt, jealousy, revenge, dissatisfaction, greed, and other human emotions and tendencies. The programming that makes you human is powerfully controlling. Until people begin to question their thoughts, they can't help how they behave. They will follow the dictates of their programming and instincts, not unlike animals. When that happens, you must forgive them "for they know not what they do" and forgive yourself as well.

When Christ Consciousness shines through the human, the human self doesn't become perfect, but it can become a vehicle for good, at least temporarily, rather than something that serves the ego and its drives and agenda. For Christ Consciousness to shine through you, your imperfections don't have to disappear; they simply need to be accepted. This doesn't mean indulging them, however. It means having compassion for them. By showering your imperfections with compassion, you become aligned with your divine self. Then those imperfections disappear for the time being.

Many imagine that being in the world but not of it means transcending the world and the ego and no longer being touched by the difficulties of the human condition. But that is not what this means. Rather, being in the world but not of it means that you fully embrace the world of form and embrace being human while knowing you are beyond all forms. To do this, you have to first love the world, including your humanness. You have to do the opposite of what the ego does, which is reject the world.

The ego rejects the world because it misperceives the world. When you stop seeing the world through the ego's eyes, you will love the world and know it as the magnificent creation and gift that it is. Then the perfection of your divine self can shine through your human self. You will be in the world but not of the world.

As long as you are in the world—as long as you are human—you will have some imperfections, issues, bad habits, and possibly addictions. These won't necessarily take you out of Presence unless you judge your human self for having them and think they shouldn't be there. Rejecting, judging, or going to war with your human shortcomings is what keeps you separate from your divine self. When you do those things, you are identified with the superego. Only the superego would go to war with the ego, because doing that accomplishes what the ego wants. It keeps people identified with the false self.

The remedy is to become aware of the interplay between these two aspects of your ego and to, instead, accept your human self. The instant you offer acceptance to your human self, you become your divine self, because the only thing that can do this is the divine self.

Sometimes you will fall short of your spiritual goals and ideals: You will not be loving, you will not be compassionate, you will not be patient, you will not be tolerant. You will gossip, lie, exaggerate, judge, blame, and get irritated. You will falter. But once you see that you've faltered and accept that, the slate is wiped clean. You are forgiven, and you can begin again.

Forgiveness is automatic as soon as you see that you have made a mistake. The seeing of the mistake is the forgiveness. Accepting that mistake will allow you to forgive yourself and move on. You are always forgiven, but if you don't forgive yourself, you'll stay stuck in the ego. Accepting that you made a mistake and that doing so is human allows you to forgive yourself. In that moment of forgiveness, you become a channel once again for Christ Consciousness.

If you have a negative tendency, such as judging or gossiping, do your best to not indulge in this. But if you do, acknowledge that you've made a mistake, accept that, have compassion for this human tendency, forgive yourself, and ask others for forgiveness if necessary. Then you will drop back into Presence, Christ Consciousness. To judge or berate yourself only keeps you separate from your divine self.

Before you can accept an imperfection, which stems from an imperfect thought, such as a judgment, you first have to become aware of that thought. That awareness is the beginning of disidentification from the ego. That little step back achieved by witnessing thought is the beginning of realignment with the divine self.

This is exactly what is practiced in meditation: You become aware of a thought, you accept that it's there, and you forgive it and yourself for having it. Doing that allows you to return to Presence. This is the way from imperfection to perfection. There is no need to do away with imperfection; all that's needed is the right relationship to your imperfections. That relationship is one of acceptance, and that makes it possible to reunite with your divine perfection. The Divine is deeply in love with the human just as it is, because the Divine created the human to be just as it is.

Acceptance is the bridge that takes you from the human condition of suffering to the freedom and love of your divine nature. Without acceptance, you are stuck in the ego and the suffering it creates. With acceptance, the ego is allowed to be as it is, while recognizing that you are not that ego. You accept that you have an ego that causes suffering, but you also know that who you are, in essence, is divine. That mysterious essence is what sees the truth about the ego.

Then, after accepting and forgiving your humanness, there's one more very important thing to do: Don't go back to the thought-stream. Stay in Presence by staying in your body and senses and noticing the vast spaciousness from which you are looking, hearing, sensing, and experiencing. Notice it and sink into it. Remain in it. The only thing that can take you out of Presence is the voice in your head.

The longer you stay in Presence, the more this spacious sense of your divine self opens up, and you discover how very satisfying and complete it is. To be happy, you don't need what the ego thinks you need. The joy of pure existence is there whenever you turn the spotlight of your attention onto it and keep it there long enough for the divine self to open, like a flower, and release its fragrance.

The proof that you are not the ego, which is why you are able to accept the ego, is that you are aware of the ego. What is aware of the ego cannot be the ego. Just as the eye can't see itself, the ego can't see itself. Only something outside the ego can see the ego. You are able to be aware of what is going on within the human condition because you are not only human.

You are, in fact, what is aware of everything: thoughts, feelings, desires, intuitions, the sense of aliveness and existence, drives, urges, inspiration, and everything in the external world that is brought to you through the sense organ that is your body-mind. This awareness is perfect, unadulterated, and cannot be harmed by any imperfection. Nothing your human self has ever done has harmed the perfection of your divine self.

When you're in touch with this perfection and know yourself as this, you act accordingly, in peace, love, and kindness towards all. When this perfection infuses and is expressed through the human self, it is very beautiful indeed. But this doesn't do away with the ego, which will rise again and seek expression. Then awareness, acceptance, compassion, and forgiveness of the ego are called for again.

This is the dance between the human self and the divine self that continues moment to moment. Always, you—the one awakening from the egoic trance—must choose what you will express, who you will be, in that moment. Will you be the ego-dominated human self or the divine-infused human self? With practice, choosing the divine self becomes much easier, but that choice must still be made. That choice eventually becomes habitual, as ego identification was once habitual. But even then, the ego still exists in potential.

Being in touch with Perfection, or Presence, is also the secret to happiness. When you're in Presence, enjoying life is natural because you have no judgments or desires for life to be any different than it is. When you have no judgments or desires, your circumstances can't upset you. You just enjoy life as it is. You fall into the moment—you lose your egoic self—and that's enjoyable enough.

It's impossible to be ego-identified and be truly happy except briefly, because the ego is the manufacturer of discontentment, and by definition, you can't be happy when you're discontent. Unless you accept life just as it is, you can't enjoy it, because you're too busy resisting or trying to change it. When you stop having that kind of relationship with life, you drop into Presence and experience the natural in-joy-ment of the divine self.

The divine self is glorying in its creation—every aspect of it. It loves the puddles, the rainbows, the garbage, the feasts, the broken things, and the shiny and new things equally. To the divine self, there is no difference between these. They are all rejoiced in. To the divine self, everything is good, everything is the Beloved, all part of itself, its own creation.

If the ego felt this way about life, there would be nothing to desire, nothing to fear, and no better future moment to strive for. In other words, there would be little left of the ego, because you could say that desiring, fearing, striving, and looking to the future are the ego. If you were to cease doing these things, you would be in Presence, and the ego would lose its power and place. The ego would still be there in the background creating a sense of individuality so that you didn't fall into the Oneness and forget you were playing at being a human being. All the ego is really needed for is that.

Now that is a deep dive into the Truth of our shared reality! As we progress toward realizing that imperfect perfection, we carry on, evolving as we go, each of us doing our best to carry out our Soul Mission, knowing that we all get to where our Creator desires us to be as we luxuriate in this full life experience.

Now back to the Declaration, its ideology, and protection of freedoms.

The first part of the second paragraph is startling and compelling, stating that all men are created equal and that this equality is derived from man's "Creator." This "Creator" provided for all of us inalienable rights because, at our core, after race, color, and gender are stripped away, we are all One and obliged to the same equal rights.

We are all the creation of an energy source that willingly allowed us to entertain the idea that we are separate to fully experience this world. When we genuinely believe we are separate and independent of one another, things can get a bit crazy! When we remember who we are, at our core, a part of the Oneness of all creation, then that Truth blossoms. We find our way forward with equanimity and goodwill toward all humans. Let us always remember who and what we actually are. We are all One! At our core, we are One and the same!

In the passage, "all men are created equal," I believe the word "humans" should be substituted for the word "men" to be more clear and to more accurately reflect our current society. Also, "created equal" does not mean created with the same abilities. We are all different and possess different skills, which should not allow for special treatment or cruel oppression. We are all made from the essence of this Creator and deserving of equal treatment; for we are all One!

With the knowledge of Oneness firmly in place, the authors of the Declaration now assert that the Creator has endowed humans with certain inalienable rights, life, liberty, and the pursuit of happiness. Since this document is over two hundred years old, it will be beneficial to ascertain the meanings of these words from the author's vernacular and historical thinking.

To this end, we turned to the website:

Source: https://constitutionus.com/constitution/rights/what-are-unalienable-rights/ (ConstitutionUS, 2023, 24 January)

Life, Liberty, and the Pursuit of Happiness

What Is Life?

The first unalienable right identified in the Declaration of Independence is the right to life. The right to life is a state of being. That is, you are either alive or dead. This does not just refer to physical life or death but also to a metaphorical idealism that one cannot fully live under the tyranny of an oppressive government.

Having been under the rule of Great Britain for more than 100 years, the Colonialists had grown weary of the concept of living merely to fulfill the purpose of the King. They wanted the right to be the masters of their own homes, their own life, and the world around them. Without the right to live as they see fit, one must consider himself to already be dead.

What Is Liberty?

The second unalienable right identified in the Declaration of Independence was the right to liberty. Under the King's rule, the Colonialists were subject to the King's laws and, therefore, the King's tyrannical courts. Under this system of rule, the average person living within the thirteen colonies could never see true justice under natural law.

The concept of liberty refers to the idealism that one has the natural right to be free from tyranny. Freedom was not a concept that the commoner could enjoy under the rule of the British Crown. <u>The King taxed just about everything</u> that a colonialist needed to survive and merely enjoy life to its fullest.

Moreover, liberty is the right to equality. Not just equality in everyday life, but every aspect of life. This means that if accused of a crime, a person has the right to defend themselves. That concept of justice is that it is blind and that one is truly innocent until his accuser can prove otherwise.

The pursuit of happiness is clearly explained by the website:

Source: https://www.civiced.org/9-11-and-the-constitution-terms-to-know
(Center for Civic Education, n.d.)

Center for Civic Education

Pursuit of Happiness

The meaning of the term "Pursuit of Happiness." In the Declaration of Independence, Thomas Jefferson announced that every human being has "certain unalienable rights," among which are those to "life, liberty, and the pursuit of happiness." What did he mean by "the pursuit of happiness"?

To answer this, we should bear in mind that in writing the Declaration, Jefferson said he was not attempting to put forth an original philosophy of his own. Rather, it "was intended to be an expression of the American mind," that is, the opinions held by most if not all Americans of his time. It is difficult, however, to say with precision what most Americans in 1776 thought "the pursuit of happiness" meant.

The history of the term "Pursuit of happiness." Since Jefferson did not invent the phrase, the best we can do is discover its source and determine what it meant to its originator. Almost surely, Jefferson read about the "pursuit of happiness" in John Locke's Essay Concerning

Human Understanding (1690), in which he discusses how the human mind operates:

As therefore the highest perfection of intellectual nature lies in a careful and constant pursuit of true and solid happiness, so the care of ourselves, that we mistake not imaginary for real happiness, is the necessary foundation of our liberty. The stronger [the] ties we have to an unalterable pursuit of happiness in general...the more are we free from [obedience to an immediate impulse for some pleasure].

What the "pursuit of happiness" is. Every day we make numerous choices in deciding what course of action will add to our well-being— what will make us happy. Making these choices is the pursuit of happiness. The results of our choices are not all equal: we soon discover that choosing some pleasures, especially following momentary impulses, leads not to happiness but to pain. But if we use our faculty of foresight, recalling past experience, we learn to postpone immediate gratification and see what choices are really in our interest. Thus, learning self-control based on experience is essential to happiness.

Pursuing happiness as an inalienable right. According to Locke, this continuous process of choosing is part of human beings' unchangeable nature. Since our nature compels us to constantly make choices about what we believe gives us well-being, such choosing is inherent in our nature—in Jefferson's terms, it is inalienable. Accordingly, our right to make these choices is inalienable, and, unless our actions attack the rights of others, it is wrong for government to interfere.

Private happiness, public happiness, and moral goodness. Locke, Jefferson, and others learned from ancient philosophers, especially Aristotle, that these choices have ethical or moral dimensions: those without moral virtue cannot be happy. Many of our choices have social consequences and therefore have a civic dimension when they enhance or subtract from "public happiness." Thus "the pursuit of happiness" must refer both to public and to private happiness.

So interesting, this pursuit of happiness is the act of making choices to further our own enjoyment and determining which options bring us true joy; after reflection.

    (How about that, the Declaration authors, encouraging our personal and spiritual evolution even while writing the Declaration of Independence; truly insightful!)

Not only are we asked to determine what truly brings us lasting happiness, but we are also asked to consider the whole of humanity while defining our happiness quotient. When we include The *All* in Truth, we are serving ourselves, for we are also a part of The *All*. (Whatsoever you do to the least of me, you also do for me. Matthew 25:40)

Further insight is provided by the website:

Source: https://news.emory.edu/stories/2014/06/er_pursuit_of_happiness/campus.html (Emory University News, 2018, 3 July)

What the Declaration of Independence really means by 'pursuit of happiness'

First, the most important thing is to realize that the happy life is about more than just me: my health, my wealth, my safety and security.

A robust understanding of human flourishing means it is *for all* and that means that our "pursuit" of happiness must transcend narrow nationalisms and thin tribalisms.

We would not permit, say, one political party to flourish and deny the chance for another to do the same. Or, to shift the imagery, we would not want our daughters to flourish but not our sons. Why, then, are we satisfied to let some neighborhoods in a city languish, or some schools in a district fail? Why are we willing to let some countries deteriorate?

Not because we are committed to the "unalienable right" of happiness, but only because we are selfishly committed to a narrow, individualized understanding of localized hedonism. But, as the positive psychology literature shows (and the biblical book of Ecclesiastes knows this too), more pleasure or more "stuff" will never bring true happiness and flourishing.

So, first and foremost, we have to think more globally, more organically. In the republic, all citizens should flourish, and in the global village, all persons should flourish.

Second, thinking about happiness as a "global village" issue shows that human flourishing will only be achieved if we take better care of our world.

This is a truly transnational issue. All humans share this planet and therefore all humans—and all governments—must take responsibility for its care, particularly in redressing the lack of care that we have exercised for far too long. Without doing so, there will simply be no place for humans to flourish. Could it be any more simple?

Third, despite the important role played by governments and law, it is increasingly clear that important things like food, medicine and safe living conditions cannot always wait for the slow movements of governments.

Positive psychology has highlighted the crucial role of *positive institutions*, including—when they function at their best—families, workplaces and communities of faith. These must be ready to do the hard work of helping others flourish when the government proves ineffectual (as it often does).

When the government is effective and rightly functioning as one such positive institution, I firmly believe we will see far less "enforcement," whether via the police or military, and far more "empowerment." I myself believe these are related: more empowerment of people—facilitating their flourishing—will mean enforcement just won't be needed anymore. It will become *passé*!

In the Bible, the prophet Isaiah has a vision along these very lines: a time where everyone will turn in their weapon and melt them all down to make more farm equipment (Isa 2:4). That is not a bad vision of thick happiness: for both humanity and the world!

I am starting to see a pattern here… When we act in a spirit of unity, harmony, and inclusivity, it becomes easier to take care of each other; for it makes the most sense. This thinking has deteriorated over time, but it is not too late to revive this mentality in our society!

This ideology seems to be firmly embedded in our governing documents.

As we awaken to these seemingly new ideas, we have the opportunity to try them out and discover their usefulness to ourselves and the whole of society.

The last part of this paragraph states that when all else has failed to regain equal treatment for all, it is time to list the grievances and declare independence from any government not representing the people satisfactorily.

The current generalized dissatisfaction with our government begs the question, do we have a list of grievances our current government seems unwilling to address? Should "We The People" take action to redress and preserve our rights? Can we make a case that warrants the abolishment of this current government? Excellent question, and we shall answer this question later in the book.

The next section is a lengthy list of grievances.

The final section summarizes all the attempts to resolve the issues civilly. And they are forced to declare their freedom from their oppressors, which means war.

Fortunately, for the current citizens of the United States, there is no need to declare war to change our government. All government representatives, except for the Supreme Court Justices, are elected representatives. "We, The People," vote for who we want to represent us in our government. And if we're going to revolt without bullets, *"We The People"* (WTP) have that option at our disposal when we go to the voting booths.

To be victorious in our revolution, WTP need to be educated on the current issues and remember the inalienable rights granted us by our Creator and vote as one people. Sending a consistent message to those that govern precisely what the American People want!

Wrapping up our discussion, here is an article detailing the lasting legacy of the Declaration of the United States of America from the website:

Source: http://ap.gilderlehrman.org/history-by-era/road-revolution/essays/declaration-independence-global-perspective (The Gilder Lehrman Institute of American History, n.d.)

The Declaration of Independence in Global Perspective

No American document has had a greater global impact than the Declaration of Independence. It has been fundamental to American history longer than any other text because it was the first to use the name "the United States of America": in this sense, the Declaration was the birth

28

certificate of the American nation. It enshrined what came to be seen as the most succinct and memorable statement of the ideals on which that nation was founded: the rights to life, liberty, and the pursuit of happiness; the consent of the governed; and resistance to tyranny. And, as the first successful declaration of independence in world history, its example helped to inspire countless movements for independence, self-determination, and revolution after 1776. One of its most enthusiastic admirers was the nineteenth-century Hungarian nationalist, Lajos Kossuth: for him, the Declaration was nothing less than "the noblest, happiest page in mankind's history."

The Declaration was addressed as much to "mankind" as it was to the population of the colonies. In the opening paragraph, the authors of the Declaration—Thomas Jefferson, the five-member Congressional committee of which he was part, and the Second Continental Congress itself—addressed "the opinions of Mankind" as they announced the necessity for

. . . one People to dissolve the Political Bands which have connected them with another, and to assume among the Powers of the Earth, the separate and equal Station to which the Laws of Nature and of Nature's God entitle them…

After stating the fundamental principles—the "self-evident" truths—that justified separation, they submitted an extensive list of facts to "a candid world" to prove that George III had acted tyrannically. On the basis of those facts, his colonial subjects could now rightfully leave the British Empire. The Declaration therefore "solemnly Publish[ed] and Declare[d], That these United Colonies are, and of Right ought to be, FREE AND INDEPENDENT STATES" and concluded with a statement of the rights of such states that was similar to the enumeration of individual rights in the Declaration's second paragraph in being both precise and open-ended:

. . . that as FREE AND INDEPENDENT STATES, they have full Power to levy War, conclude Peace, contract Alliances, establish Commerce, and to do all other Acts and Things which INDEPENDENT STATES may of right do.

This was what the Declaration declared to the colonists who could now become citizens rather than subjects, and to the powers of the earth who were being asked to choose whether or not to acknowledge the United States of America among their number.

The final paragraph of the Declaration announced that the United States of America were now available for alliances and open for business. The colonists needed military, diplomatic, and commercial help in their revolutionary struggle against Great Britain; only a major power, like France or Spain, could supply that aid. Thomas Paine had warned in *Common Sense* in January 1776 that "the custom of all courts is against us, and will be so, until by an independence, we take rank with other nations." So long as the colonists remained within the empire, they would be treated as rebels; if they organized themselves into political bodies with which other powers could engage, then they might become legitimate belligerents in an international conflict rather than treasonous combatants within a British civil war.

The Declaration of Independence was primarily a declaration of *interdependence* with the other powers of the earth. It marked the entry of one people, constituted into thirteen states, into what we would now call international society. It did so in the conventional language of the contemporary law of nations drawn from the hugely influential book of that title (1758) by the Swiss jurist Emer de Vattel, a copy of which Benjamin Franklin had sent to Congress in 1775. Vattel's was a language of rights and freedom, sovereignty and independence, and the Declaration's use of his terms was designed to reassure the world beyond North America that the United States would abide by the rules of international behavior. The goal of the Declaration's authors was still quite revolutionary: to extend the sphere of European international relations across the Atlantic Ocean by turning dependent colonies into independent political actors. The historical odds were greatly against them; as they knew well, no people had managed to secede from an empire since the United Provinces had revolted from Spain almost two centuries before, and no overseas colony had done so in modern times.

The other powers of the earth were naturally curious about what the Declaration said. By August 1776, news of American independence and copies of the Declaration itself had reached London, Edinburgh, and Dublin, as well as the Dutch Republic and Austria. By the fall of that year, Danish, Italian, Swiss, and Polish readers had heard the news and many could now read the Declaration in their own language as translations appeared across Europe. The document inspired diplomatic debate in France but that potential ally only began serious negotiations after the American victory at the Battle of Saratoga in October 1777. The Franco-American Treaty of Amity and Commerce of February 1778 was the first formal recognition of the United States as "free and independent states." French assistance would, of course, be crucial to the success of the American cause. It also turned the American war into a global conflict involving Britain, France, Spain, and the Dutch Republic in military operations around the globe that would shape the fate of empires in the Atlantic, Pacific, and Indian Ocean worlds.

The ultimate success of American independence was swiftly acknowledged to be of world-historical significance. "A great revolution has happened—a revolution made, not by chopping and changing of power in any one of the existing states, but by the appearance of a new state, of a new species, in a new part of the globe," wrote the British politician Edmund Burke. With Sir William Herschel's recent discovery of the ninth planet, Uranus, in mind, he continued: "It has made as great a change in all the relations, and balances, and gravitation of power, as the appearance of a new planet would in the system of the solar world." However, it is a striking historical irony that the Declaration itself almost immediately sank into oblivion, "old *wadding* left to rot on the *battle-field* after the victory is won," as Abraham Lincoln put it in 1857. The Fourth of July was widely celebrated but not the Declaration itself. Even in the infant United States, the Declaration was largely forgotten until the early 1790s, when it re-emerged as a bone of political contention in the partisan struggles between pro-British Federalists and pro-French Republicans after the French Revolution. Only after the War of 1812 and the end of the Napoleonic Wars in 1815, did it become revered as the foundation of a newly emergent American patriotism.

Imitations of the Declaration were also slow in coming. Within North America, there was only one other early declaration of independence—Vermont's, in January 1777—and no similar document appeared outside North America until after the French Revolution. In January 1790, the Austrian province of Flanders expressed a desire to become a free and independent state in a document whose concluding lines drew directly on a French translation of the American Declaration. The allegedly self-evident truths of the Declaration's second paragraph did not appear in this Flemish manifesto nor would they in most of the 120 or so declarations of independence issued around the world in the following two centuries. The French Declaration of the Rights of Man and the Citizen would have greater global impact as a charter of individual rights. The sovereignty of states, as laid out in the opening and closing paragraphs of the American Declaration, was the main message other peoples beyond America heard in the document after 1776.

More than half of the 192 countries now represented at the United Nations have a founding document that can be called a declaration of independence. Most of those countries came into being from the wreckage of empires or confederations, from Spanish America in the 1810s and 1820s to the Soviet Union and the former Yugoslavia in the 1990s. Their declarations of independence, like the American Declaration, informed the world that one people or state was now asserting—or, in many cases in the second half of the twentieth century re-asserting—its sovereignty and independence. Many looked back directly to the American Declaration for inspiration. For example, in 1811, Venezuela's representatives declared "that these united Provinces are, and ought to be, from this day, by act and right, Free, Sovereign, and Independent States." The Texas declaration of independence (1836) likewise followed the American in listing grievances and claiming freedom and independence. In the twentieth century, nationalists in Central Europe and Korea after the First World War staked their claims to sovereignty by going to Independence Hall in Philadelphia. Even the white minority government of Southern Rhodesia in 1965 made their unilateral declaration of independence from the British Parliament by adopting the form of the 1776 Declaration, though they ended it with a royalist salutation: "God Save the Queen!" The international community did not recognize that declaration because, unlike many similar pronouncements made during the process of decolonization by other African countries, it did not speak on behalf of all the people of their country.

Invocations of the American Declaration's second paragraph in later declarations of independence are conspicuous by their scarcity. Among the few are those of Liberia (1847) and Vietnam (1945). The Liberian declaration of independence recognized "in all men, certain natural and inalienable rights: among these are life, liberty, and the right to acquire, possess, and enjoy property": a significant amendment to the original Declaration's right to happiness by the former slaves who had settled Liberia under the aegis of the American Colonization Society. Almost a century later, in September 1945, the Vietnamese leader Ho Chi Minh opened his declaration of independence with the "immortal statement" from the 1776 Declaration: "All men are created equal. They are endowed by their Creator with certain inalienable rights, among these are Life, Liberty, and the pursuit of Happiness." However, Ho immediately updated those words: "In a broader sense, this means: All the peoples of the earth are equal from birth, all the peoples have a right to live, to be happy and free." It would be hard to find a more concise summary of the message of the Declaration for the post-colonial predicaments of the late twentieth century.

The global history of the Declaration of Independence is a story of the spread of sovereignty and the creation of states more than it is a narrative of the diffusion and reception of ideas of individual rights. The farflung fortunes of the Declaration remind us that independence and popular sovereignty usually accompanied each other, but also that there was no necessary connection between them: an independent Mexico became an empire under a monarchy between 1821 and 1823, Brazil's independence was proclaimed by its emperor, Dom Pedro II in 1822, and, as we have seen, Ian Smith's Rhodesian government threw off parliamentary authority while professing loyalty to the British Crown. How to protect universal human rights in a world of sovereign states, each of which jealously guards itself from interference by outside authorities, remains one of the most pressing dilemmas in contemporary politics around the world.

So long as a people comes to believe their rights have been assaulted in a "long Train of Abuses and Usurpations," they will seek to protect those rights by forming their own state, for which international custom demands a declaration of independence. In February 2008, the majority Albanian population of Kosovo declared their independence of Serbia in a document designed to reassure the world that their cause offered no precedent for any similar separatist or secessionist movements. Fewer than half of the current powers of the earth have so far recognized this Kosovar declaration. The remaining countries, among them Russia, China, Spain, and Greece, have resisted for fear of encouraging the break-up of their own territories. The explosive potential of the American Declaration was hardly evident in 1776 but a global perspective reveals its revolutionary force in the centuries that followed. Thomas Jefferson's assessment of its potential, made weeks before his death on July 4, 1826, surely still holds true today: "an instrument, pregnant with our own and the fate of the world."

David Armitage is the Lloyd C. Blankfein Professor of History and Director of Graduate Studies in History at Harvard University. He is also an Honorary Professor of History at the University of Sydney. Among his books are The Declaration of Independence: A Global History *(2007) and* The Age of Revolutions in Global Context, c. 1760–1860 *(2010).*

So important to reiterate that The Declaration of Independence states that in order to maintain these rights and fair treatment, WTP consent to the establishment of a government tasked with the duty to preserve these rights, and if the government is not doing a good job, it is the right and responsibility of the people to seek redress!

The government exists only because the citizens have consented to its existence.

The government's job is to represent and protect the citizens' inalienable rights. This means the maintenance of the middle class, the Unifying concept modeled and shared by the First Nation People from the first 150 years of this country.

What does that mean? The maintenance of the middle class? No individual or corporation may oppress another or attempt to elevate themselves above others! We are all in this to together. No one is left behind, and no one can wall themselves off or take advantage of the rest of the population.

Moving forward, it is less expensive to help everyone stay in the middle class than to lift someone out of abject poverty and life-threatening illnesses because of neglect.

No one is better than anyone else or more worthy! We are all created equal! We all come from the same place and we are all going back to the same place when we are done here.

Paradigm shifts are usually uncomfortable because they ask us to question long-held beliefs to determine their usefulness!

So the question of the day is:

Should we elevate the status of every U.S. citizen to be worthy of our care and protection? Our governing documents plainly state in the affirmative. What is holding us back from taking care of everyone in our family? The family of citizens of the United States of America.

The European transplants came to the new world to be free. Their freedoms, having been eroded, they fought back and went to war against their biggest oppressor, Britain.

Many times in world history, peasants revolted against their oppressors, and the results were not favorable! According to Wikipedia, world history dates between 206 BC and 1994 AD; there have been 154 peasant revolts. Resulting in:

16 Peasant victories

124 Peasant defeats

14 alternate result
(e.g. a treaty or peace without a clear result, *status quo ante bellum*, result unknown or indecisive)

So, with history stacked against the colonist, the chance for victory did not look good! However, they did have home field advantage and since we are only doing the highlights of history here, I will cut to the chase... The thirteen colonies, or what would become the United States of America won that war; granting them independence from Britain.

Chapter Two:
The Constitution

Freed from their oppressor, the colonists now had to self-govern. Their first attempt to organize and codify their system of government was called the Articles of Confederation. Eight years later, the Constitution was conceived, which gave the central government more powers to protect and serve the 13 colonies.

This new document was revolutionary, just like the Declaration, and quite a remarkable feat considering all the backward thinking that dominated this period of history. The framers of the Constitution knew they didn't want what they had before and wanted to protect what had developed over the last 150 years.

So they searched for something innovative and found inspiration in some fascinating places!

Below is a short history of some of the influences on the Constitution of the United States:

Source: https://www.ushistory.org/gov/2.asp (USHistory.org,, 2023)

Foundations of American Government

Democracy was not created in a heartbeat. In a world where people were ruled by monarchs from above, the idea of self-government is entirely alien. Democracy takes practice and wisdom from experience.

The American colonies began developing a democratic tradition during their earliest stages of development. Over 150 years later, the colonists believed their experience was great enough to refuse to recognize the British king. The first decade was rocky. The American Revolution and the domestic instability that followed prompted a call for a new type of government with a constitution to guarantee liberty. The constitution drafted in the early days of the independent American republic has endured longer than any in human history.

Where did this democratic tradition truly begin? The ideas and practices that led to the development of the American democratic republic owe a debt to the ancient civilizations of Greece and Rome, the Protestant Reformation, and Gutenberg's printing press. But the Enlightenment of 17th-century Europe had the most immediate impact on the framers of the United States Constitution.

Europeans of the 17th century no longer lived in the "darkness" of the Middle Ages. Ocean voyages had put them in touch with many world civilizations, and trade had created a prosperous middle class. The Protestant Reformation encouraged free thinkers to question the practices of the Catholic Church, and the printing press spread the new ideas relatively quickly and easily. The time was ripe for the *philosophes*, scholars who promoted democracy and justice through discussions of individual liberty and equality.

One of the first philosophes was Thomas Hobbes, an Englishman who concluded in his famous book, *Leviathan*, that people are incapable of ruling themselves, primarily because humans are naturally self-centered and quarrelsome and need the iron fist of a strong leader. Later philosophes, like Voltaire, Montesquieu, and Rousseau were more optimistic about democracy. Their ideas encouraged the questioning of absolute monarchs, like the Bourbon family that ruled France. Montesquieu suggested a separation of powers into branches of government not unlike the system Americans would later adopt. They found eager students who later became the founders of the American government.

The single most important influence that shaped the founding of the United States comes from John Locke, a 17th century Englishman who redefined the nature of government. Although he agreed with Hobbes regarding the self-interested nature of humans, he was much more optimistic about their ability to use reason to avoid tyranny. In his *Second Treatise of Government*, Locke identified the basis of a legitimate government. According to Locke, a ruler gains authority through the consent of the governed. The duty of that government is to protect the natural rights of the people, which Locke believed to include life, liberty, and property. If the government should fail to protect these rights, its citizens would have the right to overthrow that government. This idea deeply influenced Thomas Jefferson as he drafted the Declaration of Independence.

Ironically, the English political system provided the grist for the revolt of its own American colonies. For many centuries English monarchs had allowed restrictions to be placed on their ultimate power. The Magna Carta, written in 1215, established the kernel of limited government, or the belief that the monarch's rule was not absolute. Although the document only forced King John to consult nobles before he made arbitrary decisions like passing taxes, the Magna Carta provided the basis for the later development of Parliament. Over the years, representative government led by a Prime Minister came to control and eventually replace the king as the real source of power in Britain.

The Petition of Right (1628) extended the rights of "commoners" to have a voice in the government. The English Bill of Rights (1688) guaranteed free elections and rights for citizens accused of crime. Although King George III still had some real power in 1776, Britain was already well along on the path of democracy by that time.

The foundations of American government lie squarely in the 17th and 18th century European Enlightenment. The American founders were well versed in the writings of the philosophes, whose ideas influenced the shaping of the new country. Thomas Jefferson, George Washington, James Madison, and others took the brave steps of creating a government based on the Enlightenment values of liberty, equality, and a new form of justice. More than 200 years later, that government is still intact.

This short history of the influences of the Constitution from UShistory.org is fascinating in that it glosses over or ignores other important influences! And places the development of the US Constitution on the shoulders of the Europeans who came before them…

Interesting non-European influences include:

Source: https://www.pbs.org/native-america/blogs/native-voices/how-the-iroquois-great-law-of-peace-shaped-us-democracy/ (Hanson, T., 2018, 17 December)

How the Iroquois Great Law of Peace Shaped U.S. Democracy, by Terri Hansen

Much has been said about the inspiration of the ancient Iroquois "Great League of Peace" in planting the seeds that led to the formation of the United States of America and its representative democracy.

The Iroquois Confederacy, founded by the Great Peacemaker in 1142[1], is the oldest living participatory democracy on earth[2]. In 1988, the U.S. Senate paid tribute with a resolution[3] that said, "The confederation of the original 13 colonies into one republic was influenced by the political system developed by the Iroquois Confederacy, as were many of the democratic principles which were incorporated into the constitution itself."

The peoples of the Iroquois Confederacy, also known as the Six Nations, refer to themselves as the Haudenosaunee, (pronounced "hoo-dee-noh-SHAW-nee"). It means "peoples of the longhouse," and refers to their lengthy bark-covered longhouses that housed many families. Theirs was a sophisticated and thriving society of well over 5,000 people when the first European explorers encountered them in the early seventeenth century.

Graphic depiction longhouses in Haudenosaunee settlement. From Native America, Episode Two titled Nature to Nations.

The Iroquois Confederacy originally consisted of five separate nations – the Mohawks, who call themselves Kanienkehaka, or "people of the flint country," the Onondaga, "people of the hills," the Cayuga, "where they land the boats," the Oneida, "people of the standing stone," and the Seneca, "the people of the big hill" living in the northeast region of North America. The Tuscarora nation, "people of the shirt," migrated into Iroquois country in 1722.

"The Great Peacemaker[4] brought peace to the five nations," explains Oren Lyons in a 1991 interview with Bill Moyers. Lyons is the faith keeper of the Turtle Clan of the Seneca Nations, and a member of both the Onondaga and Seneca nations of the Iroquois Confederacy.

At that time, the nations of the Iroquois had been enmeshed in continuous inter-tribal conflicts. The cost of war was high and had weakened their societies. The Great Peacemaker and the wise Hiawatha, chief of the Onondaga tribe, contemplated how best to bring peace between the nations. They traveled to each of the five nations to share their ideas for peace.

A council meeting was called, and Hiawatha presented the Great Law of Peace. It united the five nations into a League of Nations, or the Iroquois Confederacy, and became the basis for the Iroquois Confederacy Constitution[5].

"Each nation maintained its own leadership, but they all agreed that common causes would be decided in the Grand Council of Chiefs," Lyons said[6]. "The concept was based on peace and consensus rather than fighting."

Their constitution, recorded and kept alive on a two row wampum belt[7], held many concepts familiar to United States citizens today.

Iroquois Confederacy and the Great Law of Peace	United States Constitution
Restricts members from holding more than one office in the Confederacy.	**Article I, Section 6, Clause 2**, also known as the **Ineligibility Clause** or the **Emoluments Clause** bars members of serving members of Congress from holding offices established by the federal government, while also baring members of the executive branch or judicial branch from serving in the U.S. House or Senate.
Outlines processes to remove leaders within the Confederacy	**Article II, Section 4** reads "The President, Vice President and all civil Officers of the United States shall be removed from Office on Impeachment for, and the conviction of, Treason, Bribery, or other High Crimes and Misdemeanors."
Designates two branches of legislature with procedures for passing laws	**Article I, Section 1**, or the **Vesting Clauses**, read "All legislative Powers herein granted shall be vested in a Congress of the United States, which shall consist of a Senate and House of Representatives." It goes on to outline their legislative powers.
Delineates who has the power to declare war	**Article I, Section 8**, Clause 11, also known as the **War Powers Clause**, gives Congress the power, "To declare War, grant Letters of Marque and Reprisal, and make Rules concerning Captures on Land and Water;"
Creates a balance of power between the Iroquois Confederacy and individual tribes	The differing duties assigned to the three branches of the U.S. Government: Legislative (Congress), Executive (President), and Judicial (Supreme Court) act to balance and separate power in government.

In 1744, the Onondaga leader Canassatego gave a speech urging the contentious 13 colonies to unite, as the Iroquois had at the signing of the Treaty of Lancaster. This cultural exchange inspired the English colonist Benjamin Franklin to print Canassatego's speech.

"We heartily recommend Union and a good Agreement between you our Brethren," Canassatego had said. "Never disagree, but preserve a strict Friendship for one another, and thereby you, as well as we, will become the stronger. Our wise Forefathers established Union and Amity between the Five Nations; this has made us formidable; this has given us great Weight and Authority with our neighboring Nations. We are a powerful Confederacy; and, by your observing the same Methods our wise Forefathers have taken, you will acquire fresh Strength and Power; therefore whatever befalls you, never fall out one with another."

He used a metaphor that many arrows cannot be broken as easily as one. This inspired the bundle of 13 arrows held by an eagle in the Great Seal of the United States.

Franklin referenced the Iroquois model as he presented his Plan of Union[8] at the Albany Congress in 1754, attended by representatives of the Iroquois and the seven colonies. He invited the Great Council members of the Iroquois to address the Continental Congress in 1776.

The Native American model of governance that is fair and will always meet the needs of the seventh generation to come is taken from the Iroquois Confederacy. The seventh generation principle dictates that decisions that are made today should lead to sustainability for seven generations into the future. And Indigenous nations in North America were and are for the most part organized by democratic principles that focus on the creation of strong kinship bonds that promote leadership in which honor is not earned by material gain but by service to others.

In the plains, there was great honor in giving your horses to the poorest members of the tribe. The potlatch still practiced in the Pacific Northwest is another example of voluntarily redistributing wealth to those who have the least.

And the Iroquois? They continue to live under their own constitution and government. Their example sparked the spread of democratic institutions across the world, as explored in "Nature to Nations," episode Two of this PBS series Native America.

Terri Hansen is an independent journalist with bylines in Indian Country Today, YES! Magazine, The Revelator, Pacific Standard, VICE, Earth Island Journal and others. She lives mainly in the wilds of the Pacific Northwest. She is a Winnebago tribal member and an unenrolled Cherokee. She has reported tribal issues since 1990, and global indigenous issues since 2009. Chat with her on Twitter @TerriHansen

---

So with the need for a stronger central government that could hold the 13 colonies together, the men of influence at this time, the Founders, drafted what would become the Constitution of the United States. They knew they didn't want a monarchy, and an oligarchy wasn't any better. The lessons learned from being in the new world and their government being half a world away encouraged them to believe that government can be run by the people being governed. This type of government is messy, chaotic, and can easily fall off the tracks, but they were determined to figure it out!

There were many issues to resolve and many ideologies and freedoms that they wanted to protect. So with the weight of the future of the United States at stake, these Founders, tragically flawed and unknowingly part of the problems we now face today, gathered together for an entire summer in 1787 and created a document that has guided the United States of America for over 230 years.

Sometimes, it seems to me that the constitution was created in a vacuum. Intended for everyone but only applied to the European newcomers. Perhaps, when it was written they all just assumed it only applied to white males, so there was no need to include that point, or they intentionally omitted that inclusion hoping that one day, it would be applied to every citizen. Either way, we have a constitution that, as written, applies to every citizen.

What is the Constitution, and what does it do?

Source: https://constitutioncenter.org/education/constitution-faqs (National Constitution Center, n.d.)

What is the U.S. Constitution?

from the National Constitution Center

The U.S. Constitution is the fundamental framework of America's system of government.

The Constitution:

- Creates a government that puts the power in the hands of the people
- Separates the powers of government into three branches: the legislative branch, which makes the laws; the executive branch, which executes the laws; and the judicial branch, which interprets the laws
- Sets up a system of checks and balances that ensures no one branch has too much power
- Divides power between the states and the federal government
- Describes the purposes and duties of the government
- Defines the scope and limit of government power
- Prescribes the system for electing representatives
- Establishes the process for the document's ratification and amendment
- Outlines many rights and freedoms of the people

Why is the Constitution so important?

In *The Constitution: The Essential User's Guide*, the Honorable Sandra Day O'Connor, former associate justice of the Supreme Court, put it this way:

"What makes the Constitution worthy of our commitment? First and foremost, the answer is our freedom. It is, quite simply, the most powerful vision of freedom ever expressed. It's also the world's shortest and oldest national constitution, neither so rigid as to be stifling, nor so malleable as to be devoid of meaning.

Our Constitution has been an inspiration that changed the trajectory of world history for the perpetual benefit of mankind. In 1787, no country in the world had ever allowed its citizens to select their own form of government, much less to select a democratic government. What was revolutionary when it was written, and what continues to inspire the world today, is that the Constitution put governance in the hands of the people."

So without further ado…

Source: https://www.archives.gov/founding-docs/constitution-transcript (National Archives, n.d.)

The Constitution of the United States.

We the People of the United States, in Order to form a more perfect Union, establish Justice, insure domestic Tranquility, provide for the common defence, promote the general Welfare, and secure the Blessings of Liberty to ourselves and our Posterity, do ordain and establish this Constitution for the United States of America.

Article. 1.

Section 1: Congress

All legislative Powers herein granted shall be vested in a Congress of the United States, which shall consist of a Senate and House of Representatives.

Section 2: The House of Representatives

The House of Representatives shall be composed of Members chosen every second Year by the People of the several States, and the Electors in each State shall have the Qualifications requisite for Electors of the most numerous Branch of the State Legislature.

No Person shall be a Representative who shall not have attained to the Age of twenty five Years, and been seven Years a Citizen of the United States, and who shall not, when elected, be an Inhabitant of that State in which he shall be chosen.

Representatives and direct Taxes shall be apportioned among the several States which may be included within this Union, according to their respective Numbers, which shall be determined by adding to the whole Number of free Persons, including those bound to Service for a Term of Years, and excluding Indians not taxed, three fifths of all other Persons.

The actual Enumeration shall be made within three Years after the first Meeting of the Congress of the United States, and within every subsequent Term of ten Years, in such Manner as they shall by Law direct. The number of Representatives shall not exceed one for every thirty Thousand, but each State shall have at Least one Representative; and until such enumeration shall be made, the State of New Hampshire shall be entitled to chuse three, Massachusetts eight, Rhode-Island and Providence Plantations one, Connecticut five, New-York six, New Jersey four, Pennsylvania eight, Delaware one, Maryland six, Virginia ten, North Carolina five, South Carolina five, and Georgia three.

When vacancies happen in the Representation from any State, the Executive Authority thereof shall issue Writs of Election to fill such Vacancies.

The House of Representatives shall chuse their Speaker and other Officers; and shall have the sole Power of Impeachment.

Section 3: The Senate

The Senate of the United States shall be composed of two Senators from each State, chosen by the Legislature thereof, for six Years; and each Senator shall have one Vote.

Immediately after they shall be assembled in Consequence of the first Election, they shall be divided as equally as may be into three Classes. The Seats of the Senators of the first Class shall be vacated at the Expiration of the second Year, of the second Class at the Expiration of the fourth Year, and of the third Class at the Expiration of the sixth Year, so that one third may be chosen every second Year; and if Vacancies happen by Resignation, or otherwise, during the Recess of the Legislature of any State, the Executive thereof may make temporary Appointments until the next Meeting of the Legislature, which shall then fill such Vacancies.

No Person shall be a Senator who shall not have attained to the Age of thirty Years, and been nine Years a Citizen of the United States, and who shall not, when elected, be an Inhabitant of that State for which he shall be chosen.

The Vice President of the United States shall be President of the Senate, but shall have no Vote, unless they be equally divided.

The Senate shall chuse their other Officers, and also a President pro tempore, in the Absence of the Vice President, or when he shall exercise the Office of President of the United States.

The Senate shall have the sole Power to try all Impeachments. When sitting for that Purpose, they shall be on Oath or Affirmation. When the President of the United States is tried, the Chief Justice shall preside: And no Person shall be convicted without the Concurrence of two thirds of the Members present.

Judgment in Cases of Impeachment shall not extend further than to removal from Office, and disqualification to hold and enjoy any Office of honor, Trust or Profit under the United States: but the Party convicted shall nevertheless be liable and subject to Indictment, Trial, Judgment and Punishment, according to Law.

Section 4: Elections

The Times, Places and Manner of holding Elections for Senators and Representatives, shall be prescribed in each State by the Legislature thereof; but the Congress may at any time by Law make or alter such Regulations, except as to the Places of chusing Senators.

The Congress shall assemble at least once in every Year, and such Meeting shall be on the first Monday in December, unless they shall by Law appoint a different Day.

Section 5: Powers and Duties of Congress

Each House shall be the Judge of the Elections, Returns and Qualifications of its own Members, and a Majority of each shall constitute a Quorum to do Business; but a smaller Number may adjourn from day to day, and may be authorized to compel the Attendance of absent Members, in such Manner, and under such Penalties as each House may provide.

Each House may determine the Rules of its Proceedings, punish its Members for disorderly Behaviour, and, with the Concurrence of two thirds, expel a Member.

Each House shall keep a Journal of its Proceedings, and from time to time publish the same, excepting such Parts as may in their Judgment require Secrecy; and the Yeas and Nays of the Members of either House on any question shall, at the Desire of one fifth of those Present, be entered on the Journal.

Neither House, during the Session of Congress, shall, without the Consent of the other, adjourn for more than three days, nor to any other Place than that in which the two Houses shall be sitting.

Section 6: Rights and Disabilities of Members

The Senators and Representatives shall receive a Compensation for their Services, to be ascertained by Law, and paid out of the Treasury of the United States. They shall in all Cases, except Treason, Felony and Breach of the Peace, be privileged from Arrest during their Attendance at the Session of their respective Houses, and in going to and returning from the same; and for any Speech or Debate in either House, they shall not be questioned in any other Place.

No Senator or Representative shall, during the Time for which he was elected, be appointed to any civil Office under the Authority of the United States, which shall have been created, or the Emoluments whereof shall have been encreased during such time; and no Person holding any Office under the United States, shall be a Member of either House during his Continuance in Office.

Section 7: Legislative Process

All Bills for raising Revenue shall originate in the House of Representatives; but the Senate may propose or concur with Amendments as on other Bills.

Every Bill which shall have passed the House of Representatives and the Senate, shall, before it become a Law, be presented to the President of the United States; If he approve he shall sign it, but if not he shall return it, with his Objections to that House in which it shall have originated, who shall enter the Objections at large on their Journal, and proceed to reconsider it. If after such Reconsideration two thirds of that House shall agree to pass the Bill, it shall be sent, together with the Objections, to the other House, by which it shall likewise be reconsidered, and if approved by two thirds of that House, it shall become a Law. But in all such Cases the Votes of both Houses shall be determined by Yeas and Nays, and the Names of the Persons voting for and against the Bill shall be entered on the Journal of each House respectively. If any Bill shall not be returned by the President within ten Days (Sundays excepted) after it shall have been presented to him, the Same shall be a Law, in like Manner as if he had signed it, unless the Congress by their Adjournment prevent its Return, in which Case it shall not be a Law.

Every Order, Resolution, or Vote to which the Concurrence of the Senate and House of Representatives may be necessary (except on a question of Adjournment) shall be presented to the President of the United States; and before the Same shall take Effect, shall be approved by him, or being disapproved by him, shall be repassed by two thirds of the Senate and House of Representatives, according to the Rules and Limitations prescribed in the Case of a Bill.

Section 8: Powers of Congress

The Congress shall have Power To lay and collect Taxes, Duties, Imposts and Excises, to pay the Debts and provide for the common Defence and general Welfare of the United States; but all Duties, Imposts and Excises shall be uniform throughout the United States;

To borrow Money on the credit of the United States;

To regulate Commerce with foreign Nations, and among the several States, and with the Indian Tribes;

To establish a uniform Rule of Naturalization, and uniform Laws on the subject of Bankruptcies throughout the United States;

To coin Money, regulate the Value thereof, and of foreign Coin, and fix the Standard of Weights and Measures;

To provide for the Punishment of counterfeiting the Securities and current Coin of the United States;

To establish Post Offices and post Roads;

To promote the Progress of Science and useful Arts, by securing for limited Times to Authors and Inventors the exclusive Right to their respective Writings and Discoveries;

To constitute Tribunals inferior to the supreme Court;

To define and punish Piracies and Felonies committed on the high Seas, and Offenses against the Law of Nations;

To declare War, grant Letters of Marque and Reprisal, and make Rules concerning Captures on Land and Water;

To raise and support Armies, but no Appropriation of Money to that Use shall be for a longer Term than two Years;

To provide and maintain a Navy;

To make Rules for the Government and Regulation of the land and naval Forces;

To provide for calling forth the Militia to execute the Laws of the Union, suppress Insurrections and repel Invasions;

To provide for organizing, arming, and disciplining, the Militia, and for governing such Part of them as may be employed in the Service of the United States, reserving to the States respectively, the Appointment of the Officers, and the Authority of training the Militia according to the discipline prescribed by Congress;

To exercise exclusive Legislation in all Cases whatsoever, over such District (not exceeding ten Miles square) as may, by Cession of particular States, and the Acceptance of Congress, become the Seat of the Government of the United States, and to exercise like Authority over all Places purchased by the Consent of the Legislature of the State in which the Same shall be, for the Erection of Forts, Magazines, Arsenals, dock-Yards and other needful Buildings;-And

To make all Laws which shall be necessary and proper for carrying into Execution the foregoing Powers, and all other Powers vested by this Constitution in the Government of the United States, or in any Department or Officer thereof.

Section 9: Powers Denied Congress

The Migration or Importation of such Persons as any of the States now existing shall think proper to admit, shall not be prohibited by the Congress prior to the Year one thousand eight hundred and eight, but a Tax or duty may be imposed on such Importation, not exceeding ten dollars for each Person.

The Privilege of the Writ of Habeas Corpus shall not be suspended, unless when in Cases of Rebellion or Invasion the public Safety may require it.

No Bill of Attainder or ex post facto Law shall be passed.

No Capitation, or other direct, Tax shall be laid, unless in Proportion to the Census or Enumeration herein before directed to be taken.

No Tax or Duty shall be laid on Articles exported from any State.

No Preference shall be given by any Regulation of Commerce or Revenue to the Ports of one State over those of another: nor shall Vessels bound to, or from, one State, be obliged to enter, clear, or pay Duties in another.

No Money shall be drawn from the Treasury, but in Consequence of Appropriations made by Law; and a regular Statement and Account of the Receipts and Expenditures of all public Money shall be published from time to time.

No Title of Nobility shall be granted by the United States: And no Person holding any Office of Profit or Trust under them, shall, without the Consent of the Congress, accept of any present, Emolument, Office, or Title, of any kind whatever, from any King, Prince, or foreign State.

Section 10: Powers Denied to the States

No State shall enter into any Treaty, Alliance, or Confederation; grant Letters of Marque and Reprisal; coin Money; emit Bills of Credit; make any Thing but gold and silver Coin a Tender in Payment of Debts; pass any Bill of Attainder, ex post facto Law, or Law impairing the Obligation of Contracts, or grant any Title of Nobility.

No State shall, without the Consent of the Congress, lay any Imposts or Duties on Imports or Exports, except what may be absolutely necessary for executing it's inspection Laws: and the net Produce of all Duties and Imposts, laid by any State on Imports or Exports, shall be for the Use of the Treasury of the United States; and all such Laws shall be subject to the Revision and Control of the Congress.

No State shall, without the Consent of Congress, lay any Duty of Tonnage, keep Troops, or Ships of War in time of Peace, enter into any Agreement or Compact with another State, or with a foreign Power, or engage in War, unless actually invaded, or in such imminent Danger as will not admit of delay.

Article II

Section 1

The executive Power shall be vested in a President of the United States of America.

He shall hold his Office during the Term of four Years, and, together with the Vice President, chosen for the same Term, be elected, as follows:

Each State shall appoint, in such Manner as the Legislature thereof may direct, a Number of Electors, equal to the whole Number of Senators and Representatives to which the State may be entitled in the Congress: but no Senator or Representative, or Person holding an Office of Trust or Profit under the United States, shall be appointed an Elector.

The Electors shall meet In their respective States, and vote by Ballot for two Persons, of whom one at least shall not be an Inhabitant of the same State with themselves. And they shall make a List of all the Persons voted for, and of the Number of Votes for each; which List they shall sign and certify, and transmit sealed to the Seat of the Government of the United States, directed to the President of the Senate. The President of the Senate shall, in the Presence of the Senate and House of Representatives, open all the Certificates, and the Votes shall then be counted. The Person having the greatest Number of Votes shall be the President, if such Number be a Majority of the whole Number of Electors appointed; and if there be more than one who have such Majority, and have an equal Number of Votes, then the House of Representatives shall immediately chuse by Ballot one of them for President; and if no Person have a Majority, then from the five highest on the List the said House shall in like Manner chuse the President. But in chusing the President, the Votes shall be taken by States, the Representation from each State having one Vote; A quorum for this Purpose shall consist of a Member or Members from two thirds of the States, and a Majority of all the States shall be necessary to a Choice. In every Case, after the Choice of the President, the Person having the greatest Number of Votes of the Electors shall be the Vice President. But if there should remain two or more who have equal Votes, the Senate shall chuse from them by Ballot the Vice President.

The Congress may determine the Time of chusing the Electors, and the Day on which they shall give their Votes; which Day shall be the same throughout the United States.

No Person except a natural born Citizen, or a Citizen of the United States, at the time of the Adoption of this Constitution, shall be eligible to the Office of President; neither shall any person be eligible to that Office who shall not have attained to the Age of thirty five Years, and been fourteen Years a Resident within the United States.

In Case of the Removal of the President from Office, or of his Death, Resignation, or Inability to discharge the Powers and Duties of the said Office, the Same shall devolve on the Vice President, and the Congress may by Law provide for the Case of Removal, Death, Resignation or Inability, both of the President and Vice President, declaring what Officer shall then act as President, and such Officer shall act accordingly, until the Disability be removed, or a President shall be elected.

The President shall, at stated Times, receive for his Services, a Compensation, which shall neither be increased nor diminished during the Period for which he shall have been elected, and he shall not receive within that Period any other Emolument from the United States, or any of them.

Before he enter on the Execution of his Office, he shall take the following Oath or Affirmation:--"I do solemnly swear (or affirm) that I will faithfully execute the Office of President of the United States, and will to the best of my Ability, preserve, protect and defend the Constitution of the United States."

Section 2

The President shall be Commander in Chief of the Army and Navy of the United States, and of the Militia of the several States, when called into the actual Service of the United States; he may require the Opinion, in writing, of the principal Officer in each of the executive Departments, upon any Subject relating to the Duties of their respective Offices, and he shall have Power to grant Reprieves and Pardons for Offenses against the United States, except in Cases of Impeachment.

He shall have Power, by and with the Advice and Consent of the Senate, to make Treaties, provided two thirds of the Senators present concur; and he shall nominate, and by and with the Advice and Consent of the Senate, shall appoint Ambassadors, other public Ministers and Consuls, Judges of the supreme Court, and all other Officers of the United States, whose Appointments are not herein otherwise provided for, and which shall be established by Law: but the Congress may by Law vest the Appointment of such inferior Officers, as they think proper, in the President alone, in the Courts of Law, or in the Heads of Departments.

The President shall have Power to fill up all Vacancies that may happen during the Recess of the Senate, by granting Commissions which shall expire at the End of their next Session.

Section 3

He shall from time to time give to the Congress Information of the State of the Union, and recommend to their Consideration such Measures as he shall judge necessary and expedient; he may, on extraordinary Occasions, convene both Houses, or either of them, and in Case of Disagreement between them, with Respect to the Time of Adjournment, he may adjourn them to such Time as he shall think proper; he shall receive Ambassadors and other public Ministers; he shall take Care that the Laws be faithfully executed, and shall Commission all the Officers of the United States.

Section 4

The President, Vice President and all civil Officers of the United States, shall be removed from Office on Impeachment for, and Conviction of, Treason, Bribery, or other high Crimes and Misdemeanors.

Article III

Section 1

The judicial Power of the United States, shall be vested in one supreme Court, and in such inferior Courts as the Congress may from time to time ordain and establish. The Judges, both of the supreme and inferior Courts, shall hold their Offices during good Behaviour, and shall, at stated Times, receive for their Services, a Compensation, which shall not be diminished during their Continuance in Office.

Section 2

The judicial Power shall extend to all Cases, in Law and Equity, arising under this Constitution, the Laws of the United States, and Treaties made, or which shall be made, under their Authority;--to all Cases affecting Ambassadors, other public Ministers and Consuls;--to all Cases of admiralty and maritime Jurisdiction;--to Controversies to which the United States shall be a Party;--to Controversies between two or more States;--between a State and Citizens of another State;--between Citizens of different States;--between Citizens of the same State claiming Lands under Grants of different States, and between a State, or the Citizens thereof, and foreign States, Citizens or Subjects.

In all Cases affecting Ambassadors, other public Ministers and Consuls, and those in which a State shall be Party, the supreme Court shall have original Jurisdiction. In all the other Cases before mentioned, the supreme Court shall have appellate Jurisdiction, both as to Law and Fact, with such Exceptions, and under such Regulations as the Congress shall make.

The Trial of all Crimes, except in Cases of Impeachment; shall be by Jury; and such Trial shall be held in the State where the said Crimes shall have been committed; but when not committed within any State, the Trial shall be at such Place or Places as the Congress may by Law have directed.

Section 3

Treason against the United States, shall consist only in levying War against them, or in adhering to their Enemies, giving them Aid and Comfort. No Person shall be convicted of Treason unless on the Testimony of two Witnesses to the same overt Act, or on Confession in open Court.

The Congress shall have Power to declare the Punishment of Treason, but no Attainder of Treason shall work Corruption of Blood, or Forfeiture except during the Life of the Person attainted.

Article IV

Section 1

Full Faith and Credit shall be given in each State to the public Acts, Records, and judicial Proceedings of every other State. And the Congress may by general Laws prescribe the Manner in which such Acts, Records and Proceedings shall be proved, and the Effect thereof.

Section 2

The Citizens of each State shall be entitled to all Privileges and Immunities of Citizens in the several States.

A Person charged in any State with Treason, Felony, or other Crime, who shall flee from Justice, and be found in another State, shall on Demand of the executive Authority of the State from which he fled, be delivered up, to be removed to the State having Jurisdiction of the Crime.

No Person held to Service or Labour in one State, under the Laws thereof, escaping into another, shall, in Consequence of any Law or Regulation therein, be discharged from such Service or Labour, but shall be delivered up on Claim of the Party to whom such Service or Labour may be due.

Section 3

New States may be admitted by the Congress into this Union; but no new State shall be formed or erected within the Jurisdiction of any other State; nor any State be formed by the Junction of two or more States, or Parts of States, without the Consent of the Legislatures of the States concerned as well as of the Congress.

The Congress shall have Power to dispose of and make all needful Rules and Regulations respecting the Territory or other Property belonging to the United States; and nothing in this Constitution shall be so construed as to Prejudice any Claims of the United States, or of any particular State.

Section 4

The United States shall guarantee to every State in this Union a Republican Form of Government, and shall protect each of them against Invasion; and on Application of the Legislature, or of the Executive (when the Legislature cannot be convened) against domestic Violence.

Article V

The Congress, whenever two thirds of both Houses shall deem it necessary, shall propose Amendments to this Constitution, or, on the Application of the Legislatures of two thirds of the several States, shall call a Convention for proposing Amendments, which, in either Case, shall be valid to all Intents and Purposes, as Part of this Constitution, when ratified by the Legislatures of three fourths of the several States, or by Conventions in three fourths thereof, as the one or the other Mode of Ratification may be proposed by the Congress; Provided that no Amendment which may be made prior to the Year One thousand eight hundred and eight shall in any Manner affect the first and fourth Clauses in the Ninth Section of the first Article; and that no State, without its Consent, shall be deprived of its equal Suffrage in the Senate.

Article VI

All Debts contracted and Engagements entered into, before the Adoption of this Constitution, shall be as valid against the United States under this Constitution, as under the Confederation.

This Constitution, and the Laws of the United States which shall be made in Pursuance thereof; and all Treaties made, or which shall be made, under the Authority of the United States, shall be the supreme Law of the Land; and the Judges in every State shall be bound thereby, any Thing in the Constitution or Laws of any State to the Contrary notwithstanding.

The Senators and Representatives before mentioned, and the Members of the several State Legislatures, and all executive and judicial Officers, both of the United States and of the several States, shall be bound by Oath or Affirmation, to support this Constitution; but no religious Test shall ever be required as a Qualification to any Office or public Trust under the United States.

Article VII

The Ratification of the Conventions of nine States, shall be sufficient for the Establishment of this Constitution between the States so ratifying the Same.

The critical part of the Constitution, in terms of protections afforded its citizens, is the Preamble.

The Preamble sets out the intention of the Constitution.

For a complete explanation of the Preamble, see the following instructional slide:

Source: https://www.independencemuseum.org/lessons/we-the-people/ (American Independence Museum, n.d.)

So what does the following mean?

We the People of the United States, in Order to form a more perfect Union, establish Justice, insure domestic Tranquility, provide for the common defence, promote the general Welfare, and secure the Blessings of Liberty to ourselves and our Posterity, do ordain and establish this Constitution for the United States of America.

- **Establish Justice:** ensures that the new government would treat its citizens fairly, and to avoid the unfair conditions created by the King of England prior to the American Revolution.

55

- **Insure Domestic Tranquility:** referred to the new government's commitment to keep peace within America's borders.
- **Provide For The Common Defense:** to keep the states safe from the threat of foreign nations (other countries) by ensuring there was a national military (army, navy, etc.).
- **Promote The General Welfare:** shows that the new government was concerned with making sure its citizens had their basic needs met (like ensuring people had adequate food, housing, and education).
- **Secure The Blessings Of Liberty To Ourselves And Our Posterity:** a promise to promote a free and fair system of government that would protect citizens' freedoms, along with those of future generations.
- **Do Ordain And Establish This Constitution For The United States Of America:** We declare this document to be the new laws of our new country, the United States of America.

I love the first line of the Preamble, "We the People of the United States." This singular phrase brings every citizen together as one entity. And as one entity, forming a more perfect union becomes a possibility. No government will be perfect, but if every citizen has a voice and is treated equally, there is a chance for a more perfect union, just like the old saying, "United we stand, divided we fall."

The whole Preamble focuses the government's attention squarely on the care and protection of the citizens of the United States. The same citizens that consented to a government in the first place.

Not once does the Constitution mention the care or protection of corporations.

The last document, in the Charters of Freedom, is called the Bill of Rights, and it is the first ten amendments that focus on the rights of the governed. Rights that were routinely not observed by the British Crown.

Before the constitution would be considered for ratification, the people wanted to be confident that their government would treat them better than their former oppressor.

Below is an article about the history of the Bill of Rights and what it does for citizens of the United States.

Source: https://www.aclu.org/other/bill-rights-brief-history (American Civil Liberties Union, 2023)

The Bill of Rights: A Brief History

"[A] bill of rights is what the people are entitled to against every government on earth, general or particular, and what no just government should refuse." –- Thomas Jefferson, December 20, 1787

In the summer of 1787, delegates from the 13 states convened in Philadelphia and drafted a remarkable blueprint for self-government—the Constitution of the United States. The first draft set up a system of checks and balances that included a strong executive branch, a representative legislature and a federal judiciary.

The Constitution was remarkable, but deeply flawed. For one thing, it did not include a specific declaration—or bill—of individual rights. It specified what the government could do but did not say what it could not do. For another, it did not apply to everyone. The "consent of the governed" meant propertied white men only.

The absence of a "bill of rights" turned out to be an obstacle to the Constitution's ratification by the states. It would take four more years of intense debate before the new government's form would be resolved. The Federalists opposed including a bill of rights on the ground that it was unnecessary. The Anti-Federalists, who were afraid of a strong centralized government, refused to support the Constitution without one.

In the end, popular sentiment was decisive. Recently freed from the despotic English monarchy, the American people wanted strong guarantees that the new government would not trample upon their newly won freedoms of speech, press and religion, nor upon their right to be free from warrantless searches and seizures. So, the Constitution's framers heeded Thomas Jefferson who argued: "A bill of rights is what the people are entitled to against every government on earth, general or particular, and what no just government should refuse, or rest on inference."

The American Bill of Rights, inspired by Jefferson and drafted by James Madison, was adopted, and in 1791 the Constitution's first ten amendments became the law of the land.

Limited Government

Early American mistrust of government power came from the colonial experience itself. Most historians believe that the pivotal event was the Stamp Act, passed by the English Parliament in 1765. Taxes were imposed on every legal and business document. Newspapers, books and pamphlets were also taxed. Even more than the taxes themselves, the Americans resented the fact that they were imposed by a distant government in which they were not represented. And they were further enraged by the ways in which the Stamp Act was enforced.

Armed with "writs of assistance" issued by Parliament, British customs inspectors entered people's homes even if they had no evidence of a Stamp Act violation, and ransacked the people's belongings in search of contraband. The colonialists came to hate these "warrantless" searches and they became a rallying point for opposition to British rule.

From these experiences came a uniquely American view of power and liberty as natural enemies. The nation's founders believed that containing the government's power and protecting liberty was their most important task, and declared a new purpose for government: the protection of individual rights.

The protection of rights was not the government's only purpose. It was still expected to protect the community against foreign and domestic threats, to ensure economic growth, and to conduct foreign affairs. It was not, however, the government's job to tell people how to live their lives, what religion to believe in, or what to write about in a pamphlet or newspaper. In this sense, the idea of individual rights is the oldest and most traditional of American values.

"Certain Unalienable Rights"

Democracy and liberty are often thought to be the same thing, but they are not.

Democracy means that people ought to be able to vote for public officials in fair elections, and make most political decisions by majority rule.

Liberty, on the other hand, means that even in a democracy, individuals have rights that no majority should be able to take away.

The rights that the Constitution's framers wanted to protect from government abuse were referred to in the Declaration of Independence as "unalienable rights." They were also called "natural" rights, and to James Madison, they were "the great rights of mankind." Although it is commonly thought that we are entitled to free speech because the First Amendment gives it to us, this country's original citizens believed that as human beings, they were entitled to free speech, and they invented the First Amendment in order to protect it. The entire Bill of

58

Rights was created to protect rights the original citizens believed were naturally theirs, including:

- **Freedom of Religion**
    - The right to exercise one's own religion, or no religion, free from any government influence or compulsion.
- **Freedom of Speech, Press, Petition, and Assembly**
    - Even unpopular expression is protected from government suppression or censorship.
- **Privacy**
    - The right to be free of unwarranted and unwanted government intrusion into one's personal and private affairs, papers, and possessions.
- **Due Process of Law**
    - The right to be treated fairly by the government whenever the loss of liberty or property is at stake.
- **Equality Before the Law**
    - The right to be treated equally before the law, regardless of social status.

"An Impenetrable Bulwark" of Liberty

The Bill of Rights established soaring principles that guaranteed the most fundamental rights in very general terms. But from the beginning, real live cases arose that raised difficult questions about how, and even if, the Bill of Rights would be applied. Before the paper rights could become actual rights, someone had to interpret what the language of the Bill of Rights meant in specific situations. Who would be the final arbiter of how the Constitution should be applied?

At first, the answer was unclear. Thomas Jefferson thought that the federal judiciary should have that power; James Madison agreed that a system of independent courts would be "an impenetrable bulwark" of liberty. But the Constitution did not make this explicit, and the issue would not be resolved until 1803. That year, for the first time, the U.S. Supreme Court struck down an act of Congress as unconstitutional in a case called *Marbury v. Madison*. Although the facts of this case were fairly mundane (a dispute over the Secretary of State's refusal to commission four judges appointed by the Senate), the principle it established - that the Supreme Court had the power to nullify acts of Congress that violated the Constitution - turned out to be the key to the development and protection of most of the rights Americans enjoy today. According to one eminent legal scholar, the independent judiciary was "America's most distinctive contribution to constitutionalism."

Cases or Controversies

The judicial branch of the new government was different from the legislative and executive branches in one very important respect: the courts did not have the power to initiate action by themselves. Congress could pass laws and the President could issue executive orders, but courts could not review these actions on their own initiative. Courts had to wait until a dispute—a "case or controversy"—broke out between real people who had something to gain or lose by the outcome. And as it turned out, the people whose rights were most vulnerable to governmental abuse had least capacity to sue.

Thus, although the power of judicial review was established in 1803, more than a century would pass before the Supreme Court even had many opportunities to protect individual rights. For 130 years after ratification, the most notable thing about the Bill of Rights was its almost total lack of implementation by the courts. By the beginning of the 20th century, racial segregation was legal and pervaded all aspects of American society. Sex discrimination was firmly institutionalized and workers were arrested for labor union activities. Legal immigrants were deported for their political views, the police used physical coercion to extract confessions from criminal suspects, and members of minority religions were victims of persecution. As late as 1920, the U.S. Supreme Court had never once struck down any law or governmental action on First Amendment grounds.

The most common constitutional violations went unchallenged because the people whose rights were most often denied were precisely those members of society who were least aware of their rights and least able to afford a lawyer. They had no access to those impenetrable bulwarks of liberty - the courts. The Bill of Rights was like an engine no one knew how to start.

In the Public Interest

In 1920, a small group of visionaries came together to discuss how to start the engine. Led by Roger Baldwin, a social worker and labor activist, the group included Crystal Eastman, Albert DeSilver, Jane Addams, Felix Frankfurter, Helen Keller and Arthur Garfield Hayes. They formed the American Civil Liberties Union (ACLU) and dedicated themselves to holding the government to the Bill of Rights' promises.

The ACLU, the NAACP, founded in 1909, and labor unions, whose very right to exist had not yet been recognized by the courts, began to challenge constitutional violations in court on behalf of those who had been

60

previously shut out. This was the beginning of what has come to be known as public interest law. They provided the missing ingredient that made our constitutional system and Bill of Rights finally work.

Although they had few early victories, these organizations began to create a body of law that made First Amendment freedoms, privacy rights, and the principles of equality and fundamental fairness come alive. Gradually, the Bill of Rights was transformed from a "parchment barrier" to a protective wall that increasingly shielded each individual's unalienable rights from the reach of government.

Enormous progress was made between 1954 and 1973, when many rights long dormant became enforceable. Today, those achievements are being heavily challenged by a movement dedicated to rolling back the reach and effectiveness of the Bill of Rights and to undermining the independence of our courts.

The development of the Bill of Rights was a pivotal event in the long story of liberty, but it is a story that is still unfolding.

Rights, But Not for Everyone

The Bill of Rights seemed to be written in broad language that excluded no one, but in fact, it was not intended to protect all the people - whole groups were left out. Women were second-class citizens, essentially the property of their husbands, unable even to vote until 1920, when the 19th Amendment was passed and ratified.

Native Americans were entirely outside the constitutional system, defined as an alien people in their own land. They were governed not by ordinary American laws, but by federal treaties and statutes that stripped tribes of most of their land and much of their autonomy. The Bill of Rights was in force for nearly 135 years before Congress granted Native Americans U.S. citizenship.

And it was well understood that there was a "race exception" to the Constitution. Slavery was this country's original sin. For the first 78 years after it was ratified, the Constitution protected slavery and legalized racial subordination. Instead of constitutional rights, slaves were governed by "slave codes" that controlled every aspect of their lives. They had no access to the rule of law: they could not go to court, make contracts, or own any property. They could be whipped, branded, imprisoned without trial, and hanged. In short, as one infamous Supreme Court opinion declared: "Blacks had no rights which the white man was bound to respect."

It would take years of struggle and a bloody civil war before additional amendments to the Constitution were passed, giving slaves and their descendants the full rights of citizenship - at least on paper:

- The 13th Amendment abolished slavery;
- The 14th Amendment guaranteed to African Americans the right of due process and equal protection of the law;
- The 15th Amendment gave them the right to vote;

But it would take a century more of struggle before these rights were effectively enforced.

This brief history helps to elucidate the intricacies of the Bill of Rights. However, the last sentence seems to be false. (But it would take a century more of struggle before these rights were effectively enforced.)

These rights still seem only to be a dream for some of our American brothers and sisters; you know it's true, and together we can lift this lid of complacency and fulfill the promises delivered to us by these documents developed over 230 years ago.

So here we have another incredible document designed to serve the people. And if we can lift this veil of assumption and allow it to apply to all people, it would be a sweeping, history-making change that would rival the creation of these enduring documents.

Not once does the Bill of Rights mention the care or protection of the rights of corporations.

History has a way of glorifying or horrifying depending on the author and their point of view. My focus is to highlight events, acts, and causes that promote unity as good for the country and good for the people of this country. And to expose events, actions, and causes that exclude, limit, punish, or deny access, to the American Dream, to the citizens of this country, no matter the color of their skin, religious or sexual persuasion, gender orientation, or anything outside the small box of white male landowners.

Clearly, the Bill of Rights and its importance to the constitution cannot be understated. Below is the document called the "Bill of Rights."

Source: https://www.archives.gov/founding-docs/bill-of-rights-transcript
(National Archives, 2023, 31 January)

The U.S. Bill of Rights

Note: The following text is a transcription of the first ten amendments to the Constitution in their original form. These amendments were ratified December 15, 1791, and form what is known as the "Bill of Rights." From the National Archives website.

Amendment I

Congress shall make no law respecting an establishment of religion, or prohibiting the free exercise thereof; or abridging the freedom of speech, or of the press; or the right of the people peaceably to assemble, and to petition the Government for a redress of grievances.

Amendment II

A well regulated Militia, being necessary to the security of a free State, the right of the people to keep and bear Arms, shall not be infringed.

Amendment III

No Soldier shall, in time of peace be quartered in any house, without the consent of the Owner, nor in time of war, but in a manner to be prescribed by law.

Amendment IV

The right of the people to be secure in their persons, houses, papers, and effects, against unreasonable searches and seizures, shall not be violated, and no Warrants shall issue, but upon probable cause, supported by Oath or affirmation, and particularly describing the place to be searched, and the persons or things to be seized.

Amendment V

No person shall be held to answer for a capital, or otherwise infamous crime, unless on a presentment or indictment of a Grand Jury, except in cases arising in the land or naval forces, or in the Militia, when in actual service in time of War or public danger; nor shall any person be subject for the same offence to be twice put in jeopardy of life or limb; nor shall be compelled in any criminal case to be a witness against himself, nor be deprived of life, liberty, or property, without due process of law; nor shall private property be taken for public use, without just compensation.

Amendment VI

In all criminal prosecutions, the accused shall enjoy the right to a speedy and public trial, by an impartial jury of the State and district wherein the crime shall have been committed, which district shall have been previously ascertained by law, and to be informed of the nature and cause of the accusation; to be confronted with the witnesses against him; to have compulsory process for obtaining witnesses in his favor, and to have the Assistance of Counsel for his defence.

Amendment VII

In Suits at common law, where the value in controversy shall exceed twenty dollars, the right of trial by jury shall be preserved, and no fact tried by a jury, shall be otherwise re-examined in any Court of the United States, than according to the rules of the common law.

Amendment VIII

Excessive bail shall not be required, nor excessive fines imposed, nor cruel and unusual punishments inflicted.

Amendment IX

The enumeration in the Constitution, of certain rights, shall not be construed to deny or disparage others retained by the people.

Amendment X

The powers not delegated to the United States by the Constitution, nor prohibited by it to the States, are reserved to the States respectively, or to the people.

So with the Bill of Rights proposed as the first ten amendments, the new Constitution is ratified by a majority of the states, and the United States of America is up and running for better or worse. And now, with the European newcomers firmly entrenched in the New World, freed from their previous oppressor, with a new form of government, their dominance in the new world seems unlikely to shift hands anytime soon. So, unable to roll back time to allow the American Indians to live in peace or to leave

African people undisturbed on their native soil, the only option available is to forge ahead with these new conquering people in the new world.

Fortunately, they created a form of government that, on paper, promised to include protections and civil liberties for all citizens. This new government was created to protect what they had learned and benefitted from during their first 150 years in the New World. It was tasked with bringing this new American Dream to every citizen for generations to come. That promise has been nothing short of an enormous struggle for most non-white and sometimes even for white people and most women, who do not have the advantage of accumulated wealth.

So there you have it, the three documents that make up the basis for the system of government in the United States. For a more in-depth study of how and why the framers of the Constitution believed they had developed a credible form of government, please refer to the Federalist Papers. They were written to help citizens understand the Constitution, so that the ratification process would come from a place of knowledge as opposed to any form of coercion.

The purpose of presenting the history of the United States, as such, is to set the context with a broader lens, allowing for all sides to be considered. Hopefully, our shared history of mistakes and successes will be a reminder of the importance and duty allotted to each and every citizen.

In the interest of brevity, we now skip ahead over two hundred years of history to our current time to discuss how we got off track and how to get back on track. Some argue it has been a rocky road right from the start, and I tend to agree. I also believe that these ideas presented in this book, if adopted would certainly help create a more perfect union!

Before we discuss how to create a more perfect union, we have commentary on the worst form of government:

Source: https://blogs.fcdo.gov.uk/petermillett/2014/03/05/the-worst-form-of-government/ (Foreign, Commonwealth and Development Office, 2014, 5 March)

Peter Millett

Ambassador to Libya, Tripoli

Part of UK in Jordan

5th March 2014

The Worst Form of Government

Winston Churchill once said that; "democracy is the worst form of government – except for all the others that have been tried." His cynicism was perhaps justified after the British people voted him out from his position as Prime Minister within months of winning the Second World War.

Whether it is the worst form of government or not, there is little doubt that the alternatives are worse. Suppressing people's views through dictatorship or tyranny means the rule of a narrow minority over the rest. Imposing stability through fear is not the best way to provide the security, prosperity and growth that will make people's lives better.

True stability means giving people a voice in the way they are governed, to back the individuals and the policies that they deem capable of making their lives better; and to remove governments that fail to deliver. That connection between the people and their government is pivotal, especially at difficult times.

Democracy is not only about elections: it is also about creating and encouraging the building blocks of an open and fair society: the rule of law, protection of minorities, strong political parties, liberty, a free media, a strong role for civil society and action against corruption.

Building these democratic institutions takes time. Countries like the United Kingdom have been doing it for hundreds of years. England went through a vicious civil war 350 years ago which culminated in Parliament executing the King. France went through a bloody revolution over 200 years ago and also ended up guillotining the monarch.

These are not necessarily great examples for other countries to follow! But they illustrate the fact that democracy takes time. It is a process not an event. There will inevitably be bumps along the road. And it will mean continually adjusting to new demands for better ways to deliver governments that can govern effectively.

Evolution is better than revolution. And peaceful protest is better than rebellion. The Arab world has seen revolutions and rebellions in the last three years in Tunisia, Egypt, Libya and the ongoing tragedy of Syria.

It has been those countries that have accepted the need for incremental change, like Jordan and Morocco that have retained their stability. A common theme in all these countries has been the demand for dignity: that people should not be humiliated by violent suppression, but participate effectively in their governance. Responding to this demand is essential.

Change takes time. There will always be resistance: those people who have been used to political and economic privileges are not always keen to give them up. But it is impossible to keep all the people happy all the time. Responding to the demands and aspirations of people for reform is a fundamental component of stability. Equally, democracy requires people to have the freedom to challenge policy and criticise those who are driving it.

The conspiracy theorists seem to believe that countries outside the Arab world want to interfere in the way countries develop their democracies. Interference is wrong: each country has to respond to the demands of its people in its own way. There is no Western model. Democracy must be built on the history, traditions and political culture of each country in its own way.

What other countries can do is share experience. Bring lessons of what worked and what didn't. Show that achieving lasting positive change is the work of many generations. And illustrate the fact that it is worth the effort: that each country can achieve, not the best form of government; nor the worst; but the one that works for them.

Can you imagine the level of civil unrest necessary before, during, and after the decapitation of the head of your country?

What must we do to avoid going through such a traumatic event? Can we create a government that actually serves and protects its citizens? Is it worth the effort?

The following report delineates the ingredients for good government.

Source: https://www.lawyersforgoodgovernment.org/mission (Lawyers for Good Government, n.d.)

By Lawyers for Good Government

Lawyersforgoodgovernment.org

Mission & Principles

What "good government" means and why it matters

Our mission is to protect and strengthen democratic institutions, resist abuse of power and corruption, and defend the rights of all those who suffer in the absence of "good government."

7 Principles of Good Government

We believe "good government" requires, at minimum:

1. Equality

A "good government" is grounded in the principle that all people are equal and may not be discriminated against because of their race, religion, ethnic group, gender, or sexual orientation.

2. Citizen Participation

A healthy democracy cannot exist without citizen participation in government - including running for office, voting in elections, staying informed, debating issues, protesting, sitting on juries, etc.

3. Free and Fair Elections

In a healthy democracy, elected officials must be chosen and peacefully removed from office in a free and fair manner. Obstacles should not exist which make it difficult for people to vote. Election districts should not be drawn in a manner designed specifically to disadvantage members of a particular political party, race, religion, or any other group.

4. Protection of Human Rights and the Environment

In a "good government," the rights of the minority are protected even though the "majority rules" in a democracy. Human rights, including (but not limited to) those explicitly protected by the Constitution, must be respected and defended. The environment must be protected for the sake of all human beings and for future generations relying on those in power to ensure a safe, healthy, and sustainable environment. Government decisions should reflect a deeply rooted respect for human life and human dignity.

5. Accountability to the People

A "good government" is accountable to the people, not to special interests, corporate interests, or the self-interest of elected and appointed officials. Government officials must make decisions and perform their duties based on the best interests of the people. To ensure accountability to the people, a "good government" is as transparent as possible - holding public meetings and allowing citizens to attend, providing information to the press, and being clear about what decisions are being made, by whom, and why.

6. Control of the Abuse of Power

A "good government" prevents elected officials or groups of people from misusing or abusing their power. Corruption, conflicts of interest, failure to respect the legitimate authority of other branches of government, acting outside the bounds of one's own authority, and other abuses must be prevented or at the very least, identified and addressed quickly. To ensure that abuses of power can be controlled, the checks and balances contemplated by our Constitution must be able to operate as intended.

7. Rule of Law & Due Process

In a "good government," no one is above the law; this includes members of Congress, Justices of the Supreme Court, and the President of the United States. The law must be enforced equally, fairly, consistently, and with respect for human life and dignity.

The above ingredients for "Good Government" seem to line up with the original documents created over two hundred years ago.

Did the Framers miss something? How did everything get off-track?

The following are quotes from Thomas Jefferson concerning good government:

Source: https://famguardian.org/Subjects/Politics/ThomasJefferson/jeff0650.htm (Family Guardian Fellowship, n.d.)

Thomas Jefferson on Politics & Government

Good Government

"Government should be judged by how well it meets its legitimate objectives. Good government is that which most effectively secures the rights of the people and the fruits of their labor, promotes their happiness, and does their will."

"The care of human life and happiness and not their destruction is the first and only legitimate object of good government." –Thomas Jefferson to Maryland Republicans, 1809. ME 16:359

"The only orthodox object of the institution of government is to secure the greatest degree of happiness possible to the general mass of those associated under it." –Thomas Jefferson to M. van der Kemp, 1812. ME 13:135

Even though many of the framers of the Constitution were slave owners and considered their wives to be their property, the documents they created seem to be unique and sufficient to manage the invaders from Europe. Yet, in 2023, there is so much strife, inequality, homelessness, disregard for the environment, and such a laissez-faire attitude toward corporations and the upper class.

The care and protection of our citizens have decayed to the point of reckoning! "We The People" seem ready to do something to change this but are continually stymied by a system that pretends to care but only procrastinates on their agreed-upon responsibilities to protect.

What is the missing ingredient that would solidify and congeal this Republic into a consistent, efficient, classless, and protective arm of our society? The trouble is not with the documents but with the individuals involved. Not only the individuals doing the actual governing but the people being governed also bear some responsibility.

What is a government to do with an angry mob of citizens hell-bent on lynching people? And what happens when the citizens governing these people agree that lynching is okay; the lynching proceed without prosecution.

Below is a report on the history of lynching in the United States of America from Smithsonian Magazine.

Source: https://www.smithsonianmag.com/smart-news/nearly-2000-black-americans-were-lynched-during-reconstruction-180975120/ (Fox, A. 2020, 18 June)

Nearly 2,000 Black Americans Were Lynched During Reconstruction

A new report brings the number of victims of racial terror killings between 1865 and 1950 to almost 6,500

Alex Fox
Smithsonian Magazine
Correspondent
June 18, 2020

Just over a year after the end of slavery in the United States, New Orleans hosted a convention of white men seeking to ensure Louisiana's new constitution would guarantee voting rights for black residents.

Virulently racist opposition by the local press, which denounced both the convention's attendees and its intent, preceded the July 1866 gathering. And when black men from the surrounding area staged a march in support of the convention, a mob of white men and police enacted a horrific scene of racial terror.

"For several hours, the police and mob, in mutual and bloody emulation, continued the butchery in the hall and on the street, until nearly two hundred people were killed and wounded," wrote a Congressional committee tasked with investigating the massacre. "How many were killed will never be known. But we cannot doubt there were many more than set down in the official list in evidence."

This incident is one of nearly 2,000 white supremacist massacres and killings recorded in a new report from the Equal Justice Initiative (EJI), an Alabama-based nonprofit dedicated to combating racial inequality. The survey details nearly 2,000 racial terror lynchings of black men, women and children during the Reconstruction era of 1865 to 1876.

In 2015, EJI researchers released a report documenting more than 4,400 lynchings that took place between 1877 and 1950. The new study, titled *Reconstruction in America: Racial Violence After the Civil War*, brings the overall death toll between 1865 and 1950 to nearly 6,500.

"We cannot understand our present moment without recognizing the lasting damage caused by allowing white supremacy and racial hierarchy to prevail during Reconstruction," says Bryan Stevenson, EJI's founder and director, in a statement.

As Safiya Charles writes for the *Montgomery Advertiser*, Reconstruction-era lynchings, as well as thousands of largely unprosecuted acts of assault and terrorism during the period, "were used to intimidate, coerce and control Black communities with the impunity of local, state and federal officials—a legacy that has once again boiled over, as nationwide protests sparked by multiple police killings and extrajudicial violence against Black Americans call for an end to centuries of hostility and persecution."

The names of more than 4,000 lynching victims are written in stone at EJI's National Memorial for Peace and Justice. Since opening in Montgomery in 2018, the memorial and its accompanying museum have welcomed around 750,000 visitors, reports Campbell Robertson for the *New York Times*.

Stevenson tells the *Times* that building the museum and memorial made EJI's team realize that the 12-year period following the Civil War saw a disproportionate number of killings of black Americans and therefore warranted special attention.

"If there was any period of time where white animus toward blacks was omnipresent, particularly in the South, it was certainly during the time of Reconstruction," Derryn Moten, a historian at Alabama State University, tells the *Montgomery Advertiser*. "That was the dawning of African Americans' new freedom. ... [But it] was also the time period when the Klan and other terror groups came into fruition."

The white supremacist terrorism perpetrated against black Americans during Reconstruction effectively nullified constitutional

72

amendments designed to provide black people with equal legal protections and ensure their right to vote, according to the report. As Stevenson explains to the *Guardian*'s Ed Pilkington, American institutions ranging from local sheriffs to the Supreme Court—which passed decisions that blocked efforts to enact further legal protections for black U.S. citizens—failed to protect the rights outlined in these landmark amendments.

"It's only because we gave in to this lawlessness and abandoned the rule of law and decided that these constitutional amendments would not be enforced that it was possible to have nearly a century of racial terror," Stevenson tells the *Times*.

The thousands of racial terror lynchings documented in the report likely represent just a fraction of the carnage's true scope: "[T]housands more were attacked, sexually assaulted, and terrorized by white mobs and individuals who were shielded from arrest and prosecution," the study's authors write.

Speaking with the *Montgomery Advertiser*, Stevenson adds, "Our continued silence about the history of racial injustice has fueled many of the current problems surrounding police violence, mass incarceration, racial inequality, and the disparate impact of COVID-19."

In 2016, Jordan Steiker, a law professor at the University of Texas, told the New Yorker's Jeffrey Toobin that the legacy of lynching continues to influence the criminal justice system today—particularly in the case of capital punishment.

"In one sense, the death penalty is clearly a substitute for lynching. One of the main justifications for the use of the death penalty, especially in the South, was that it served to avoid lynching," Steiker said. "The number of people executed rises tremendously at the end of the lynching era. And there's still incredible overlap between places that had lynching and places that continue to use the death penalty."

EJI's new report, as well as its memorial and museum, seeks to expose Americans to their nation's history of white supremacy and the acts of racial terrorism it inspired.

"It's important that we quantify and document violence," Stevenson tells the *Times*. "But what's more important is that we acknowledge that we have not been honest about who we are, and about how we came to this moment."

Alex Fox
Alex Fox is a freelance science journalist based in Washington, D.C. He has written for *Science, Nature, Science News*, the *San Jose Mercury News* and *Mongabay*. You can find him at Alexfoxscienoo.oom.

No one comes out of the womb with hatred for another of a different color. That hatred is encouraged by fear and taught to our young. The clear and persistent message I am receiving from the Light is to teach only Love.

Can people of differing ethnic and skin color groups ever get along? What is it about humans that propel them to ostracize people dissimilar to themselves? Fear and fear alone fuel this behavior. The fear of the unknown is well documented as the source of much discomfort that besets humanity. The existence of another human being that is very dissimilar can seem to be unsettling, but does that make it okay to hate that for which you are unfamiliar?

Wouldn't the proper response be an interest and a curiosity to investigate the differences and look for the commonality? Are we not all humans? Do we not all come from one Creator? Who are we to judge who the favored group of people is? What purpose would there be for a preferred group of people? How would that serve the Creator? Favoritism is an assumption, pure and simple, and only attempts to serve the ones who indulge it, but without favor.

Humans have many liabilities and shortcomings, are we doomed to hang on to them, like rats on a sinking ship? We are free to change, grow, and evolve. This evolution is not only good for the persecuted but good for the persecutors as well! For to live a life full of hate binds you to a state of hate that is hard to break. We have all experienced Love, and we all know its sweet taste… Allowing it to enter our lives fully will help us melt the chains that bind us to anything that is not love. We are all free to live in a state of Love.

The fact that humans have free will and the ability to judge their experiences, good or bad, gives them dominion over the kind of life they will experience; this is good news! The difficulty is that humans frequently judge most situations as bad or wrong. The mind begins justifying that decision as soon as they judge. At the same time, they use any rationale at their disposal, even if the evidence is erroneous. Once the assessment has been rendered, the mind must mount the evidence to relieve the stress caused by the judging in the first place.

Does anybody remember, "Judge not lest ye be judged" (Matthew 7:1)?

A free-floating fear lurks in the minds of most unaware individuals; the fear that they are being judged. To combat this fear, people judge, as a way to defend against this fear, a sort of, first-strike-defense theory. It all happens so fast, this mental mind manipulation that constricts and binds one to their imaginary fears. The proof, to prove these fears correct, comes flooding in so fast that it has to be true and correct. Any behavior selected can be rationalized, up to and including lynching.

It doesn't have to be this way, even though it has been this way for a long time. We can move past this limited way of thinking only if we are so inclined.

Are you familiar with the concept of an angel on one shoulder whispering into your ear and a devil on your other shoulder whispering into your other ear?

As an adult human being, you have to ask yourself, what kind of person do I want to be? I know there are all kinds of reasons people use to justify siding with their lower nature. Destroying another person's life just because of a free-floating fear is no longer defensible. It's just not okay to behave in this manner. Once everyone in our society understands this concept and believes it to be unjust, this behavior will also fade out of existence and become a part of history, a history that future people will wonder, "How could they have ever done that to other people back in those days?"

For a more updated and in-depth explanation of the angel/devil theory, please see the article below:

The Illusory World Created by the Mind and Ego

This is one of eight talks from Gina Lake's online course Moving Beyond Ego, which is about the ego and how to free yourself from the voice in your head and what it's like to live unencumbered by this voice.

Because we're identified with our thoughts, we misperceive the world, and this creates an illusory or false sense of the world—a misperception of the world. The thoughts that I'm talking about are the thoughts that come from the ego, or egoic mind, the thought-stream, the voice in our head. This voice is the illusion generator. It's the ongoing commentary in our head that centers around "me, myself and I," particularly tho me in the past and in the future: "What am I going to do? What did they think of me? What will happen to me?"

This is the kind of commentary that goes on in people's minds, which creates the false self. From these thoughts, you get the ideas about yourself that you believe to be true. And we believe these thoughts simply because we're programmed to believe them. And so, that is how the illusion of being a separate self is created—simply by the thought-stream that pours into each of our minds from who knows where.

Where do these thoughts come from? They come out of nowhere, and yet, they're taken to be who we are. They seem to be who we are, but these thoughts don't even belong to us. We didn't choose them, and they don't really describe us—not our true self. They describe the false self, a character who feels a certain way, who thinks a certain way, who's been programmed to believe certain things.

The thought-stream wouldn't be a problem if our attention wasn't constantly glued to it. Not only do we believe the thoughts in the thought-stream, we are fascinated by them. We can hardly take our attention off of them.

If we don't take our attention off of them, what results is an illusory sense of ourselves and the world. Like a cloud or fog, our thoughts cover over reality, and we're unable to see clearly. We live in a virtual reality, one created by our thoughts about life and ourselves.

This thought-stream distorts our perception. It blinds us to the truth and the beauty of the world—because another feature of this thought-stream, which is problematic, is that it's generally negative: It makes you feel fearful, insecure, lacking, and not good enough.

The ego is a survival mechanism, and although we need to have some remnant of ego to function, we don't need the thought-stream. The thought-stream is archaic and dysfunctional. When you first see this about the thought-stream, it's pretty shocking. But those who are awake or enlightened no longer refer to their thought-stream for how to live their lives.

They use the rational mind, the intellect, to problem-solve, to read, to follow directions, and to navigate life. The rational mind is very different from the thought-stream. The thought-stream is the voice in your head that talks to you. That voice is what is outmoded. And although some of the conditioning reflected in the thought-stream may be helpful or neutral, a lot of it is simply lies.

What you discover after awakening is that your body and the intelligence embedded in it already knows what you need to know. The conditioning you need is already in your body-mind. It's already known to you. So, to keep yourself safe, you don't need to refer to the thought-stream, which essentially just repeats things you already know. It's also quite amazing to see that.

You don't need any of those thoughts, and it took me a long time to realize this. It took a lot of investigation of the thought-stream to see that I don't even need a thought like, "Take the pot off the stove now! It's boiling over." We don't need a thought like that because the body moves to the stove and takes the pot off when it sees what's happening.

So, the mind takes credit for telling you what you already know. It seems like we need those thoughts, those seemingly helpful, safety-oriented thoughts. But the truth is that knowing moves the body, and the thoughts come later. And we just think we needed those thoughts to tell us what to do.

This is really good news—that you don't need the thought-stream—because that means you don't have to go sorting through your thoughts to find the important ones, the necessary ones. It means you can disregard the thought-stream and put your attention on something else. This is a radical teaching: You can disregard the thought-stream! But you have to find that out for yourself through investigation and little by little, letting go of each thought as you see how useless it is. And keep doing this until you're convinced that the entire thought-stream is useless.

This takes a willingness to look at your thoughts and discover the truth about them. Most people are so identified with their thought-stream that they aren't examining or questioning it. They're just believing it, and their lives are run accordingly. Their thoughts say, "Go here. Do that," and that's what they do. And that's the right experience earlier on in our human evolution. There's nothing wrong with that.

It is as it's meant to be until we reach a point in our evolution when we begin to wake up and see that we don't need to live like that any longer. But until then, it's perfectly fine to be lost in the illusion. The illusion serves evolution—until it no longer does. It's all just fine the way it is.

But I'm speaking to you, and you're here because it's time for you to wake up. So, how do we begin to see through the illusion and break free of it? I frankly don't know any better way than a practice of meditation, which trains you to detach from the voice in your head so that you can begin to see this voice for what it is. I will be saying more about meditation in a later talk.

We automatically believe our thoughts, so unless we can get some distance from that programming, there's no choice but to believe them. That distance, the ability to notice our thoughts, gives us some choice around them—to believe them or not. Without that distance, we automatically believe our thoughts, and we're run by them, by our programming.

Overcoming that programming doesn't just happen, and it doesn't happen overnight. It takes effort, and that effort is usually in the form of meditation or some other spiritual practice that develops our ability to be aware of and at a distance from our thoughts.

Our default is to believe our thoughts and identify with them ("This is who I am!") and let them run our life. Waking up is about changing that default and coming into some control and choice around our thoughts.

We have to step out of the thought-stream long enough to discover that there's something else guiding us and living our life and always has been. The being that we are allows the egoic mind—the voice in our head—to run our life until it's time for us to awaken. And then, some mysterious force arises within us and says, "Wait a minute. This can't be right. I'm making myself miserable. Everyone's making themselves miserable. What is this voice in my head? How do I release myself from this suffering?"

You finally ask those questions, and you discover that the answers to those questions have been available throughout history from spiritual masters and mystics, enlightened beings who knew the way out of suffering.

And so, the beautiful, wonderful, good news is that there's something at the core of life other than all of our thoughts about it. There is one being behind all of life, and you are an expression of that. The only thing that's ever been living your life is this awesome, magnificence that you are. And the only thing that has ever interfered with this magnificence expressing in life is thoughts about yourself—the false self. Isn't that amazing that thoughts are powerful enough to obscure our divine nature?

Your divine nature, your true self, has never wavered. It is the only thing here. It's the only thing that has ever looked out of your eyes, moved your body, breathed your lungs, and beat your heart. It's the only thing. And it's the same in everyone. So, our work here, as spiritual beings who are waking up, is to remove the obscurations to this beautiful fact, to this beautiful truth, so that we can begin to see the world through eyes that are clear and pure, ones that see life and the world as it truly is, as the beautiful and magnificent creation that it is.

Once we drop out of the thought-stream, that is our experience. The experience is that the world is one of wonder, awe, and beauty, very similar to how many of us remember experiencing the world as a child: every moment fresh and new. That is the true self's experience. That is the true experience. And the only thing that has ever kept you from that experience is your thoughts, particularly thoughts about yourself.

Those are the biggest obstacles—all of the "I" thoughts: "I need this. I want this. I'm too scared. I never do anything right. I have to have this." All of the ideas you have about "I" are a lie. If you just say, "I," that's not a lie. That's about as true a statement as you can make. Or you could say, "I am." That's true too. But anything you add after that is likely to be a lie. It's too small a truth to be true. It's too incomplete to be true.

Of course, language is necessary, but language, by its nature, creates separation. Language is more often the tool of the ego than of the divine self. Nevertheless, we're here to learn to speak in a way that is not egoic but expresses truth. We're here to learn to move in a way that is not egoic but expresses our true nature and our true beingness and what it wants for us in this lifetime.

Each and every one of you has a plan, a certain destiny, that your soul set out to accomplish in this lifetime, and by attuning to your true self, you find your way to that. The egoic mind can take you away from that, and it often does. But the beauty is that the divine self has so many ways of contacting us that most people don't entirely lose their way.

Most people are living a dance between their egoic self and their divine self: They identify with their ego, and then they say something wonderful and loving. Then, they identify with their ego again, and then they say something loving and wise. Eventually, we become more aligned with our spiritual self and speak and act more in alignment with that and less in alignment with the ego.

It's a long process. Breaking our identification with the ego and learning to live from a deeper place doesn't happen overnight. The trick to living from this deeper place is learning to attune to the subtle realm and the true self's subtle communications, which for the most part, doesn't come in the form of words.

Now, I'm a channel, so I do receive guidance in the form of words in my head, but that's a rarity for most people. When someone does receive such guidance, it doesn't feel like the thought-stream. It feels clean and clear, and it's also very short. It doesn't go on and on like the thought-stream. The egoic mind is quite a chatterbox, and it's all about "I." Your deepest self doesn't communicate with you that way.

If you're looking for guidance, you won't find it in your mind. You'll find it in the more subtle realm, in the subtle urges and drives that come from deep within yourself, which arise suddenly out of the moment: Suddenly, you're moved to call someone. Suddenly, you're excited about creating something. Suddenly, you say something true and meaningful, and it feels good to everyone—to you as you speak it and to others as they receive it.

This is how the true self operates. Moment-to-moment, it shows you how to live. It doesn't let you know what your life will be like in the future. It's all about learning to live moment-to-moment. And since each moment is complete just as it is, you don't need a future. The ego needs a future because the ego makes us so unhappy in the present that we need a pretend, happier future to try to get to. But if you're present, the moment-to-moment experience and guidance you receive is enough. The experience of the moment is enough. It's full, it's complete.

I can't stress enough the importance of meditation for getting some distance from the mind. It's nearly impossible to get beyond a lot of negativity or negative feelings without some kind of practice of meditation and, also, some healing work. A negative mind is very difficult to detach from because it feels alarming. Negative thoughts feel like you have to pay attention to them or you won't be safe.

That's why there's so much emphasis in spiritual circles on changing negative thoughts to positive ones. If your thought-stream is more neutral or positive, you'll be able to drop into Presence more easily. Eventually, with a lot of meditation and inquiry into the mind, your thought-stream does become more benign, more neutral, less troublesome, and less compelling and sticky. And so, it's important to do whatever you can to minimize that negativity. There are lots of different tools for that: affirmations, inquiry, Bryon Katie's work, and various methods of healing.

Writing down your negative thoughts, I think, is really helpful to clearly see what's in the thought-stream. When people do this, they're often surprised at how negative their own mind is. There's something about putting those thoughts down on paper that gives you power over them. They're just words. They have no reality, but the illusion gives them reality—and they can become self-fulfilling prophecies.

If you believe your negative thoughts, they do create a negative reality. They create a negative internal climate that, in turn, creates a negative external climate, as people respond negatively towards your negativity. If you live in a negative internal climate, others feel that and are repelled by that, so you don't get the love, support from others, and opportunities you'd like to have.

So, anything you can do to become more aware of your thoughts and make them more positive will be really helpful. Inquiry into your thoughts to see if they are true and useful is especially helpful. You will always, I guarantee, discover that the thoughts in your thought-stream are not useful or even true. They have such a small amount of truth in them that they can't really be considered true. I think Byron Katie's inquiry process, which she calls "The Work," is some of the best cognitive work you can do.

If you have a lot of negative emotions or trust issues due to an abusive or a neglectful childhood, it can feel scary to drop into Presence and stay there. So, you may have to work on those issues first with a therapist, an energy healer, or some other kind of healer. Your deepest self will bring various tools and people into your life to help you heal. Notice what kinds of healing methods you're intuitively drawn to. I'm all for psychotherapy if you can find a good transpersonal psychotherapist, someone who acknowledges the spiritual side of life. Most people need to do some Inner Child work at some point, which I've written about in a number of my books.

A question I'm being asked now in the chat window is, "Is thinking a decision?" If you're talking about using your intellect, your rational mind, then that type of thinking is a decision. We consciously decide to think about something: We decide to plan our next vacation or plan what we'll make for dinner. But the thinking that goes on in the thought-stream just happens to us, at least initially: A thought pops into our mind from out of nowhere. But then we may jump on the bandwagon and purposely think more about that initial thought. That initial thought is not a decision, but to continue to think thoughts along the same line is likely a decision, although an unconscious one for most people. We consciously or unconsciously agree with certain thoughts and reinforce those thoughts with more of the same.

It takes a certain amount of spiritual development and awareness of your thoughts to get to the point where you can make a conscious decision to not join the thought-stream. Most people are unconsciously and automatically identified with their thought-streams, so they don't feel they have a choice. Meditation will help you feel you do have a choice and you don't have to jump on that thought train and get lost in it.

Here's another question: "When the ego is purged, what, if anything, takes its place?" What takes its place is what's been here all along; it just doesn't express itself through words in your head. It is the silent presence that is who you are, the silent presence that is hearing these words, the silent presence that is sitting, listening, seeing, sensing, and intuiting. It experiences a thought. It experiences a feeling. It experiences sensations. What's left when the ego has fallen into the background is the Experiencer, but I hesitate to use the term as a noun like that. It's better to say that what's left is pure experiencing, absent of any evaluation.

Who you are is the Noticer, the Experiencer, the Witness. But what's left isn't a thing. It isn't an entity or individual. It is all of life living through you. What you experience in the space between your thoughts or when the thought-stream quiets down is who you are. You are that silence. You are that experiencing, that awareness, that awakeness, that Presence. That being that is experienced in between your thoughts has always been there, but it allows your thoughts to take you over.

And here's a nice comment from somebody sharing something: "One day, when I saw a bird, I didn't think of the bird. I was the bird. One day, when I was able to love all creation, I had no thoughts of creation. Rather, I was part of all creation. Duality was absent. Oneness had taken its place."

That's beautiful, and that's the experience of dropping into your being. That is how your true self experiences life. It experiences a connection to all of life in that way.

The desire for oneness is the one desire that is worth keeping. You don't really need the rest of your desires. To get what we need in life, we don't need our desires. Life is taking care of us. We are being held in God's hands. It's very beautiful that way. If we could only trust that, then we'd be able to discover that. But it takes trust to move out of the egoic mind, which does not trust life. You have to have enough trust to move out of the egoic mind to discover that life is benevolent and provides everything we need.

One last question: "Do you think your experience came from your practice? Does practice really do anything?"

I think that practice is extremely important. I practiced meditation for over twelve years, one or two hours a day, before I awakened. I think awakening is grace. It's not necessarily something we can order up or cause to happen through practice. But I think that the sincerity and intention you bring to a practice and the training of your brain that creates a foundation for awakening, so that if awakening does occur, you'll have a stable experience. People who awaken without practices often have a destabilizing experience after awakening. In any event, whether you awaken or not, meditation will lead to a happier and better life for you and everyone around you.

Clearly, the oppression we all face daily starts in our minds. For those individuals unaware of this option to choose negativity or love, fall in step with the negativity, for it is so insistent. Most people are unaware there is a choice. If everyone around you is screaming for a lynching and you are ten years old, what will you do? Naturally, you will go along to get along.

Societies indoctrinate their young. Right or wrong, we pass along what we believe, the good and the bad. Change usually comes from the younger generations. Sometimes they are unwilling to go along to get along, and they band together to initiate change. The Baby Boomers were responsible for a massive movement of change when they were young. Are they willing to take another look at the oppression we are now holding onto and release it before we pass it on to the next generation? The opportunity to consistently choose Love is within our grasp! It is a tremendous opportunity for a giant leap forward in the evolution of our species.

I am just saying. Why not?...

So how do I choose Love?

How do I take my attention off the thought stream from my ego?

Where can I find a meditation class? I am ready to go within!

This idea was around two thousand years ago… "The Kingdom of Heaven is Within" …

Somehow it was hijacked, and we are no longer encouraged to go within, to discover, evolve, wake up, and know the Truth of our

83

Reality. The Truth is still there waiting to be discovered, and it will still set you free if only you will seek it.

I am just saying… Why not…
Thank you for being a part of this experiential journey! Now, please, let's return to my worldly thread of thought.

The following story is a part of the history of the New World and has its roots in Europe. The Salem Witch Trials exemplify people not generally beguiled by such monkey business. So sad how they fell prey to the mass hysteria of the mob mentality. People were willing to believe in false evidence convicting innocent people. Eventually, the rule of law began to be applied, false accusations were no longer believed, and the whole concept was released and became a part of history that is no longer practiced.

Source: https://www.law.berkeley.edu/research/the-robbins-collection/exhibitions/witch-trials-in-early-modern-europe-and-new-england/ (Berkeley Law, 2008)

Witch Trials in Early Modern Europe and New England

Legal Basis for Witch Trials

Historians have identified a number of crucial legal developments that led to the panic surrounding—and subsequent trials of—witches in Early Modern Europe. One was the idea of "heretical fact," put forth by Pope John XXII (1316-1334), which allowed heresy to be viewed as a deed and not just an intellectual crime. Another step was the establishment of a link between witchcraft and heresy, a link that had not existed before the end of the 15th century, which emerged thanks to a new theory of "diabolical witchcraft" that held that the practice of **malefice** (such as using religious objects to curse one's neighbor) in fact involved an active pact with the Devil and was therefore a heretical act and not just a ritual performed by misguided country folk. This view of witchcraft was spread throughout Europe by handbooks like the *Malleus Maleficarum*.

Malleus Maleficarum

The height of the German witch frenzy was marked by the publication of the *Malleus Maleficarum* ("Hammer of Witches"), a book that became the handbook for witch hunters and Inquisitors. Written in 1486 by Dominicans Heinricus Institoris and Jacobus Sprenge, and first published in Germany in 1487, the main purpose of the *Malleus* was to systematically refute arguments claiming that witchcraft did not exist, to refute those who expressed skepticism about its reality, to prove that witches were more often women than men, and to educate magistrates on the procedures that could find them out and convict them. The main body of the *Malleus* text is divided into three parts; part one demonstrates the theoretical reality of sorcery; part two is divided into two distinct sections, or "questions," which detail the practice of sorcery and its cures; part three describes the legal procedure to be used in the prosecution of witches. The *Malleus* was republished 26 times in the Early Modern period and remained a standard text on witchcraft for centuries.

Legal and Geographical Discrepancies in European Witch Trials

Differences in the development of legal systems in Early Modern Europe had a profound influence on the course the witch trials took in different countries. The relatively few prosecutions of witches in Spain, Italy, and France, for example, can be attributed to the fact that neither the Spanish nor the Roman inquisition believed that witchcraft could be proven. England likewise saw relatively few prosecutions due to the checks and balances inherent in the jury system. It was only in places like Scotland, the Alpine lands, and in South German ecclesiastical principalities that witch panics and actual prosecutions proliferated. In those regions, made up of small, weak states, secular courts actively and successfully prosecuted heresy cases. Another important reason for the active conviction of witches in the German states was the Holy Roman Empire's adoption of the *Constitutio Criminalis Carolina* in 1530, which not only instituted prosecution at the judge's initiative, thus putting the accused witches at the mercy of a magistrate who was at once judge, investigator, prosecutor, and defense counsel, but also provided for the secret interrogation of the accused, denied him or her counsel, required torture in order to extract a confession, and specified that witches be punished with death by burning.

Witch Hunts in Early Modern Europe

The height of the witch hunting frenzy in Early Modern Europe came in two waves: The first wave occurred in the 15th and early 16th centuries, the second wave in the 17th century. Witch hunts were seen across all of Early Modern Europe, but the most significant area of witch hunting is considered to be southwestern Germany, where the highest concentration of witch trials occurred during the years 1561 to 1670.

Salem Witch Trials: Beginnings

The 1692-1693 Salem Witch Trials were a brief outburst of witch hysteria in the New World at a time when the practice was already waning in Europe. In February 1692 a girl became ill, and at the same time her playmates also exhibited unusual behavior. When a local doctor was unable to cure the girls, a supernatural cause was suggested and suspicions of witchcraft emerged. Soon three townswomen were accused of witchcraft: Tituba, a slave, Sarah Good, a poor beggar and social misfit, and Sarah Osborne, a quarrelsome woman who rarely attended church. While the matter might have ended there with the three unpopular women serving as scapegoats, during the trial Tituba—possibly to avoid being unfairly prosecuted—declared she was a witch and that she and the other accused women flew through the air on poles. With skeptics silenced, witch hunting began in earnest.

Court of Oyer and Terminer

Before long, accusations of witchcraft abounded and the jails filled with suspects who confessed to witchcraft, seeing it as a means to avoid hanging. The provincial governor created court of "oyer and terminer" which allowed judges to hear "spectral evidence" (testimony by victims that the accused witch's specter had visited them) and granted ministers with no legal training authority to guide judges. Evidence that would be disallowed today—hearsay, gossip, unsupported assertions—was routinely admitted, while defendants had no right to counsel or appeal. Through the rest of 1692, in a climate of fear, accusations flew, many were convicted, and a number were put to death.

Decline and Closure of Salem Witch Trials

By the fall of 1692 the witch hunting hysteria began to die down as more and more people began to doubt that so many people could be guilty of witchcraft. People urged the courts not to admit spectral evidence and to rely instead on clear and convincing testimony. Once spectral evidence was no longer admissible, acquittals abounded, and the three originally convicted women were pardoned. In May of 1693 the remaining accused and convicted witches were released from prison. Over the course of the Salem witch hysteria, of the 150 people who were arrested and the 26 who were convicted, 14 women and 5 men were executed. The Salem Witch Trials only lasted a little over a year and had very little practical impact on the Colonies at large. However, the trials and executions had a vivid afterlife in the American consciousness, giving rise to a wealth of scholarship and an abundance of cultural artifacts including paintings, novels, plays, and films.

The Salem witch trials are another example of human being's total disregard for another person's civil liberties. Fortunately, for some accused of witchcraft, calmer heads finally prevailed and convinced the populace of the fallacy of this type of discrimination.

Hopefully, we will find peace in all other areas of discrimination too. The documents to freedom from these injustices have already been written, and now it is up to us, "We The People," to manifest this freedom from the hate that still persists in our communities.

The Framers deliberately inserted safeguards to our citizen's civil liberties in the Constitution and, if followed closely, would negate all of this type of behavior and protect these citizens from harm. So why are certain groups of individuals still suffering from injustice in our society today

What can be done to fulfil the promises proposed in the Constitution?

I assume "We The People" still want all of these protections?

What must we do to enact this reform and ensure our safety and general welfare?

How far are "We The People" willing to go to provide for our safety?

For those that are willing, there is a way!

Education is the first step! First, all citizenry must know and understand the tenets of all three documents, called the Charters of Freedom.

When "We The People" know our rights, we can stand up for ourselves and protect others who are too weak to defend themselves.

When we understand what good government is, we will be able to choose conscientious representatives that will enforce the protections and liberties of the Constitution.

When we understand the importance of good government, upholding the Constitution's ideals will become a noble challenge. That will spur women and men to enter the political arena to meet that challenge and bring forth the best interpretations to serve and protect all people.

After two hundred years, the consensus for what is good government still follows the Constitution's guidelines.

So let us spread the good news! With a bit of patience, diligence, and understanding, we can all live, laugh, and love free from hate, persecution, and ill will! There is still hope for us and our country.

Chapter Three:
Education and Democracy

The European invaders showed up on the shores of this New World un-announced and eventually unwelcome. Their lasting legacy has given us an experiment in democracy unrivaled in world history and is currently unraveling.

How can we get this democracy experiment back on track? The first thing that needs to happen is a robust reform in the education of our citizens.

The following is a report on how to put democracy back into public education.

Source: https://tcf.org/content/report/putting-democracy-back-public-education/ (The Century Foundation, 2016, 10 November)

RICHARD D. KAHLENBERG AND CLIFFORD JANEY

Putting Democracy Back into Public Education

November 10, 2016

Throughout U.S. history, Americans have pivoted between whether the central priority of public education should be to create skilled workers for the economy, or to educate young people for responsible citizenship. Both goals are important, of course, but with the recent rise of a global economy, the emphasis has shifted away from preparing citizens and toward serving the needs of the marketplace.

On one level, this change of priorities is understandable. As we celebrated two hundred years of a continuous, improving democracy, the need for schools to emphasize the civic portion of public education began to feel less urgent to many leaders and educators. In a globalized economy, competition from foreign nations such as China appeared a more imminent threat than domestic challenges undermining our democratic values.

But new evidence suggests that American democracy is under severe strain. In a recent survey, two-thirds of Americans could not name all three branches of the federal government.[1] Only a third could identify Joe Biden as the vice president or name a single Supreme Court justice.[2] Declining proportions say that free elections are important in a democratic society.[3] The crisis came to a head in the 2016 presidential election, in which a candidate with authoritarian leanings captured the presidency of the United States. Moving forward, the question has become: How can our public schools do a better job of educating children for our pluralistic democracy?

This report proceeds in four parts. The first part articulates the ways in which the founders believed that public education was critical to protecting the republic from demagogues. The second part discusses the tilt toward market values and away from democratic norms in recent years in both the courses we teach children directly and the way we model (or do not model) democratic practices in schooling. The third part outlines the considerable costs of failing to emphasize democratic values and embrace democratic practices. And the last part makes public policy recommendations for restoring the right balance in our schools at the state, local and federal levels. Throughout the report, we seek to synthesize the practical experiences of one of us (Janey), who served as superintendent of public schools in Rochester, New York (1995–2002), Washington, D.C. (2004–2007), and Newark, New Jersey (2008–2011), and the scholarly work of one of us (Kahlenberg), who has researched and written about school integration and is the biographer of teacher union leader Albert Shanker.[4]

The Role of Public Education in Supporting American Democracy

Since the founding of public education in the United States, public schools have been charged not only with giving future workers skills for the private marketplace, but also with preparing students to be citizens in a democracy.

The American Founders were deeply concerned with finding ways to ensure that their new democracy, which provided ultimate sovereignty to the collective views of average citizens through the franchise, not fall prey to demagogues. The problem of the demagogue, the Founders believed, was endemic to democracy.[5]

One answer to the threat of demagogues and rule by the "mob" in a democracy, the Founders suggested, was America's elaborate constitutional system of checks and balances. The potential rise of a demagogue is attenuated by dividing power between three branches of government (executive, legislative and judicial); between federal and state governments; and between government and a host of free civic institutions—an independent press, religious congregations, business groups, and labor unions—that check the power of government. The U.S. Senate, in particular, was designed as the "saucer" to cool the piping hot tea boiled by the populist House of Representatives—a metaphor George Washington was said to have used in discussion with Thomas Jefferson.[6]

But the Founders believed that another layer of protection was needed. The Constitution, after all, can be amended (though with difficulty) by the mob. Likewise, a demagogue, appealing to passions rather than reason, can use democratic means to win office, and, once in power, chip away at rival sources of authority—such as an independent press, and an independent judiciary—that stand in his way. Early leaders such as George Washington did not know how this system would work out. "The preservation of the sacred fire of liberty and the destiny of the republican model of government," he said in his first inaugural address, "are justly considered, perhaps, as deeply, as finally, staked on the experiment entrusted to the hands of the American people."[7]

For the experiment to succeed, the Founders knew, a second fundamental bulwark against demagogues needed to be created: an educated populace. Thomas Jefferson argued that general education was necessary to "enable every man to judge for himself what will secure or endanger his freedom."[8] Jefferson noted, "if a nation expects to be ignorant and free, in a state of civilization, it expects what never was and never will be."[9]

The Founders wanted voters to be intelligent in order to discern serious leaders of high character from con men who do not have the nation's interests at heart. Beyond that, public education in the United States was also meant to instill a love of liberal democracy: a respect for the separation of powers, for a free press and free religious exercise, and for the rights of political minorities. In this way, demagogues who sought to undermine those institutions would themselves be suspect among voters. Educating common people was the answer to the oligarchs who said the average citizen could not be trusted to choose leaders wisely. The founder of American public schooling, nineteenth century Massachusetts educator Horace Mann, saw public education as fundamental to democracy "A republican form of government, without intelligence in the people, must be, on a vast scale, what a mad-house, without superintendent or keepers, would be on a small one."[10]

The centrality of public education to American democracy was not just the quaint belief of eighteenth- and nineteenth-century leaders. In 1916, John Dewey's *Democracy and Education* explained that "a government resting upon popular suffrage cannot be successful unless those who elect and who obey their governors are educated."[11] In 1938, when dangerous demagogues were erecting totalitarian regimes in many parts of the world, Franklin D. Roosevelt noted: "Democracy cannot succeed unless those who express their choice are prepared to choose wisely. The real safeguard of democracy, therefore, is education." He continued: "It has been well said that no system of government gives so much to the individual or exacts so much as a democracy. Upon our educational system must largely depend the perpetuity of those institutions upon which our freedom and our security rest. To prepare each citizen to choose wisely and to enable him to choose freely are paramount functions of the schools in a democracy."[12] And in a 1952 Supreme Court case, Justice Felix Frankfurter, noting the central role of public schools in our system of self-governance, said teachers should be regarded "as the priests of our democracy."[13] All nations, the late historian Paul Gagnon noted, provide an excellent education to "those who are expected to run the country" and the quality of that education "cannot be far from what everyone in a democracy needs to know."[14]

Teaching students to be good democratic citizens had two distinct elements: (1) providing student the analytical and critical thinking skills necessary to be well informed and make sound decisions in elections; and (2) instilling in students an appreciation for the benefits of liberal democracy as a system of governance, thereby guarding against demagogues who would undermine democratic principles. In the United States, as Jennifer Hochschild and Nathan Scovronick argue, schools have been charged with teaching values that "include loyalty to the nation, acceptance of the Declaration of Independence and the Constitution as venerable founding documents, appreciation that in America, constitutional rights sometimes trump majority rule and the majority rule is supposed to trump intense desire, belief in the rule of law as the proper grounding for a legal system, belief in equal opportunity as the proper grounding for a social system [and a] willingness to adhere to the discipline implied by rotation in office through an electoral system."[15]

While many Americans take these values as self-evident, they are not in-born and must, as American Federation of Teachers president Albert Shanker noted, be taught and cultivated anew in each generation. At bottom, that is the fundamental purpose of public schools, he said: "to teach children what it means to be an American," transmitting "common values and shared culture," in a unique process known as "Americanization." He explained: "one is not born into something that makes you an American. It is not by virtue of birth, but by accepting a common set of values and beliefs that you become an American."[16]

Americanization means becoming a part of the polity—becoming one of us.

To be sure, the concept of "Americanization" has at times been mis-construed in U.S. history to justify horrific practices, such as seeking to "civilize" indigenous children and undermine their heritage. As the late Barbara Jordan noted in 1995, Americanization "earned a bad reputa-tion when it was stolen by racists and xenophobes in the 1920s. But it is our word, and we are taking it back. Americanization means be-coming a part of the polity—becoming one of us." Jordan argued, "The United States has united immigrants and their descendants around a commitment to democratic ideals and constitutional principles. People from an extraordinary range of ethnic and religious backgrounds have embraced these ideas."[17]

There are two primary ways to encourage children to discover the genius of democracy: by telling them explicitly, and by showing them implicitly. A curriculum of rigorous courses in history, literature, and civics can cultivate knowledge of democratic practices and a belief in democratic values. The classes should tell America's stories—warts and all—and include the ways in which groups have used democratic means to improve the country. Children should also be taught what it is like to live in nondemocratic countries in order to appreciate what they might otherwise take for granted. But that is not enough.

In addition to teaching democratic values directly, we must also address the hidden curriculum—what is taught to students implicitly, through how we conduct ourselves as a society, perhaps most important being how we choose to run our schools. As Century Foundation policy asso-ciate Kimberly Quick has noted, our schools "not only reflect our current values as a nation, but also reveal the values that we anticipate passing along to the next generation of Americans."[18]

Are the voices of parents and community members heard as a part of decision-making, or are they shut out by state takeovers and bil-lionaire philanthropists who bankroll reform efforts? Are teachers, parents, and students involved in determining how schools are run, or do principals get the only voice? Do students have access to economically and racially integrated schools where they are treated equally, or are they segregated into separate and unequal schools or tracks within schools? These are all critical questions, because no matter what the explicit curriculum says about democracy, as

Rochester union leader Adam Urbanski has noted, "You cannot teach what you do not model."

Shifting Emphasis Away from Democracy to Marketplace Skills

In recent decades, as the nature of the American economy changed to require greater knowledge and skills from workers, and as democratic capitalism spread after the collapse of the Soviet Union, educators shifted their emphasis strongly toward the role of schools in promoting private skills rather than civic education. This shift occurred both in the explicit curriculum of schools and the "hidden curriculum" that schools impart through example. Fixing the civics curriculum is relatively straightforward. But getting the hidden curriculum right will require extensive efforts over time.

Education reformers from both major political parties reduced the grand two-fold purposes of American public education to a narrower focus on workplace skills. As part of this effort, reformers have tended to emphasize the economic value of education to individual students using a particular focus on reading and math test scores as the salient metric of success. Students, the mantra pronounced, must be "career and college ready."

President Barack Obama highlighted the idea that "A world-class education is the single most important factor in determining not just whether our kids can compete for the best jobs but whether America can out-compete countries around the world. America's business leaders understand that when it comes to education, we need to up our game. *That's* why we're working together to put an outstanding education within reach for every child."[19] (Emphasis added.) The language of education leaders became infused with the dialect of the marketplace, and the need to garner a "return on investment." In a telling sign, in 2013, the governing board of the National Assessment for Educational Progress (NAEP) dropped fourth- and twelfth-grade civics and American history as a tested subject when it needed to save money.[20]

As civics instruction was curtailed, some education reformers went further in their push toward market-based policy, saying that there was too much democracy in the public education system itself. Many reformers took their cue from scholars John Chubb and Terry Moe, whose book, *Politics, Markets and America's Schools*, argued that "direct democratic control" over public education appears to be "incompatible with

94

effective schooling."[21] This motif was made manifest in four emerging trends: state takeovers of urban districts; efforts to reduce workplace democracy in schools; diminishment of school integration as a valued goal; and adoption of a new marketplace theory of charter schools. Critics noted that these efforts to reduce democratic control of schools not only sent an unfortunate signal to students about democratic norms; they also frequently failed to improve educational outcomes.

State Takeovers

One popular strategy embraced by education reformers is state takeovers of struggling urban districts. These efforts have sometimes been aided by well-meaning philanthropists, who put faith in technocratic solutions and see community input as a hindrance to getting things done. In Newark, New Jersey, for example, journalist Dale Russakoff chronicled the effort of Governor Chris Christie and Mayor Cory Booker to improve educational opportunities with a $100 million gift from Facebook billionaire Mark Zuckerberg in 2010. Although Newark schools had been under state control since 1995 with little positive effect, Booker told Zuckerberg that he "could flip a whole city." Zuckerberg and Booker's stated goal, says Russakoff, "was not simply to repair education in Newark but to develop a model for saving it in all of urban America—and to do it in five years."[22]

This transformation would be accomplished not by reducing poverty or school segregation—strong predictors of academic achievement—but by a series of top-down reforms: closing failing schools, expanding charter schools, and weakening teacher tenure. These reforms were adopted with little input from public school teachers, with whom Christie regularly feuded, or from the community.[23] Christie, who noted "I got maybe six votes in Newark," felt free to ignore local opinion.[24] Christopher Cerf, Christie's education commissioner, told a group of philanthropists, "We still control all the levers."[25] At a fundraising party, Zuckerberg was asked who the new superintendent in Newark would be; Zuckerberg replied, "Anyone we want."[26]

Outside technocrats, wrote journalist Sarah Carr in the *Washington Post,* were given "nearly dictatorial power" in Newark.[27] Cerf consistently overrode the votes of a democratically elected advisory board, leading Shavar Jeffries, a civil rights attorney who was a strong supporter of reform, to warn, "Education reform comes across as colonial to people who've been here for decades."[28]

Thoroughly undemocratic, the reforms also failed to produce positive results for students, as test scores declined in math and literacy during the tenure of Christie's hand-picked superintendent Cami Anderson. Anderson, who was forced by Christie to resign, was left to complain that the state tests were "fatally flawed."[29]

The Newark experience is not unique. State takeovers of local districts, writes John Jackson of the Schott Foundation, rarely achieve their stated goal of raising academic outcomes for students. Moreover, by removing local democratic control over schools, they "should sound the same alarm" as efforts to deny individuals the right vote, especially since takeovers frequently occur in low-income communities of color, Jackson argues.[30]

Another common motif among education reformers is that democratically elected teacher union leaders are seen not as vehicles for workplace democracy, but rather as stubborn impediments to doing right by school children. No one has embodied this philosophy more clearly than Michelle Rhee, the chancellor of Washington, D.C., public schools from 2007 to 2010, who went on to found Students First, an organization meant to counter the influence of teachers unions.

Rhee argued that public schools in Washington, D.C. were in such bad shape that extraordinary measures were required. She even proposed the idea of getting a congressional declaration of emergency, so that she would not have to bargain with the elected representatives of teachers at all. "Cooperation, collaboration, and consensus-building," she argued, "are way overrated."[31] Rhee held veteran teachers in disdain, and famously posed on the cover of *Time* magazine with a broom in her hands. As chancellor, she once told a film crew, "I'm going to fire somebody in a little while. Do you want to see that?" Her widespread dismissal of teachers was found to violate due process rights. In 2011, an arbitrator reinstated seventy-five educators fired by Rhee in 2008, after determining that she had neither explained why they were being terminated nor given them a chance to respond to charges.[32] Not only were her methods found to be autocratic; critics noted that they, and those of her anointed successor, Kaya Henderson, did not promote equal opportunity. "Despite all the promises made by Rhee and Henderson," journalist John Merrow wrote in 2015, "the 'achievement gap' between well-to-do kids and poor kids has widened."[33]

The U.S. Supreme Court's landmark 1954 decision *Brown v. Board of Education* held that separate schools for black and white are inherently unequal; and subsequent research also suggested that separate schools for rich and poor are a recipe for inequality.[34] The *Brown* decision explicitly underlined "the importance of education to our democratic society," noting that schooling "is the very foundation of good citizenship." Integrated schools underline the democratic message of equality, while segregated schools can teach the opposite: that some citizens are more deserving than others.

Integrated schools underline the democratic message of equality, while segregated schools can teach the opposite: that some citizens are more deserving than others.

But education reformers have often walked away from the democratic lessons of *Brown*. Intimidated by the political challenges to racial and socioeconomic integration, they argue that we should instead devote our efforts to improving high-poverty schools as best we can.[35] Indeed, some charter schools boast of the fact that they are segregated and have "the highest octane mix of poor and minority kids," notes the American Enterprise Institute's Frederick Hess, "even though just about every observer thinks that" integrated schools are "good for kids, communities, and the country."[36]

The evolution of the charter school phenomenon nicely illustrates the education reform community's shift away from a focus on democracy toward an emphasis on market-based policy. Democracy was at the center of the early concept of charter schools that American Federation of Teachers president Albert Shanker outlined in a 1988 speech to the National Press Club and subsequent writings. Shanker saw charters as a vehicle for workplace democracy—where rank and file teachers could suggest ideas on how schools could be run better. He also believed charters offered the opportunity for socioeconomic, racial, and ethic integration of students, drawing upon the example of a school he visited in Cologne Germany that educated Turkish immigrant students alongside native Germans. These laboratory schools would then share lessons with traditional public schools.[37]

But as the charter school movement grew, the idea shifted markedly from a democratic vision of teacher empowerment, school integration, and collaboration to one that suggested "charter schools are a vehicle for infusing competition and market forces into public education," in the words of one leading charter advocate.[38] Charter schools became seen as a way to bypass elected teacher union leaders; they purposefully located in segregated neighborhoods; and they were pushed as a way to whip traditional public schools into shape. A 2013 review of charter school laws found that providing competition was the most widely cited purpose of charter school legislation.[39]

Across a variety of policy areas, then, the education reform community helped to radically shift the focus of public education. Being career and college ready became much more important than training students to become citizens. It seemed safe to focus on producing skilled workers for a market economy because America's highly successful experiment in self-governance appeared stable and firmly ensconced.

Cost to Ignoring Democracy's Role

Today, however, we are seeing the costs of an unbalanced approach to public education that focuses on markets far more than democracy: dangerously low levels of civic knowledge, and a reduced faith in democratic values among Americans. These developments are particularly troublesome because they have occurred alongside two larger societal trends that undermine our democracy: a decline in labor unions, and increased political polarization by residential areas, all of which we explore below.

Americans' knowledge of basic civics is frighteningly scant. A 2015 survey conducted by the Annenberg Public Policy Center of the University of Pennsylvania found that only 31 percent of Americans can name all three branches of government, and 32 percent cannot identify a single one. (See Figure 1.) The survey found that only 53 percent of Americans understood that a 5–4 decision by the U.S. Supreme Court constitutes law and must be followed; 15 percent believed that a 5–4 decision is sent back to Congress for reconsideration, and 13 percent thought that the decision would be returned to lower courts and decided there.[40]

Performance among students on the 2010 National Assessment of Educational Progress (NAEP) was also disturbingly low. Only 27 percent of fourth-graders, 22 percent of eighth-graders, and 24 percent of twelfth-graders performed at or above the proficient level in civics. Thirty-six percent of twelfth grade students failed to even reach the basic level in civics, signifying that they were unable to describe forms of political participation in a democracy, or draw simple conclusions from basic graphs, charts, maps, or cartoons.[41]

What is particularly disturbing is that civic literacy has not risen despite considerable gains in educational attainment. As scholar William Galston observed in 2003, "Although the level of formal schooling in the United States is much higher than it was fifty years ago, the civic knowledge of today's students is at best no higher than that of their parents and grandparents."[42] Among college graduates, older respondents perform significantly better than younger ones according to the

American Council of Trustees and Alumni. While over 98 percent of college graduates over 65, for example, knew that the president cannot establish taxes, only 74 percent of graduates aged 25–34 understood this concept.[43]

If schools are doing a poor job of imparting civic knowledge, they are also doing a poor job of inculcating an appreciation for the democratic values embodied in the Bill of Rights. In the 2015 Annenberg Survey, for example, over one-quarter of people (26 percent) would vote to alter or eliminate the Fifth Amendment so that courts could require a person testify against herself. Almost half (46 percent) opposed a prohibition on "double jeopardy"; the same percentage of people believe that the government should be permitted to prohibit a peaceful march down a main street if those marching expressed offensive views; and only half of respondents thought that the government should not be able to prohibit practice of a religion if a majority of voters perceived it to hold "un-American" views.[44]

The problem has grown over time, giving rise to some startling attitudes. Columnist Catherine Rampell points out that Americans have become, "steadily more open to anti-democratic, autocratic ideals."[45] As researchers Roberto Stefan Foa and Yascha Mounk note, trends in the World Values Survey show that Americans have shown a declining trust in institutions, including democracy.[46] When asked whether democracy is a good or bad way to run a country, 17 percent said bad or very bad, up from 9 percent in the mid-1990s. Among those ages 16 to 24, about a quarter said democracy was bad or very bad, an increase of one-third from a decade and a half earlier (see Figure 2).

Some 25 percent of millennials said it is "unimportant," that in a democracy, people should "choose their leaders in free elections." Among U.S. citizens of all ages, the proportion who said it would be "fairly good" or "very good" for the "army to rule," has risen from one in sixteen in 1995, to one in six today.[47] Likewise, a June 2016 survey by the Public Religion Research Institute and the Brookings Institution found that a majority of Americans showed authoritarian (as opposed to autonomous) leanings. Moreover, fully 49 percent of Americans agreed that "because things have gotten so far off track in this country, we need a leader who is willing to break some rules if that's what it takes to set things right."[48]

The decline of public schools' emphasis on democracy has been particularly disturbing because it has been accompanied by a parallel decline of labor unions, which serve as critical civic associations in healthy de-mocracies. From the 1950s to today, union membership fell precipi-tously, from one in three to one in ten. This decline is closely associat-ed with the hollowing out of the American middle class, which thriving democracies need to survive. But the drop in labor membership also has reduced the role of unions as incubators of democratic practice. Throughout much of the twentieth century, labor unions served as what Harvard political scientist Robert Putnam calls "schools for democra-cy."[49] Being involved in workplace decisions and collective bargaining, and voting for union leadership are important drivers of "democratic acculturation." Union members also staff phone banks and go door to door recruiting voters, which increases civic participation among union members and nonmembers alike.[50] Relatedly, research shows that unions played an important role in countering "an authoritarian streak" among working-class voters. Seymour Martin Lipset found that orga-nized labor made workers more inclined to embrace democratic norms by inculcating "civic virtues in its members."[51] That critical force is great-ly diminished today.

Finally, the crisis in civic education in our public schools comes at a time of increasing political polarization—including by residential areas—that makes it harder for democracy to operate well. Part of the democratic process is the education of citizens—by neighbors and news sources—that will help them consider a wide range of views and make up their minds about candidates and policy issues. But that continuing lifelong education through dialogue in a democracy no longer works the way it used to in the United States.

But that continuing lifelong education through dialogue in a democracy no longer works the way it used to in the United States.

Sociologist Robert Cushing and political analyst Bill Bishop have found that Americans have become increasingly likely to live in close proximi-ty to those who share a political ideology. In the presidential election of 1976, 27 percent of voters lived in so called "landslide counties"—coun-ties in which the winning presidential candidate won by twenty points or more. By the 2004 election, that number had reached 48 percent.[52] In 2016, a poll of Virginia voters found that more than half of Hillary Clin-ton supporters said they had no close friends of family voting for Donald Trump, and vice versa.[53]

We also are increasingly engaging with news sources and social media that confirm our preexisting hunches, creating political echo chambers that inhibit critical thinking. According to the Pew Research Center, con-sistently liberal voters are most likely to block, un-follow, or defriend someone on social media because they disagreed with that person's political stance. Meanwhile, consistent conservatives do the same and tend to receive their news from one conservative source, *FOX News*.[54] In this way, political polarization is helping compound the ineffectiveness of schools in making us good citizens.

Case Study: Donald Trump's Presidential Candidacy—A Twenty-First-Century Sputnik Moment

These anti-democratic developments came to a head in the 2016 election and the disturbing rise of an authoritarian presidential candidate, Donald Trump, who ran on a platform that consistently rejected mainstream liberal democratic norms that historically have been embraced by Republicans and Democrats alike and nevertheless managed to win the presidency. The rise of a candidate who questioned several elements of constitutional democracy—including freedom of religion, freedom of the press, the rule of law, the independence of the judiciary, and the peaceful transition of power following elections—should serve as a Sputnik moment for civics education and the need to model democratic values in how our schools are run. Just as Soviet technological advances triggered investment in science education in the 1950s, the 2016 election should spur renewed emphasis on the need for schools to instill an appreciation for liberal democratic values.

Against a backdrop in which the American public school system has deemphasized democratic citizenship, and in which Americans have demonstrated less commitment to democratic institutions, Trump called for a series of attacks on liberal democratic values. While candidates have often been chided by the opposing party for rejecting constitutional norms, Trump's candidacy was different in kind. Fellow Republicans repeatedly had to distance themselves from their own standard-bearer for rejecting essential democratic norms.

Michael Gerson, a former speechwriter for President George W. Bush, said that with Donald Trump, "we have reached the culmination of the founders' fears: Democracy is producing a genuine threat to the American form of self-government."[55] Peter Wehner, another veteran Republican official, wrote of Trump's candidacy: "The founders, knowing history and human nature, took great care to devise a system that would prevent demagogues and those with authoritarian tendencies from rising up in America. That system has been extraordinarily successful. We have never before faced the prospect of a political strongman becoming president. Until now."[56] What set Trump apart, wrote University of Texas historian Jeffrey Tulis, is that "no other previous major party presidential candidate has felt so unconstrained by . . . constitutional norms."[57] Consider:

- *Freedom of Religion.* The First Amendment provides for the free exercise of religion, yet during the campaign, Trump proposed a religious test on immigration, calling for "a total and complete shutdown of Muslims entering the United States."[58] He called for heavily surveillance of Muslim communities and their houses of worship, which Anthony Romero of the ACLU noted "would infringe upon American Muslims' First Amendment right to exercise their religion freely without fear or intimidation."[59] While these policies were widely rejected by mainstream Republican leaders, Trump's announcements, disturbingly, were associated with his rise in the polls.
- *Freedom of the Press.* The free press is essential for holding government officials accountable, which is why the U.S. Supreme Court more than a half century ago suggested special protection from libel suits brought by public figures.[60] During the campaign, however, Trump promised to "open up" the nation's libel laws. He revoked the press credentials of critical reporters from newspapers such as the *Washington Post* and *Politico*, "an almost unheard-of practice for a modern presidential candidate."[61]
- *Rule of Law.* While President George W. Bush and Vice President Dick Cheney were criticized for engaging in water-boarding of terrorism suspects, Trump suggested he would do "a hell of a lot worse than waterboarding."[62] Trump also called for murdering family members of terrorists, which is a violation of the Geneva Conventions.[63] When Trump was asked by a Fox News host what would happen if the military refused to follow orders to torture, Trump responded, "They're not going to refuse me." Such "impatience with constraints placed on democratic governments," Dalibor Rohac of the American Enterprise Institute notes, is the hallmark of "authoritarianism."[64]
- *An Independent Judiciary.* During the campaign, Trump famously criticized a federal judge presiding over a lawsuit against Trump University. He suggested an Indiana-born jurist of Mexican heritage, Gonzalo Curiel, was incapable of being neutral in the suit. Paul Ryan, Republican Speaker of the House, said, "Claiming a person can't do their job because of their race is sort of like the textbook definition of a racist comment."[65] Trump was scolded by Republican judge and former Attorney General Michael Mukasey, who called Trump's position, "baseless and squalid."[66]

- *Scapegoating Minorities.* More generally, Trump used the classic tactic of demagogues seeking to enhance their own power by whipping up animosity against society's minorities. Trump focused mostly on Muslims and immigrants from Mexico, whom he broad brushed as "rapists."[67] The founders warned against a "tyranny of the majority" that overrode the rights of minorities. Some of the founders were particularly concerned about the rights of elites who owned property, but Trump used the classic ploy of going after elites who allegedly "coddle minorities."[68]
- *Celebrating the Violence of the Mob.* Authoritarians often rely on violence to intimidate. During the campaign, when Trump was asked what would happen if he were denied the Republican nomination, he responded, "I think you'd have riots." When protesters interrupted his rallies, Trump mused, "In the old days, protesters would be "carried out in a stretcher."[69] Journalist Andrew Sullivan observes, "No modern politician who has come this close to the presidency has championed violence in this way."[70] For Trump, violence is linked to the promise of strength, says Brookings Institution scholar Robert Kagan. "What [Trump] offers is an attitude, an aura of crude strength and machismo, a boasting disrespect for the niceties of the democratic culture that he claims, and his followers believe, have produced national weakness and incompetence."[71]
- *Imprisoning Political Opponents.* The hallmark of authoritarian regimes, Dana Milbank notes, is the imprisonment of political opponents, which is what made chilling the constant refrain from the Republican National Convention's lynch mob regarding the presumptive Democratic presidential nominee: "Lock her up!"[72] Donald Trump then doubled down on this idea, telling Hillary Clinton in the second presidential debate that if he wins, he would "instruct my attorney general to get a special prosecutor to look into your situation," and adding that "you'd be in jail," if he ran the country. "It's a chilling thought," said Michael Chertoff, head of the Justice Department's criminal justice division in the administration of George W. Bush. "It smacks of what we read about tin-pot dictators in other parts of the world, where when they win an election their first move is to imprison opponents," he said.[73]
- *Threatening Not To Respect Election Results.* Before the ultimate outcome of the election was known, during the third presidential debate with Clinton, Trump astounded observers by refusing to say he would respect the results of the election, a hallmark of American democracy for centuries. Trump would not commit to this principle despite the plea of the moderator, Chris Wallace of *FOX News*, who noted, "But sir, one of the

prides of this country is the peaceful transition of power and that no matter how hard-fought a campaign is, that at the end of the campaign that the loser concedes to the winner."[74] John McCain, the 2008 Republican presidential nominee, noted that while he did not like losing the election, he had "a duty to concede." He said, "A concessions isn't just an exercise in graciousness. It is an act of respect for the will of the American people."[75]

- *Strongman to the Rescue.* Like a Central American strongman, Trump claimed in his acceptance speech at the Republican National Convention, "I am your voice." He declared, "Nobody knows the system better than me, which is why I alone can fix it."[76] This sentiment, that Trump was the "man on the horseback to save a frightened and supine nation," wrote Gerson, is a notion the founders would have held "in utter contempt."[77]

- *A Preference for Authoritarians.* During the campaign, Trump famously and repeatedly showered admiration on Vladimir Putin, at one point saying the Russian dictator was "a leader far more than our leader." Russian chess champion Garry Kasparov responded, "Vladimir Putin is a strong leader in the same way that arsenic is a strong drink." He continued: "Praising a brutal K.G.B. dictator, especially as preferable to a democratically elected U.S. president, whether you like Obama or hate him, is despicable and dangerous."[78] Trump also expressed admiration for Iraq's dictator Saddam Hussein, Kim Jong Un of North Korea, and the Chinese leaders behind the Tiananmen Square massacre.[79] "There is no precedent for what Trump is saying," notes former Mitt Romney advisor Max Boot. "George McGovern was not running around saying 'what a wonderful guy Ho Chi Minh is!'"[80] Trump is not a totalitarian, Eric Chenoweth, an expert on democracy notes, because he does not have a fixed ideology. But he does seem to identify with authoritarians, who gain "political power with a clear aim to dominate and control the state."[81]

The 2016 election stood apart from other elections, Chenoweth wrote. Historically, both parties, while differing on the size of government, regulation, taxation, and other issues "have remained within a broad democratic range and commit themselves to adhering to America's constitutional foundations that establish and protect basic rights and a democratic system of governance." During the midst of the 2016 campaign, however, we faced "an abnormal situation: one of America's two major parties has nominated an explicitly authoritarian candidate for the presidency," which posed "a present danger to American democracy."[82]

Reflecting on Trump's campaign through July, Chenoweth wrote that the candidate "adopted many parts of the authoritarian toolkit from the last century: chauvinism, preying on people's fears of national decline, promising an idyllic vision for the future based on a unique individual's ability to lead the people and encouraging mass adulation for a political savior of the nation."[83]

Running on this platform, Trump, a newcomer to politics, stunningly defeating sixteen other candidates for the Republican presidential nomination, several of them respected governors and senators with decades of political experience between them.[84] Along the way, he won more primary votes than any other Republican candidate in the party's history.[85] America has long seen demagogues who rejected civil rights and civil liberties —from Huey Long to Father Charles Coughlin, and from Joseph McCarthy to George Wallace—but never before has a major political party nominated for presidency an individual who so thoroughly questioned widely accepted democratic norms of their era. "In terms of liberal democracy and constitutional order," Andrew Sullivan wrote, "Trump is an extinction-level event."[86] And then the unthinkable happened: Trump was elected president of the United States.

It has been broadly noted that Donald Trump performed particularly well with working-class white voters who lack college degrees. In a July 2016 poll, for example, this group supported Trump over Clinton 60 percent to 33 percent, compared with college-educated whites who polled 43 percent for Trump, 42 percent for Clinton.[87] Working-class whites constituted Trump's base, providing between 58 percent and 62 percent of his overall support.[88] At one point during the primaries, Trump himself memorably observed that he loved "the poorly educated," who supported him so strongly.

Of course, these voters have every right to make the political choices they would like in a democracy. And they have a right to be angry about a political establishment that has ignored their economic needs and created a vacuum for right-wing populism.[89] To be clear, people can legitimately agree or disagree with candidates on a variety of issues. Trump may be right or wrong on world trade, American involvement in NATO, taxes, gun control, or abortion. What sets this election apart, however, is the attack on the very principles of liberal democracy. And an authoritarian candidate's resonance with less-educated voters in particular raises the critical role public education can play in supporting democratic values and norms. The point, then, is not that Trump supporters are all "deplorable"; rather, what is deplorable is the failure of our education system to instill an essential belief in the values of constitutional democracy.

Policy Recommendations for Putting Democracy Back into Public Education

On the heels of a presidential election in which an authoritarian candidate captured the country's highest office—with especially strong support from less-educated voters—we are faced with an urgent question: Moving forward, how can public schools do a better job of educating students to be responsible citizens who sustain America's experiment with constitutional government for future generations? Put differently, how can we put democracy back into education?

Below we outline several ideas for state, local, and federal policy makers. The first set of ideas has to do with directly improving the civics curriculum that students are taught; the second set of proposals has to do with improving the "hidden curriculum"—the messages sent to students about democracy by the critical choices we make about how we value and treat parents, community members, teachers, and students in our education system.

To begin with, schools must do a much better job to directly enhance students' appreciation for liberal democratic values. Exposure to existing civics classes is not enough. Ninety-seven percent of twelfth-grade students already report taking a civics or government class in high school.[90] State policies on civics have not been found to be associated with greater informed political participation by young adults.[91]

But quality of instruction does matter. Research finds that "done right, school-based civic education can have a significant impact on civic knowledge," notes William Galston, and that such knowledge, in turn, "enhances support for democratic principles and virtues, promotes political participation, helps citizens better understand the impact of public policy on their concerns, gives citizens the framework they need to absorb and understand new civic information, and reduces generalized mistrust and fear of public life."[92] Three reports—one from the Albert Shanker Institute, one from the Education Commission of the States and the National Center for Learning and Civic Engagement, and one from social psychologist Jonathan Haidt—provide important guideposts for improving civics education.

In 2003, the Albert Shanker Institute outlined a strategy for civics education that remains compelling today. The blueprint was endorsed by a wide variety of civil rights advocates, business and labor leaders, and public officials from various ideological backgrounds who were all committed to supporting democratic values. Signatories included progressives such as Bill Clinton, Henry Cisneros, Wade Henderson, John Lewis, and Richard Riley, but also conservatives such as Frederick Hess, Harvey Mansfield, and Norman Podhoretz.[93] The group eschewed relativism by declaring their conviction "that democracy is the worthiest form of human governance ever conceived." They went on to suggest that because we are not born democrats, "we cannot take its survival or its spread—or its perfection in practice—for granted. We must transmit to each generation the political vision of liberty and equality that unites us as Americans, and a deep loyalty to the political institutions put together to fulfill that vision."[94]

The group asked: how will young people be instilled with "an understanding of and an appreciation for their stunning political heritage? How do we educate citizens? How do we raise democrats?"[95] The Shanker Institute outlined a four-part strategy that called for:

1. *A robust history/social studies curriculum, starting in the elementary years and continuing through every year of schooling;*
2. *A full and honest teaching of the American story;*
3. *An unvarnished account of what life has been and is like in nondemocratic societies; and*
4. *A cultivation of the virtues essential to a healthy democracy.*[96]

The first prong—a robust history curriculum—is critical. "A serious engagement with history is essential to the nurturing of the democratic citizen," the Shanker Institute noted. "Only history can give students an appreciation for how long and hard and tangled the road to liberty and equality has been."[97] Through history classes, students learn to recognize the realities of human nature that protects them from "utopian fantasies" that mask antidemocratic ideas. Mastering a common core of American history can also bind us together and create "a common civic identity based on a patriotism of principle."[98]

The second prong—telling the American story in an honest way—also helps prepare democratic citizens. This historical accounting should include the warts—slavery, the *Dred Scott* decision, the Triangle Shirt Waist fire, the Chinese Exclusion Act, Japanese internment, lynching, the persecution of gays, among others—but also discuss the movements to abolish slavery, to gain women's suffrage, to establish worker safety, and to promote civil rights. The Shanker Institute notes,

From the accounts of these transformations—and of the individuals, the organizations, the movements that fought for them—students will recognize the genius of democracy: When people are free to dissent, to criticize, to protest and publish, to join together in common cause, to hold their elected officials accountable, democracy's magnificent capacity for self-correction is manifest.[99]

In the past, textbooks have failed at this balance: in the early years, providing a whitewashed celebration of America; and in recent years, suggesting America's sins are its essence, the Shanker Institute notes, leaving students concluding that the world is a hopeless place. A new balance must be struck.

The third prong—teaching students what life is like in non-free countries—will give students something to which American society can be compared. Children should be taught to realize that in many societies, there is no assumption that leaders should be chosen by the people, that governments can be freely criticized, or that trials must be fair. Exposure to these realities will generate questions among students—"How could these things happen?"—and will also provide students with "armor against antidemocratic ideas."[100]

The fourth prong—cultivating the virtues essential to a healthy democracy—recognizes that formal democratic institutions are not enough for the survival of self-governance; we also need a citizenry equipped to grapple with important moral questions. History, literature, and biography can train "the heart as well as the head"; it can help students avoid the moral relativism that suggests it is only a matter of opinion whether, say, Hitler's gas chambers are to be condemned. While religious instruction is forbidden in the public schools, moral education is critical as "the basic ideas of liberty, equality, and justice, of civil, political and economic rights and obligations are all assertions of right and wrong, or moral values."[101]

A 2014 report of the Education Commission of the States and the National Center for Learning and Civic Engagement also provides important guidelines on practices that can make for effective civic learning.[102] The groups suggest incorporating discussions of current issues—such as global warming, gun control, racial profiling, and immigration—into the classroom to make civics feel relevant to the lives of young people. The organizations say service projects and extracurricular activities, such as speech and debate and school newspaper, should be encouraged. Students also should be given the opportunity to participate in school governance. In New York, for example, students took on a project to reverse budget cuts to programs they deemed important—and won.

Finally, 2016 research by social psychologist Jonathan Haidt of New York University and Australian political scientist Karen Stenner sheds light on how civics education can help nurture democracy—and thwart authoritarian appeals—by emphasizing what we have in common as Americans. As Robert Pondiscio of the Fordham Institute notes, research by Haidt and Stenner suggest that the "authoritarian button on our foreheads" is pushed when people believe that society is "coming apart."[103] While the old civics emphasis on the "melting pot" has serious problems, Pondiscio notes, swinging to the other extreme, where students only learn about differences, can feed a frightening backlash that promotes white nationalism and undermines inclusive democratic norms. While it is important to respect and honor ethnic, racial and economic differences, Pondiscio suggests, democratic impulses are fed when schools teach all the things that bind Americans together as well.

Modeling democratic practices is as critical as explicitly teaching them in the curriculum. To reinforce the message of the civics book, students should able to see firsthand that parents and community members and teachers have a role in democratic decision-making in schools; and that students are given genuinely equal opportunity.

Do students see that parents and community members have input on key issues such as where new schools are built, or does a remote state actor or outside consultant make these decisions unilaterally? Below are three examples of inclusion.

- *The D.C. Compact.* In the years before Washington, D.C. schools chancellor Michelle Rhee implemented her motto that "collaboration is overrated," district schools took a more democratic approach. As explained below (see Washington, D.C. case study), in 2004, Clifford Janey created the D.C. Education Compact (DCED), made up of government leaders, community activists, foundation officials, business leaders, teachers, unions, and teachers and concerned citizens to be part of a dialogue for improving education and informing the district's strategic plan.[104] The group was given major responsibility for adopting in D.C. a version of the highly rated Massachusetts standards and accountability system. Michelle Rhee subsequently disbanded the DCED.
- *Newark Public Engagement Strategy.* In Newark, New Jersey, where residents felt disenfranchised by a state takeover of the district schools in 1995, Superintendent Janey sought to build community trust through an extensive public engagement strategy. (See Newark case study). Although the district had an elected school board that exercised only advisory power, Janey honored the group by meeting with them to discuss key decisions. His successor, Cami Anderson, by contrast, stopped attending

advisory board meetings in the final year of her tenure as super-intendent.[105]

- *St. Paul's Inclusive Bargaining.* Parents often feel excluded from important decisions made in collective bargaining agree-ments between teachers and management, and in prepara-tion for the 2011 negotiation, the St. Paul, Minnesota teachers union sought to remedy that concern. The union met with par-ents to find out what sort of provisions they would like to see in the union-district contract and incorporated community goals into the bargaining process. In the negotiations, teachers sought smaller class sizes, less standardized testing, and the hiring of librarians, nurses, social workers, and counselors to better serve students. Although management initially rebuffed these concerns, calling them a matter of management pre-rogative, community support of a threatened teachers strike allowed the community and educators to prevail on the key issues at stake. [106]

Do students see that teachers are part of democratic decision-making or is power concentrated in a single person—the principal? Are demo-cratically elected teacher union leaders key players, or are they publicly denigrated? What do students observe?

- *Inclusion of Employees and Unions in Decision-Making in New-ark.* Some leaders routinely vilify teacher unions and seek to bypass them. By contrast, in Newark, Clifford Janey treated the union as a valued partner and every employee—whether a principal, teacher, or custodian—was invited to make sug-gestions and toward a comprehensive strategic plan for the schools (see Newark case study).
- *Peer Review in Toledo, Ohio and Rochester, New York.* An-other powerful way to model democracy for students—and im-prove educational outcomes—is through peer assistance and review programs for teachers.[107] Teacher union leader Albert Shanker acknowledged that "some teachers are excellent, some are very good, some are good, and some are terrible."[108] But how can schools weed bad teachers out of the profession without giving undue power to principals who often have very little knowledge of a teacher's particular field and might play personal favorites? In places such as Toledo, Ohio, and Roch-ester, New York (see Rochester case study), expert teachers from outside a school work with struggling teachers in the same fields, seeking to provide assistance where possible, but ulti-mately recommending termination of employment in certain circumstances.[109]

The idea of teachers—and their unions—being involved in recommending termination of colleagues is controversial. Some critics liken union involvement in firing teachers to the fox guarding the hen house, while some hardline unionists object to a practice that chips away at teacher solidarity. But unions need a credible answer to the charge that they protect incompetent teachers; and in practice, teachers have been even tougher on colleagues than administrators have been in several jurisdictions, from Cincinnati, Ohio to Montgomery County, Maryland.[110] And in places that have peer review, students see workplace democracy in action: where teachers, like professors, doctors and lawyers, have a strong say in how their profession is policed.

- *Teacher-Run Schools in Newark, New Jersey and Elsewhere.* In Newark, New Jersey, Henderson, Minnesota, and elsewhere, teachers extend the democratic principle of peer review in the area of dismissals to virtually every realm of school affairs: teachers make decisions about hiring, curriculum, scheduling, and many other facets of schooling that are left to principals in most schools. Under his tenure in Newark, for example, Clifford Janey arranged for a contract waiver for teachers to start the Brick Avon Academy, a teacher-led traditional public school in which rank and file staff members elect fellow teachers to make decisions about curriculum, budget, hiring, and other school governance issues.[111] (See Newark case study.) The school, which draws on Newark's poorest community, saw steep test score increases in subsequent years.[112] At teacher cooperatives such as Minnesota New Country School in Henderson, Minnesota, and Avalon School in St. Paul, teachers are given unparalleled say in running their schools. "Twenty-four brains are undoubtedly more powerful and smarter than one," said one teacher at Avalon. The schools perform well academically, and the emphasis on democracy and collaboration filters through to students.[113]

Do students see that classmates of all races and economic backgrounds have access to the best schools and the most academically advanced tracks or do race and class appear to be highly predictive determinants of opportunity? Does the assignment of students to schools and academic tracks send the message that in a democracy, people of all backgrounds are equally valued, or that some are more worthy than others?

- *School Integration in Cambridge, Massachusetts; Rochester, New York; and Elsewhere.* The socioeconomic and racial integration of schools is important to the health of a democracy for three distinct reasons: (1) integrated schools underline the democratic message that in America, we are all political equals; (2) integrated schools promote tolerance and acceptance and make demagogic appeals that scapegoat minorities less likely to be effective, and (3) the opportunity to attend integrated schools raises educational attainment, which, in turn, is directly correlated with democratic participation rates.

One key principle undergirding American democracy is that we all have not only an equal vote in elections but also an equal right to feel a part of the nation's democratic heritage. Because Americans are bound not by blood but by a set of democratic ideals, everyone—no matter what race or national origin or religion or length of time in this country—can lay equal claim on the ideas of Jefferson and Madison and Washington.[114] Of course, American history is riddled with examples of these ideals being trampled for certain groups, which is why it is important that we as a nation remain vigilant in the fight to preserve these ideals for all Americans. When American schoolchildren are educated in what are effectively apartheid schools—divided by race and class—the democratic message of equal political rights and heritage is severely undermined.

Likewise, demagogues can more effectively inflame passions against those they deem as "others"—Muslims, Mexican immigrants, or African Americans—when there are large audiences who do not personally know many members of these groups, partly because they were raised in communities and schools that were almost exclusively white and Christian. The profound lesson of the gay rights movement, for example, is that only when gay Americans openly came out as neighbors, coworkers, and classmates did efforts to demonize homosexuals lose their potency. So too, a large body of research finds that integrated schools can reduce prejudice and racism that stems from ignorance and lack of personal contact.[115] As Thurgood Marshall noted in one case, "Unless our children begin to learn together, then there is little hope that our people will ever learn to live together."[116]

Providing an excellent, integrated education also promotes democracy by improving educational attainment, which increases political participation. Controlling for family socioeconomic status and academic achievement, a 2013 longitudinal study found that students attending socioeconomically integrated schools are as much as 70 percent more likely to graduate high school and enroll in a four-year college than those attending high-poverty schools [117] Political philosopher Danielle Allen has suggested that denying an adequate education to low-income and minority students, as we routinely do, is another form of "voter suppression," given the strong correlation between educational attainment and voter participation. In 2012, Census data show that 72 percent of adults with a bachelor's degree or more voted, compared with less than 32 percent of those with less than a high school education.[118]

Today, one hundred school districts and charter schools consciously consider socioeconomic status as a factor in student assignment, up from two in 1996.[119] In 2001, for example, Cambridge, Massachusetts adopted a plan to produce economic diversity through school choice. The schools have also proven remarkably integrated by race. Graduation rates in Cambridge for low-income, African American, and Latino students are as much as 20 percentage points higher than in nearby Boston (see Figure 3). A similar choice program for socioeconomic diversity has been adopted in Rochester, New York, among other districts (see Rochester case study).

- *Addressing Within-School Integration in Rochester, New York.* In many communities, school building are integrated by race, socioeconomic status, and special education status, but individual classrooms are not, a phenomenon which often denies opportunity to disadvantaged students and runs counter to the democratic message that public schools are designed to impart. In the early 1980s, for example, most students with disabilities in Rochester, New York schools were taught in separate classroom, triggering a complaint to the Office of Civil Rights at the U.S. Department of Education and, ultimately, a consent decree. In 1997, the inclusion rates were still below 20 percent, and superintendent Janey set a goal of 70 percent inclusion.[120] Between 1999 and 2002, the inclusion of students with disabilities into regular learning environments rose from 32.8 percent to 71.4 percent, and performance of students with disabilities in fourth grade English Language Arts exams exceeded similar students statewide.[121] Strong efforts were also made to make sure that special education and minority students had access to rigorous AP and International Baccalaureate classes (see Rochester case study).
- *Giving Students a Chance to Practice Democracy in Newark, New Jersey; the State of Maryland; and Elsewhere.* Students throughout the country are taught democracy and civic engagement by running for office in student government, writing for school newspapers, and engaging in volunteer activities to strengthen the community. In the state of Maryland, for example, Kathleen Kennedy Townsend spearheaded the first effort nationally to require all students to engage in community service as a requirement for high school graduation.[122]

In Newark, New Jersey, many people had for years held low expectations for disadvantaged students, but under Superintendent Janey, the district placed a major emphasis on speech and debate and service learning. The school district converted an old high school sheet metal shop into a distinguished courtroom with mahogany furniture and hosted mock trials so students could learn the judicial process. Debate was expanded to every high school in the district. Students, who were stereotyped as gang members, volunteered in local hospitals in a service program that was nationally recognized (see Newark case study).

Finally, there are a small but growing number of charter schools that are fulfilling Albert Shanker's original vision as vehicles for promoting democratic values by giving teachers voice and integrating students of different socioeconomic and racial backgrounds. My colleague Halley Potter and I profile several of these schools in our book, *A Smarter Charter: Finding What Works for Charter Schools and Public Education.*

One such school is City Neighbors Charter School in Baltimore, which opened in 2005. The schools' founder, Bobbi Macdonald, explains that "democracy and public education" are at the heart of the schools' philosophy. Teachers are part of a union (as are all charter teachers in Maryland), which is something Macdonald embraced rather than resisted. And teachers are represented on the board of the charter, providing them with substantive voice. Most key decisions are made through collaborative committees that include teachers, parents and administrators. The school also intentionally located in a diverse neighborhood. Today, the student body is richly diverse by race (54 percent black, 42 percent white) and income (42 percent low income).[123] While charters are generally more likely to be segregated and less likely to provide teacher voice than traditional public schools, City Neighbors stands as an example of how charters can embody the best democratic ideals.

It is unclear whether a Department of Education under Trump will urge reforms in civic education. But in the long haul, what steps can be taken to strengthen the civic health of the nation? How can we expand the focus of public education to include not only being "college and career-ready" but also "civic-ready"?[124] Broadly speaking, federal policies should support the state and local efforts outlined above—to prioritize a rich curriculum in civics education; and to encourage schools to model democratic practices for students, by giving parents and communities voice in school governance, enabling teachers to participate in workplace democracy, and ensuring students are given access to integrated schools and integrated classrooms. Meeting those various goals will take sustained effort, but in addition, we outline three specific recommendations that can be acted upon in the years to come: (1) federal and state accountability measures should include civic knowledge alongside math, reading, and science; (2) schools should be rewarded when adults model democratic practices for students; and (3) federal charter school programs should encourage those schools that promote democratic practices.

If we believe the role of public schools in sustaining our democracy is important, then civic literacy should be given equal weight to that provided to math, reading, and science test scores in education accountability schemes. No Child Left Behind defined success very narrowly, but the passage of the Every Student Succeeds Act (ESSA) allows states to broaden the concept of what makes a school a success, an important step in the right direction (see below).

When the underlying federal law—the Elementary and Secondary Education Act (ESEA)—is next reauthorized, Congress could elevate the importance of civics education. In the meantime, the National Assessment of Educational Progress (NAEP) should restore civics education testing for the fourth and twelfth grades. It is critical to know, as soon as reasonably possible: Do students have civics knowledge? In the long term, it would also be good to begin tracking a more robust set of outcomes: Do graduates of a school vote, volunteer, and get involved in democratic activities, such as public service and political campaigns? A democracy cannot thrive without active citizens, so just as there is a push to link schools to wage outcomes, so too, we should find creative ways to track post-high school civic participation.

ESSA requires, for the first time, that schools be judged not only by standardized test scores, but also based on "School Quality or Student Success Measures" that might include items such as student engagement, student access to and completion of advanced coursework, school climate and safety, or "other indicators" that might include measures such as physical fitness, access to the arts, climate surveys, and social-emotional skills.[125] This development involves a proper recognition that reducing schools to a few test score results fails to capture the rich set of goals which public schools are charged with meeting.

In the future, states should develop—and the U.S. Department of Education should approve—assessments that measure the degree to which schools are modeling democratic practices for students. How involved are teachers in decision making? Parents? Community members? How racially and socioeconomically integrated are the schools?[126] Is access to a high-quality curriculum and AP classes widely available, or constrained mostly to advantaged students? We cannot expect public schools to do a good job of teaching students to be thoughtful citizens who embrace democracy if the schools do not themselves reflect democratic values and norms.

The federal government provided $333 million to charter schools in fiscal year 2016, and has provided more than $3 billion since charter schools were first created in the 1990s.[127] Federal funding properly focuses on schools that are likely to improve academic achievement and work skills, but little recognition is provided to the role that charter schools can play in promoting democratic values. Do students observe a democratic structure in which their teachers, parents, and broader members of the community have a say in how the school is run? Do students enjoy a racially and economically integrated environment? Alongside academic criteria, this hidden curriculum about democratic values should be a part of what the federal government supports in charter schools.

Do students observe a democratic structure in which their teachers, parents, and broader members of the community have a say in how the school is run? Do students enjoy a racially and economically integrated environment?

Federal funds for starting up new charter schools should provide a priority to those that (a) are likely to promote academic achievement; (b) provide teachers with democratic voice in the workplace (either by providing an automatic opportunity to vote to bargain collectively and/ or provide teachers a role on the charter government board); and (c) have plans to promote socioeconomic and racial integration (such as enrolling students across a region, employing targeted recruitment, or using a weighted lottery to ensure student diversity).[128]

Conclusion

Public education in the United States has always been justified in large measure for its role in supporting America's grand experiment in self-governance. In recent years, we have let that goal slip as economic concerns have all but subsumed the democratic purposes of public education. The 2016 presidential election should serve as a powerful impetus for action. New policies and investments are needed to ensure that our nation, which has been a shining example of democratic values for the world, can continue to play that role for generations to come. (Please refer to the article online for footnotes)

This report makes clear the need for civics education for all citizens.

While this country was developing, Thomas Jefferson was ardent in his profession that only an educated populace could maintain this new Republic.

Below are a couple of articles with quotes attributed to Thomas Jefferson.

Source: https://democracyeducationjournal.org/cgi/viewcontent.cgi?article=1084&-context=home (Carpenter, J., 2013)

Thomas Jefferson and the Ideology of Democratic Schooling

James Carpenter (Binghamton University)

Later, in his First Inaugural Address in 1801, Jefferson specified that even a republican government need be limited. For though majority rule must be the norm, Jefferson pointed out that "that will to be rightful must be reasonable; that the minority possess their equal rights, which equal law must protect and to violate would be oppression" (Peterson, 1984, p. 493). Jefferson's exact understanding of a republic, as he explained it to John Taylor in 1816, was "a government by its citizens in mass, acting directly and personally according to rules established by the majority" (Lipscomb & Bergh, 1903, Vol. XV, p. 19).

To promote justice effectively and protect the rights of all citizens meant that people must be encouraged, morally obligated in Jefferson's opinion, to discuss issues and to make judgments "at the bar of the public reason" (Peterson, 1984, p. 495). It was their republican duty to be prepared to engage in such public debate. This necessitated the education of all citizens, not just the ruling classes. This education, Jefferson wrote to Madison, would facilitate the people's "good sense" on which "we may rely with the most security for the preservation of a due degree of liberty" (Lipscomb & Bergh, 1903, Vol. XV, p. 918).

By being informed, citizens could act freely in ways that would allow them to exercise their own rights while being mindful of the rights of others. In 1817 Jefferson wrote to George Ticknor, the Boston educator and author, that "knolege is power, that knolege is safety, and that knolege is happiness" (Lee, 1967, p. 114). In other words, knowledge would enable a citizen to fulfill the ideals Jefferson stated in the Declaration of Independence in 1776: to protect their "inalienable rights" of "life, liberty and the pursuit of happiness."

In a republican government there could be no other role for citizens, since they were responsible for the government that made the laws by which all were to abide. As Jefferson would maintain persistently, it was the duty of citizens to provide the security against abuse that governments, even elected governments, might succumb. A citizen's responsibility was to protect his own freedom and that of his neighbor as well. (I use the masculine pronouns to conform to Jefferson's narrow definition of participatory citizens.) This responsibility was common to all citizens, be they wealthy or poor, tradesman or farmer.

This was the job primary schools, both public and private, were to do. In 1818 he wrote that one of the objectives of education was "to instruct the mass of our citizens in these, their rights, interests and duties, as men and citizens" (Peterson, 1984, p. 459). This would be the common bond uniting all citizens regard- democracy & education, vol 21, no- 2 feature article 4 less of class, occupation, geography or other divisive characteristics

---

Source: https://www.monticello.org/the-art-of-citizenship/the-role-of-education/ (Jefferson Monticello, n.d.)

The Role of Education

Thomas Jefferson believed **only educated citizens could make the American experiment in self-government succeed**. He proposed a system of broad, free, public education for men and women alike that was radical in his day and his founding of the University of Virginia partially achieved his larger goals.

What did Thomas Jefferson say about education and democracy?

Source: https://www.tandfonline.com/doi/abs/10.1080/00131729709335239?-journalCode=utef20 (Jewitt, T.O., 2008, 30 January)

Thomas Jefferson and the Purposes of Education

That democracy cannot long exist without enlightenment; That it cannot function without wise and honest officials; That talent and virtue, needed in a free society, should be educated regardless of wealth, birth or other accidental condition; That other children of the poor must thus be educated at common expence.

What did Thomas Jefferson say about good government?

Source: https://founders.archives.gov/documents/Jefferson/03-01-02-0088#:~:-text=To%20the%20Republicans%20of%20Washington%20County%2C%20Maryland,-The%20affectionate%20sentiments&text=that%20the%20great%20%26%20leading%20measure,be%20doubted%20by%20candid%20minds. (National Archives, n.d.)

Thomas Jefferson to the Republicans of Washington County, Maryland …

The care of human life & happiness, & not their destruction, is the first & only legitimate object of good government. I salute you, fellow citizens, with every wish for your welfare, & the perpetual duration of our government, in all the purity of its republican principles. Monticello Mar. 31.

Here is the last report confirming that education and democracy go together:

Source: https://www.educatingforamericandemocracy.org/wp-content/uploads/2021/02/Educating-for-American-Democracy-Report-Excellence-in-History-and-Civics-for-All-Learners.pdf (Educating for American Democracy, 2021, 2 March)

America's Constitutional Democracy Requires Better Civic and History Education

A self-governing people must constantly attend to historical and civic education: to the process by which the rising generation owns the past, takes the helm, and charts a course toward the future. The United States is the longest-lived constitutional democracy in the world, approaching its 250th anniversary in 2026. This occasion calls for both celebration and fresh commitment to the cause of self-government for free and equal citizens in a diverse society. Education in civics and history equips members of a democratic society to understand, appreciate, nurture and, where necessary, improve their political system and civil society: to make our union "more perfect," as the U.S. Constitution says.

This education must be designed to enable and enhance the capacity for self- government from the level of the individual, the family, and the neighborhood to the state, the nation, and even the world. The word "civic" denotes the virtues, assets, and activities that a free people need to govern themselves well. When civic education succeeds, all people are prepared and motivated to participate effectively in civic life. They acquire and share the knowledge, skills, and dispositions necessary for effective participation. Equity also is essential. High-quality education must be delivered to all, for our form of government necessarily invests in all young people the chance to become civic and political leaders. Yet civic and history education has eroded in the United States over the past 50 years, and opportunities to learn these subjects are inequitably distributed.

Across the same time period, partisan and philosophical polarization has increased. A recent surge in voter participation has been accompanied by dangerous degrees of misinformation and tension, even rising to violence. Dangerously low proportions of the public understand and trust our democratic institutions. Majorities are functionally illiterate on our constitutional principles and forms. The relative neglect of civic education in the past half-century is one important cause of our civic and political dysfunction. Excellence in civic and history education represents a part of the solution; it should be a foundation of our national civic infrastructure.

Civics and History Have Been Neglected

Dedicated educators and organizations work hard and well every day to teach American history and civics, and some states have implemented admirable policies. Yet recent waves of federal education reform—from the

No Child Left Behind Act of 2002 to the Race to the Top grants of 2009—have largely neglected these subjects. Over the last three decades, governments at all levels—from federal to local—have provided scant support for curriculum development, teacher professional development, assessment, and research and development in civic and history education.

Nevertheless, state legislatures and departments of education often pass mandates to teach specific topics in these disciplines. This dynamic often results in incoherent standards at once lengthy and superficial, and too extensive to be taught in the limited time and with the scant resources allocated for social studies. In an era of high-stakes accountability, social studies—commonly the home of much civic education—has often gone untested. This drives declining investment of time and other resources in these disciplines. Students and educators are left to confront often fraught and controversial topics without adequate intellectual support, instructional time, and guidance.

Curricula and instructional practices alike reflect this neglect. Although some well-resourced students have access to high-quality civic learning in and out of school, others are left behind due to economic constraints or geographic inaccessibility. Research consistently shows that low-income and underserved students flourish when they receive innovative and student- centered educational approaches to civic learning that require investments not always available in their classrooms.

The consequence? Generations of students have not received the high-quality education in history and civics that they need, and deserve, to prepare them for informed and engaged citizenship.

We have done a poor job regarding civics education for our youth.

The following report exemplifies how some educational tracts keeps citizens out of the democratic process by disallowing entrance.

Source: https://www.huffpost.com/entry/why-many-inner-city-schoo_b_5993626 (Singer, A, 2014, 15 December)

Alan Singer, Contributor

Social studies educator, Hofstra University, my opinions, of course, are my own

Why Many Inner City Schools Function Like Prisons

I've come to realize that Common Core and its high-stakes assessments are just another piece in the school-to-prison pipeline.

In June 2014 I was <u>interviewed</u> by <u>Susan Modaress</u> of *Inside Out* for a feature video on the school-to-prison pipeline in the United States. Since then I visited and spoke with graduates of the pipeline at the <u>Green Haven Correctional Facility</u> in Stormville, New York.

Since the early 1970s, the United States <u>prison population</u> has quadrupled to 2.2 million. It is the largest prison population in the world. According to the <u>International Centre for Prison Studies</u>, China is number two at 1.7 million people, Iran is number 8 at 217,000 people, and the United Kingdom is number 17 at 85,000. Fourteen million people are arrested every year and over two million are sent to jail. Approximately 65 million people in the United States, or more than twenty-five percent of the adults population, has a criminal record.

The U.S. <u>incarceration rate</u> is five to ten times the size of other democratic countries. It is over 700 prisoners for every 100,000 people compared to 149 for England and Wales, 143 for Spain, 102 for France, 90 for Italy, 81 for Germany, and 57 for Sweden.

Meanwhile, more than half of state prisoners are in jail for <u>nonviolent crimes</u>. Mass incarceration has destructive impact on families, communities, and state and local budgets. It cost $80 billion a year to keep all these people in prison and more than $250 billion to pay for all the additional police and court expenses. According to the human rights group Human Rights Watch, while prison should be a last resort, in the United States "it has been treated as the medicine that cures all ills."

In 2000, over two million American children had a <u>parent</u> in prison. I saw the impact of this on young people at a <u>conference</u> at the City University of New York. Eight students who attend a school for teenagers already involved in the criminal justice system discussed how they grew up in families where parents were incarcerated and its impact on them as children.

Conditions in New York City's Rikers Island prison and scandals in the city's criminal injustice system have repeatedly made headlines in the last year. Correction officers were arrested for corruption and brutality. Mentality ill inmates were routinely mistreated. One mentally ill inmate died in an over-heated cell.

People were detained without trial of conviction for years. Kenneth Creighton was jailed on Rikers Island from 2006 until 2011 while awaiting trial until charges against him were finally dropped. Seventeen-year-old Kalief Browder was arrested in the Bronx and confined on Rikers Island for three years before being released without ever being convicted of a crime. While in Rikers, he spent weeks at a time in solitary confinement. The New York City Correction Department now promises to end solitary confinement for prisoners ages 16 and 17 by the end of 2014.

I have written about the school-to-prison pipeline and Michelle Alexander's book *The New Jim Crow: Mass Incarceration in the Age of Colorblindness* in previous Huffington Posts. The more I thought about it before the interview, the more I realized that Common Core and its high-stakes assessments are just another piece in the school-to-prison pipeline. This post is based on my notes for the video interview, which can be viewed online.

What role do the school's play in the school-to-prison pipeline?

I work at Hofstra University as a teacher educator now, but I was a high school teacher in New York City for fourteen years working in some very difficult schools. I have also been a guest instructor at Rikers Island, the last stop on the New York City school-to-prison pipeline.

There is a lot of talk about how schools can transform society. The Bush administration's education policy declared "No Child Left Behind," but of course many children are still left behind. Barack Obama demanded that schools lead his "Race to the Top," but it is not clear what direction he wants the schools and students to run. The reality is that schools reflect and reinforce society; they do not transform it. In the United States dating back to the 1920s high schools were organized on factory models to prepare working class immigrant youth for the tedium of factory work and harsh discipline.

Since the 1970s factory jobs in the United States have been shipped overseas. Companies do not need students prepared for factory work, so schools have evolved to perform a new social role. In inner city minority neighborhoods especially Black and Latino young people attend schools organized on the prison model where they are treated as if they were criminals.

Students enter buildings through metal detectors. If tho device gnes off they are bodily searched. Armed police stand guard. Uniformed security crews that report to the police sweep the halls. Students are forced to sit in overcrowded uncomfortable classrooms doing rote assignments geared to high-stakes Common Core assessments. Stressed out teachers, fearful that they will be judged by poor student performance on these tests, use boredom and humiliation to maintain control of the classroom.

When young people react to these conditions they are disciplined. The ultimate goal of school policy is to sort them out with a few destined for success, some to menial jobs, and others for imprisonment. When these pipeline schools do their jobs well, the young people who fail are convinced they failed because it was their own fault and that they deserve their punishment.

When did this "school-to-prison pipeline" process start?

Multiple forces were at work producing a perfect storm. Starting in the 1960s working class blue-collar jobs disappeared and vocational training in schools largely ended. During the 1970s economic downturn inner city minority schools became chaotic as a result of cuts in funding that have really never been restored. In the 1980s the crack epidemic undermined families in inner city communities and began to fill up the jails. In a world without work, crime became the main employer. Instead of addressing social problems, our society stiffened laws and stuffed people into cells. Private companies went into the prison business and became hungry for profits and raw materials. In the 1990s a conservative coalition that blamed the victims cut into government social welfare programs that were keeping families afloat and the situation worsened. A new zero-tolerance ideology justified tougher laws, mandatory sentences, and stricter treatment in schools. Following 2001, new police tactics like stop and frisk and new technologies that were supposed to protect the country from terrorist attack were used to systematize the punitive nature of inner city minority schools and school-to-prison connection. Add to the mix curriculum organized around boring Common Core test prep drills. The overall affect was to accelerate the exodus of students of color from schools.

What role do gangs play in this cycle?

Gangs are a symptom of the problem. Poverty, unemployment, racism, and government indifference are the problem. Young people turn to gangs when they are driven out of school by oppressive policies, neighborhoods are in decay, they need protection from other gangs, and crime is the major growth industry in their community.

Why is it so hard for these kids to escape from the juvenile justice system?

One, because wealthy people are making money off of their incarceration. Another is deep-seated racism in the United States. Conservative groups use fear of Black and Latino youth to mobilize White voters and win elections. Blacks were outraged by the Trevor Martin murder, they feared for their children. But most Whites accepted the not guilty verdict because they believe Black youth wearing hoodies are potential threats. But the underlying problem is the unwillingness of anyone in government to recognize that the economic system is not working. These young people are surplus - there are no jobs for most of them.

I am not excusing individual behavior and individual choices. Every inner-city Black and Latino youth does not end up engaging in criminal behavior and spending time in prison. Some escape by joining the military. But I am saying that socio-economic circumstances and political decisions by those in power stack the deck against them.

Why are the majority of youths funneled into this system Black and Hispanic?

In impoverished rural communities prisons are the employer of last resort. White men are hired to guard incarcerated Blacks and Latinos. If the prison population more evenly reflected demographics, it would be harder to mobilize White voters to support the system and it would be easier to challenge economic inequality.

Are there specific areas in which we see a higher concentration of this "school-to-prison pipeline" epidemic?

We are looking at inner city minority communities across the nation, but I think the problem is greater in the old Confederate states of the south where public school is at its worst and school performance is at its lowest. Young Black and Latino men are arrested on petty charges and told if they plead guilty they will be released back into the same communities and conditions. If they get picked up for the same petty offenses they are sent to prison for violating the condition of their release. Even if they stay clear of the criminal injustice system, they often lose many of their citizenship rights, including the right to vote.

Why were zero tolerance policies initially implemented?

Zero tolerance ideology takes hold in the 1990s to pacify White voters, justify the entire school to prison incarceration system, and provide raw material to fill the private jails.

Can you attribute a lot of neighborhood youth violence and crime to those who have dealt with the juvenile justice system?

The main job training in prison is how to be a better criminal. You get to network with other criminals, you become dependent on gang connections, and they become your family and employer when you are released.

How can we better rehabilitate the youth who have had this experience?

Our society will have to address the lack of opportunity for inner city minority youth if it wants to improve education and close the tap on the school to prison pipeline. I need to use a four-letter word here. J-O-B-S. Without jobs there can be no real education and no rehabilitation. Without jobs young people are going to turn to crime and return to jail. So-called training programs that do not lead to guaranteed employment are just another fraud so private companies can steal government funds.

How can police change their behavior?

When I was a young teacher I too frequently got into battles of will with resistant students. I had to learn I was the adult in the classroom and that the best way to deal with a tense situation was to ratchet down the tension, to calm the student so we could resolve the conflict. This is hard to do in the school and it is even harder in the street, but if police can be trained to ratchet down the tension, I think fewer young Black and Latino young men would be drawn into the pipeline.

What could states do to reduce the financial incentive for keeping youths incarcerated?

The first step is to immediately end the privatization of prisons. But we also need to deal with underlying social and economic problems facing the United States. I am not sure how, but the country must deal with residual racism. The federal Justice department needs to investigate unequal school funding and disproportionate arrest and incarceration rates as examples of racial prejudice and a violation of the 14th amendment. But more fundamentally, the nation must address income inequality. That means tax the wealthy and corporations to improve schools and communities and it means at the completion of school or training everyone is guaranteed a job. That was the dream of Martin Luther King. We need to turn that dream into reality.

After reading this article, the indignity of having to endure such a system is so humiliating that I feel nauseated! Imagine watching your child suffer through this type of dilemma. It is no wonder that children trapped by these institutions perform poorly in school, have low graduation rates, and find illicit employment to make ends meet for themselves and their families.

I am sending out a siren of alarm! This situation needs to be corrected immediately. Nothing is more important than giving every single child a proper education that enables them to participate in our democracy and choose the profession that matches their desires and passions! Education will bring greater joy to each individual and assure the safety and protection of all children and future generations.

From a purely economic view, it is much more cost-effective to educate children and set them up to be sustaining members of our community than to house them for the rest of their lives in prison. Privately run prisons are not interested in rehabilitation. To make more money, they need more prisoners. How much longer are we willing to let this injustice stand?

To illustrate the cost difference, educate citizens, or maintain prisoners, please see the article below.

Source: https://finance.yahoo.com/news/america-spends-much-more-prisoners-090300648.html (Anderson, J. 2019, 22 May)

America Spends Much More on Prisoners Than Students — Here's Why

Joel Anderson
May 22, 2019

A new study from GOBankingRates found that prison spending in the U.S. is outpacing that of what should be one of society's highest priorities: education. Almost every state spends more money per prisoner than it does per student in public schools—and in 20 states, the difference between per-inmate and per-student spending is more than $24,000. Overall, education spending in America loses out to tho <u>huge amounts of money flowing into prisons</u>.

From the same article, here are the top three states with the most significant difference between pupil and prisoner spending.

---

3. Connecticut

- **Per-Pupil Spending:** $18,957.84
- **Average Cost per Inmate:** $62,159
- **Difference:** $43,201.16

At nearly $19,000 a year, per-pupil spending in Connecticut is good for the second-highest rate overall in the United States. However, because Connecticut spends over $62,000 a year to house each prisoner, it's still less than a third of the state's per-prisoner spending.

2. New York

- **Per-Pupil Spending:** $22,366.37
- **Average Cost per Inmate:** $69,355
- **Difference:** $46,988.63

New York is one of the <u>richest states in America</u> and spends the most on its public school students compared to the rest of the country. However, New York also spends the most on each prisoner at nearly $70,000 a year.

1. California

- **Per-Pupil Spending:** $11,495.33
- **Average Cost per Inmate:** $64,642
- **Difference:** $53,146.67

California spends the most on its prison system of any state in the country at $8.6 billion. And, although California also spends the most on its public schools, it's also the most populous state in America—meaning those expenditures only come out to $11,495.33 per student, good for 22nd overall. California can afford to send more than five kids to school for every person it keeps in jail or prison.

It is fiscally irresponsible to continue neglecting the education of our youth in this country!

After hearing all of the information about education and democracy, it is evident that they go together. WTP should demand a proper education for all children. I argue that an amendment to the constitution is appropriate.

Of course every citizen needs introductory civic courses to understand how this governmental system operates, but it goes deeper than that! The basic understanding of who is in charge is backward. The assumption that the government is in charge needs to be corrected! The government serves at the pleasure of *"We The People"* of these United States.

WTP has tasked the government with establishing Justice, ensuring domestic Tranquility, providing for the common defense, promoting the general Welfare, and securing the Blessings of Liberty to ourselves and our Posterity. And if the government is failing in these duties, WTP must demand it from our government.

As a citizen of the United States, I have to understand how our governmental system operates so that I can be a part of the system. Understanding the system and voting is just the minimum participation level in a Constitutional Democracy. To elevate into more advanced levels of participation, one must be willing to get more involved by joining the group of people that become elected representatives and serve the people of the United States or become an active member of *"We The People."*

To become an active member of *"We The People"* (WTP), one only needs to engage with others on critical issues. Many people believe they are actively involved in this process but merely complain about the state of the government and do nothing to change the situations they find objectionable. Discourse without a call to action is just people standing around shooting the shit. Nothing wrong with that, but it is not what I would call being an active member of WTP.

To actively engage others on a subject with enthusiasm and ideas for change requires courage, a depth of understanding, and a willingness to be challenged. This ability requires discipline, knowledge of your subject, and listening to others to refine and define your subject. Once the issue has been thoroughly clarified, a call to action becomes the next obvious step. I refer to this process as genuine discourse. It can and should be taught to everyone, along with introductory civics courses.

What is Genuine Discourse? Genuine discourse is a rare bird, and our only path through the morass of issues WTP faces today. Here is a quick definition found on Wikipedia:

Source: https://en.wikipedia.org/wiki/Discourse_ethics (Wikipedia, n.d.)

Public discourse ethics

This type of ethics consists of conversations about ideas in civic or community contexts marked by diversity of perspectives requiring thoughtful public engagement. This discourse is made up of differing insights that helps to shape the public's engagement with one another. [3] This type of discourse is meant to protect and to promote the public good. For public discourse ethics to be successful there must be an effective level of civility between people or persons involved. It was Sigmund Freud who once said, "civilization began the first time an angry person cast a word instead of a rock" and that statement is something that continues to be seen in society today.

What is civility, and why does it matter?

Civility Defined. Merriam-Webster defines civility as "polite, reasonable and respectful behavior." (Mirriam-Webster, n.d.) The first rule of George Washington's "Rules of Civility and Decent Behavior in Company and Conversation" states that "every action done in company ought to be with some sign of respect to those that are present." (Washington, G., Toner, J. M., ed., 1888) Civility is being polite and respectful, but is it more?

The Institute for Civility in Government defines civility as "more than just politeness, although politeness is a necessary first step. It is about disagreeing without disrespect, seeking common ground as a starting point for dialogue about differences, listening past one's preconceptions and teaching others to do the same. Civility is the hard work of staying present even with those with whom we have deep-rooted and fierce disagreement." (The Institute for Civility in Government, n.d.)

Without civility, debate or discourse seldom reaches its final destination of resolution.

The following is the way back to civil discourse:

Source: https://www.claremontlincoln.edu/engage/claremont-core/three-cs-golden-rule/ (Aranda, E. 2017, 17 March)

Claremont Lincoln University

The Three Cs that Make the Golden Rule

CLU President Dr. Eileen Aranda

March 17, 2017

The level of discontent in this country has visibly risen. Discourse has been reduced to extremes and name calling. Regardless of your political position, this trend is troubling and highly unproductive.

People *do* differ mightily on issues somewhat peacefully—just as long as they avoid personalizing the discussion. With the insertion of the simple word "you" followed by a negative statement, useful talk abruptly ends. The discussion has moved away from the issue and now to the person and, as they used to say in the Old West, "them's fightin' words". It is short-sighted to think this practice of negative exchange is simply rhetoric and we will get over it. It has become the way we deal with each other. Today's insulting discourse is now a habit. Unfortunately, history has taught us that, when there is not an opportunity for productive dialogue, people often turn to violence as an outlet of their frustration.

Are we hopelessly in a negative spiral towards a violent deadlock over the issues that divide us? Not if we learn another way to engage with each other. We learned to be nasty; we can re-learn to be respectful.

There are three elements needed to move us into position to resolve the issues facing us: civility, common good and curiosity.

Civility – What you say and how you say it does matter

"Political correctness" is currently under attack. There seems to be a sense that we should not be compelled to be respectful, spare another's feelings, or be gracious. Somehow, this ability to be well-mannered has become a *lesser* skill to being boorish – which really seems to take no skill at all.

If we want people to listen to us, to hear our thoughts and ideas, we must present those ideas in a way that can be heard. **We must revive the art of dialogue**. Dialogue is an intentional conversation, a space of civility and equality, where people who differ can speak and listen together. At Claremont Lincoln, we believe that dialogue is an essential skill for all change-makers, so much so that we have made it a part of our core curriculum.

To have productive civil discourse, here are some guidelines to keep in mind:

- **While we need not agree, we must listen to understand**. Make open ended comments like "tell me more" or "help me understand" rather than arguing. In dialogue, there is no winner.
- **Create an empty space for resolution**, rather than choosing an already-crafted resolution. Together, build a solution – that way, no one has to "give in".
- **Allow yourself to wonder** – "what if" is an inclusive and permissive statement. Relax your grip on certainty; think about what is possible.

The trouble with much of what passes for communication today is that it's all crosstalk. It's a din, not a dialogue. We fire salvos of information across the Internet, or shoot each other text messages, or blog or Twitter about ourselves. But is anyone paying attention? And if they are, do they catch our drift?

Self-interest has become the norm. *I want what I want and too bad for everyone else.* This is the path to fascism. As a society, we are dependent on each other. Ethics – the right thing to do – must become the *norm*, with the **common good** as the prevailing *focus* if we are to thrive.

If we work together, we can maximize our shared resources. If we divide ourselves and hoard what we believe to be "ours," we will perish in scarcity, unable to address the problems that need attention – education, jobs, natural resources, and our role in the world. We cannot survive alone.

So what can we do to refocus on common good?

- **Look at things with a view to abundance.** Think in terms of "and" not "or"; ideas are a renewable resource and we can find ways that will result in <u>mutual gain.</u>
- **Consider other perspectives** – step back, consider how others might view things. Can you authentically articulate their points of view?
- **Think of the second and third level consequences of self-interest.** In a long-term view, what are the implications of given actions? Who might be harmed?

Firstly, to help resolve crucial societal issues, **one must be willing to be curious.**

Fundamentalism—that view that concludes that "I" possess the truth, the one right answer—leads to inertia. Because when one "knows" or when one believes they have that one right answer, at that moment, one stops <u>thinking.</u>

Because our problems today are complex, there is never a single right answer. In fact, there is seldom *an* answer. We need many different perspectives to understand how we might <u>resolve our difficult issues</u>. We need to be curious about the possibilities, not stuck in the status quo.

"What else could we do" is much more fertile than "I have the answer." It is a much more inclusive statement and, therefore, more likely to lead to collaboration and mutual benefit.

Curious people are:

- Willing to challenge their assumptions and imagine a different reality.
- Not unsettled by uncertainty and find joy and wonder in not knowing the answers to everything.
- Mobilized by change as an opportunity to try new things.

Forbes <u>also emphasized</u> curiosity as a crucial quality for leaders to "enable their companies to navigate complexity and be future-ready.

All three of these elements of respectful engagement—civility, the common good, and curiosity—draw from the Golden Rule: to treat

someone as you would like to be treated. We all want to be spoken to in a way that suggests we have value. We want our needs to be considered as important. We want our ideas to be heard and found to have merit. It may appear that there is no other way to engage than our current habit, but we can change how we interact. We can work our way out of this funk by:

- Getting past arguing – listen don't talk; it is amazing what you can learn. There is always time to make your point.
- Putting our feet in someone else's shoes – what is another point of view. No need to agree just understand another person's perspective.
- Looking for the next right answer – relax into the joy of not knowing and explore options.

Creating a society based on the Golden Rule is one of the Core Values at Claremont Lincoln University and is integral to our mission to lead positive social change. We teach our students these three elements of the Golden Rule every day through the Claremont Core™, our Core curriculum. In fact, a previous student even wrote about what the Claremont Core taught him.

Source: https://www.claremontlincoln.edu/engage/claremont-core/claremont-core-taught-me/ (Flores, E. 2016, 10 November)

This Is What the Claremont Core Taught Me

Student Contributor

November 10, 2016

This student post was written by M.A. Social Impact alumnus, Ely Flores. Please see author bio at the end of post.

At the beginning of my Social Impact Master's Program, I believed that I exemplified Claremont Lincoln's tenets of *Mindfulness, Change, Collaboration*, and *Dialogue*.

The Claremont Core, with these four tenets, "takes you through a process of self-awareness and steadily evolves towards engagement with others and society at large."

As I began diving deeper into the courses, I quickly understood that these principles are not just words that should be used in passing.

But rather, they are values that should be pursued as a way of life and a commitment to transformational leadership.

I had always prided myself in understanding dialogue but, in learning about its profound simplicity as a process in which people engage with each other to try and see the world from the other's perspective, I opened up to a deeper transformational process.

To engage in true dialogue requires becoming a leader that is **mindfully** present.

Mindfulness is one of those things that is easier said than done like meditation. Meditation is hard because our minds lack in focus and won't stop thinking.

Mindfulness is similar in that we want to jump and attach ourselves to the first emotion that arises from a conversation. Then, we are quickly distracted by another emotion without truly understanding why we are becoming emotional in the first place.

A dialogue requires us to pay attention and be mindfully present. It asks you to not judge what is coming out of the other person's mouth, but, rather, to try to see the world from the other person's perspective.

The Claremont Core challenged me to continue to grow as a transformational leader, but, most importantly, it has inspired and dared me to be a driver of change through dialogue and mindfulness.

Thus, the people around me feel valued and validated when, as a leader, I am able to engage in a genuine exchange of experiences.

About the Author

Ely Flores is a recent graduate of Claremont Lincoln University's Social Impact Program.

He is founder and executive director of his own nonprofit, Leadership through Empowerment, Action, and Dialogue Inc. (LEAD), which has trained more than 200 youth in California and established a school that empowers underserved young adults from 18 to 24 to complete their high school education, prepare for college and/or career and become leaders in their communities.

He also works as outreach coordinator and manager for GRID Alternatives of Los Angeles, assisting low-income communities through the Single-Family Affordable Solar Homes Program.

Thus, we truly believe that by embracing the Golden Rule and its three Cs of civility, common good, and curiosity, we can all work towards a society of purposeful engagement.

What are some ways you do that today? How often do you practice civility, the common good, and curiosity? How can we collectively create a society based on these facets of the Golden Rule?

Below is the Golden rule explained:

Source: https://www.scarboromissions.ca/golden-rule/understanding-the-golden-rule (Scarboro Missions, n.d.)

Understanding the Golden Rule

Ethic of Reciprocity

The Golden Rule, known also as the *Ethic of Reciprocity*, is arguably the most consistent, most prevalent and most universal ethical principle in history. Many regard it as the most concise and general principle of ethics.

The Golden Rule is found in numerous cultures, religions, ethical systems, secular philosophies, indigenous (Native) traditions, and even in the mathematical sciences (e.g. the golden mean). And because it crosses so many traditions and philosophies, the Golden Rule possesses tremendous moral authority and reveals a profound unity underlying the diversity of human experience. The Golden Rule also emphasizes values of mutuality, interdependence and reciprocity.

Given its omnipresence across history, the Golden Rule is often described as a *universal ethical principle*. To reflect on the Golden Rule is to reflect from the perspective of a universal wisdom. Accordingly, the Golden Rule is not just a moral ideal for relationships between people but also for relationships among nations, cultures, races, sexes, economies and religions.

The Golden Rule, with roots in a wide range of the world's religions and cultures, is well suited to be a standard to which different cultures could appeal in resolving conflicts. As the world becomes more and more a single interacting global community, the need for such a common standard is becoming more urgent. Clearly, the Golden Rule has the capacity to be the ethical cornerstone as the human family works together to build a peaceful, just and sustainable global society.

Its appeal is augmented by the fact that its message is simple, universal and powerful. In July 2000, Scarboro Missions published the Golden Rule Poster featuring the Golden Rule in 13 religions in a striking and attractive 4-colour format. Scarboro Missions has been stunned by the success of the poster – this piece of multifaith art is making its way around the world. Everywhere it goes, it performs its magical task of healing, unity and reconciliation.

Statement from Jeffrey Wattles

*Jeffrey Wattles is a philosopher who teaches at Kent State University in Ohio, USA. Wattles has published one of the best books ever written on the Golden Rule ("**The Golden Rule**" Oxford Press, 1996). The two-page conclusion of Wattles' book is an excellent statement about the meaning of the Golden Rule. We are privileged to reprint it here (with permission of author). To facilitate the reading of the Statement, two sub-headings have been added:*

The Golden Rule is, from the first, intuitively accessible, easy to understand; its simplicity communicates confidence that the agent can find the right way. The rule tends to function as a simplified summary of the advocate's moral tradition, and it most commonly expresses a commitment to treating others with consideration and fairness, predicated on the recognition that others are like oneself.

The Golden Rule is offered to those among whom a minimal sincerity may be presupposed – the hearer will not manipulate the rule in defense of patently immoral conduct. The Golden Rule is not best interpreted as an isolated principle in a value vacuum, to be examined as a candidate for the role of sole normative axiom in a formalized ethical theory. Nevertheless, the rule is a principle in a full sense.

Even before it is formulated, its logic operates in the human mind. Once formulated, it shows itself to be contagious and quickly rises to prominence. It functions as a distillation of the wisdom of human experience and of scriptural tradition. It serves the needs of educated and uneducated people alike, and stimulates philosophers to codify its meanings in new formulations. Given the equal, basic worth of each individual, the rule implies a requirement of consistency; as philosopher Samuel Clarke puts it: "Whatever I judge reasonable or unreasonable for another to do for me; that, by the same judgment, I declare reasonable or unreasonable, that I in the like case should do for him." In addition, this principle of a philosophy of living carries implications for social, economic, and political realms.

An Expression of Human Kinship

Much of the meaning of the rule can be put into practice without any religious commitment, since it is a nontheologic principle that neither mentions God nor is necessarily identified with the scriptures or doctrines of any one religion. The rule is an expression of human kinship, the most fundamental truth underlying morality. From a religious perspective, the Golden Rule is the principle of the practice of the family of God, and it means relating with other people as a brother or sister. At the limit, it involves conduct patterned on a divine paradigm, extending to others the same attitude of service that one would welcome as the recipient of someone else's divinely parental love in the same kind of situation.

The rule cannot be captured in a static interpretation for it engages the thoughtful doer in a process of growth. To follow it to the end is to move from egoism to sympathy, to sharpen moral intuition by reason, and to find fulfillment beyond duty-conscious rule following in spontaneous, loving service. In the process of identifying maturely with others, adopting the other's perspective imaginatively may be helpful, along with every other technique of understanding and cooperating with others. Thus the unity of the rule, amid its wide diversity, is its life as a symbol of this process of growth.

Identifying with Others

Whoever practices the Golden Rule opens himself or herself to a process of change. Letting go of self to identify with a single other individual, or with a third-person perspective on a complex situation, or with a divine paradigm, one allows a subtle and gradual transformation to proceed, a transformation with bright hope for the individual and the planet. The rule begins by setting forth the way the self wants to be treated as a standard of conduct; but by placing the other on a par with the self, the rule engages one in approximating a higher perspective from which the kinship of humanity is evident. To pursue this higher perspective is to risk encountering the divine and the realization that every step along the forward path is illumined by the Creator....

Confronting the problems of modern civilization, superficial thinking looks for a panacea. A simple word of wisdom, however, cannot help with a complex problem unless its simplicity expresses a life that comes from being connected with a universal network of truths. The more deeply the Golden Rule is grasped, the less it seems an easy answer. But those who learn to practice it fully, conjoining material sympathy with moral reason under the guidance of spiritual love, will point the way toward a brighter future.

"Do to others as you want others to do to you" is part of our planet's common language, shared by persons with differing but overlapping conceptions of morality. Only a principle so flexible can serve as a moral ladder for all humankind.

(End of Jeffrey Wattles' Statement)

Can civility bring back a government that functions well and adequately serves the people?

Can an understanding of the Golden Rule and a determined effort to utilize this undervalued proverb help unlock the gears of Government that have ground to a halt?

The answer is a definite yes, only if those doing the governing remember their position as a representative for the majority of the people that elected them and not an individual with their own agenda.

So what is Majority Rule before we go on? See below for a full explanation:

Source: https://www.worldcat.org/title/understanding-democracy-a-hip-pocket-guide/oclc/64510833 (Patrick, J.J. 2016)

From *Understanding Democracy: A Hip Pocket Guide* by John, J. Patrick.

Majority Rule and Minority Rights

The essence of democracy is majority rule, the making of binding decisions by a vote of more than one-half of all persons who participate in an election. However, constitutional democracy in our time requires majority rule with minority rights. Thomas Jefferson, third President of the United States, expressed this concept of democracy in 1801 in his First Inaugural Address. He said,

All . . . will bear in mind this sacred principle, that though the will of the majority is in all cases to prevail, that will to be rightful must be reasonable; that the minority possess their equal rights, which equal law must protect and to violate would be oppression.

In every genuine democracy today, majority rule is both endorsed and limited by the supreme law of the constitution, which protects the rights of individuals. Tyranny by minority over the majority is barred, but so is tyranny of the majority against minorities.

This fundamental principle of constitutional democracy, majority rule coupled with the protection of minority rights, is embedded in the constitutions of all genuine democracies today. The 1992 constitution of the Czech Republic, for example, recognizes the concepts of majority rule and minority rights. Article VI says, "Political decisions shall stem from the will of the majority, expressed by means of a free vote. The majority's decisions must heed the protection of the minorities." The Czech constitution is filled with statements of guaranteed civil liberties, which the constitutional government must not violate and which it is empowered to protect.

Majority rule is limited in order to protect minority rights, because if it were unchecked it probably would be used to oppress persons holding unpopular views. Unlimited majority rule in a democracy is potentially just as despotic as the unchecked rule of an autocrat or an elitist minority political party.

In every constitutional democracy, there is ongoing tension between the contradictory factors of majority rule and minority rights. Therefore, public officials in the institutions of representative government must make authoritative decisions about two questions. When, and under what conditions, should the rule of the majority be curtailed in order to protect the rights of the minority? And, conversely, when, and under what conditions, must the rights of the minority be restrained in order to prevent the subversion of majority rule?

These questions are answered on a case-by-case basis in every constitutional democracy in such a way that neither majority rule nor

minority rights suffer permanent or irreparable damage. Both majority rule and minority rights must be safeguarded to sustain justice in
a constitutional democracy.

Majority rules seem like a simple concept, and it is! Minority rights are
also simple yet less understood. The minority has a right to their opinion. Even though they lack the numbers to enact public policy or laws,
their rights also need to be safeguarded, lest we have oppression by the
majority, which can become tyrannical if left unchecked.

Lately, the problem with majority rules is that there needs to be
respect for the outcome of the vote. Why the lack of respect? Simply
human foibles. People like to be correct, they want to win, and when
they are not winning, some will resort to unscrupulous means to achieve
their desired outcome. This behavior does not serve WTP.

The concept of majority rules has been observed in nature and
many types of herd animals; here is one example.

Please see the summary below:

Source: https://www.biologicaldiversity.org/news/center/articles/2012/moth-
er-nature-network-11-04-2012.html (McLendon, R, 2012, November 4)

From the, Center for Biological Diversity

Red deer

The red deer of Eurasia live in large herds, spending lots of time either
grazing or lying down to ruminate. Some deer are ready to move on
before others are, and scientists have noticed that herds only move
when 60 percent of the adults stand up—essentially voting with their
feet. Even if a dominant individual is more experienced and makes
fewer mistakes than its underlings, herds typically favor democratic
decisions over autocratic ones.

A major reason for this, according to research by biologists Larissa
Conradt and Timothy Roper, is that groups are less impulsive: "Democratic decisions are more beneficial primarily because they tend to

produce less extreme decisions, rather than because each individual has an influence on the decision per se."

Majority rules work very well when a herd of red deer tries to decide in which direction to look for a new grazing area. The minority is not oppressed. Their desire to remain with the herd for protection influences their willingness to capitulate to the majority.

Now imagine, for a moment, one of the deer, in the minority, is unhappy with the herd's decision. That deer steps onto a mound of dirt and begins to evangelize the reasons not to go along with the majority. This deer promotes the minority opinion, even after the majority has made their will known. I know it seems ridiculous, but it happens in human politics. Presidential candidates contest the vote, special interest groups lobby the public to sway them to their opinion, and wealthy citizens purchase TV and radio stations to promote their views. This behavior does not serve WTP. Majority rules and minority rights should be included in all appropriate civics courses!

Inclusion promotes participation, and participation promotes a society that freely examines the institutions that provide for their protection, minimizing oppression, injustice, and discrimination. Understanding these concepts and processes encourages involvement. We want as many members as possible to participate to ensure the proper representation of all members. Disenfranchised members or members unaware of the process end up not being represented. Their experience with the democratic system may end with a negative result. They distance themselves from WTP, often becoming a distracting burden to the whole.

Oppression, injustice, and discrimination negate the possibility of life, liberty, and the pursuit of happiness. For our continued evolution, it is the duty of the citizens of these United States to initiate change, for it will not trickle down from government on its own accord.

The government gets its marching orders from us – WTP!

WTP must let the government know what we want.

If we leave anyone behind, it limits us all.

I appreciate the extraordinary efforts put forth on my behalf to enjoy these inalienable rights. The more people with access to these rights, the more unfettered our society can become, releasing us from the demoralizing effects of oppression, after which we are all free to blossom into and enjoy the full vision our Creator has planned for each and every one of us.

There are some among us able to enjoy that blossoming now. These people have a creative spark and intuitive knowing that is more profound and vivid than most. They can blast through the density that is our society's culture and outdated belief systems to live a life unhindered by the fear that grips most people.

This creative spark comes from deep within and is available to all who seek it. Desire sets your course upon this path. Developing this relationship opens you to the possibility of this intuitive knowledge of your Creator, in a co-creator relationship, spreading light, love, and beauty throughout the world, no matter your position in life, be you, prince or pauper.

What percentage of people can elevate to this place of peace and unity? Can we increase this percentage? By what means do we improve this percentage? Everyone has an innate ability. Desire is the driving force that carries you home. Are you interested in a beautiful relationship with your Creator?

Throughout history, epochs of time are marked by an influx of creativity in many of the different creative arts. Whether it be poetry, music, or new thought brought about by stimulated intellectual discourse and there have been eras of deep oppression that have made life a constant struggle.

Are we at a point in the history of the human race where we can identify, nurture and cultivate the components that make up a society, burgeoning with citizens that understand and follow their Soul's Path to self-fulfillment and have not only the freedom to do so but the encouragement of culture and community at large to do so? I would call this a "Full Expression Society."

All citizens in a Full Expression Society are encouraged to develop a deep connection and knowledge of the Energy Source that animates us all. From this place of awareness, one can find their own path to self-fulfillment.

Everyone is at least vaguely familiar with this place, deep inside their beings, for it has been observed and encouraged by many different societies and cultures all across the planet. Our culture has yet to promote its development on a grand scale. See below for some interesting revelations:

Source: https://www.tm.org/blog/enlightenment/kingdom-of-god-is-within-you/
(Pearson, C, 2010, 12 June)

The Kingdom of God is Within You

From the TM Blog

This inner treasure of life has had many names. Plato refers to it as *the Good* and *the Beautiful*, Aristotle as *Being*, Plotinus as *the Infinite*, St. Bernard of Clairvaux as *the Word*, Ralph Waldo Emerson as *the Oversoul*. In Taoism it is called the *Tao*, in Judaism *Ein Sof*. Among Australian aborigines it is called the *dreamtime*, among tribes of southern Africa *Hunhu/Ubuntu*. The names may differ, but the inner reality they point to is one and the same.

In every case, it's understood that this inner, transcendental reality can be directly experienced. This experience has likewise been given different names. In India traditions it is called *Yoga*, in Buddhism *Nirvana*, in Islam *fana,* in Christianity *spiritual marriage*. It is a universal teaching based on a universal reality and a universal experience.

Is there something to this Energy Source? Can it help us find fulfillment? Can it transform our society? Were the Founding Documents for this country pointing us in this direction? Are we now just realizing the potential of what could be – or what we could do?

What would it be like living in a Full Expression Society? How would that be different from what we have now?

Currently, we live in a fear-based society, meaning that most of our drives and reasons for doing things stem from fear.

Examples:

Be a good person or go to hell

Go to church or go to hell

Follow the Ten Commandments or go to hell

Believe in the Savior or go to hell

Go to the proper church, or go to hell

You were born a sinner; you probably go to hell anyway

Pay for a university degree or end up jobless and homeless

Keep your low-paying job or end up homeless

Be a good husband or wife or end up divorced, jobless, and homeless

Follow the rules of our society or go to jail

Play it safe. Living life dangerously could cause early death

Eat healthy food or die early

Be first, or you are a loser

Never give a sucker a break

Be handsome or pretty, or no one will like you

Maintain a large budget for military preparedness or lose a war

This list could go on and on.

No matter the country you are born into, you acquire the basic assumptions of your society and culture as you grow up. These assumptions become deeply embedded and become beliefs. True or false, these beliefs become a driving force. They compel you to find evidence of their existence.

With the assumptions listed above, the citizens will invariably be self-righteous and hyper-focused on only their own needs. They may become depressed if they don't measure up, blaming others for their shortcomings or reject all assumptions and live a felonious life. They may become very competitive and potentially unscrupulous about winning and gaining an advantage. They may judge others who they deem better than them harshly so they can feel better about themselves. It does not sound like a life I would want to live!

Of course, there is the option to try and be a good person against all odds. I felt that desire to be a good person growing up. It emanated from my insides and made me feel good about being nice to others. And then I started my educational tract at the local Church school; everybody was so mean, especially the teachers!

And then, the teachers began to explain my relationship to the cosmos, and I was desperately confused. I was stressed beyond the breaking point. My inner knowing continuously communicated with me, contradicting all of the information I was receiving from my teachers, society, and culture. How was I to know that my insides were just trying to stay focused on the Truth, and all of the outside influences, just ushering in the normal human experience of separation?

I was taught that I was born a sinner. My very Being was created with a tragic flaw. That flaw was the propensity to lie, cheat, and steal. I was informed that it was my duty to try and not indulge in these pastimes or else be sentenced to the eternal flames of hell, from which there is no escape. Fortunately for me and all others, there was a human not born into sin, and his sacrifice, upon the cross, was payment for my sins. Freed from the penalties of my sins, through no effort of my own, I was now free to go to heaven...

Provided I follow the rules of this new governing body, surrounding the teachings of this human, not born into sin. All I had to do was accept and believe in these facts, and I was assured a place in heaven. This meant I had to disavow everything my insides were communicating with me, completely severing me from myself, making self-actualization, enlightenment, and the discovery of my Soul Mission exponentially more difficult.

Nevertheless, here I am, writing a book and sharing great truths as they are being revealed to me. I would not change a thing. It has been a great ride, from separation to salvation, or the rediscovering, of the knowing, of my unity with The All.

We all come to this physical realm seeking salvation, among many other things, but to place the burden of salvation, for all of us, on one human is very misleading and deceptively detrimental to discovering our purpose for coming to this earth plane. This journey to salvation is a Hero's Journey – one that is meant for each and every one of us. This one human set the example, as others have, that it can be done. His Light and Love are a shining beacon, showing the way. In his own words, "*The Kingdom of God Is Within You.*"

He found his way through the ego barriers of a separate self, to the core of his being. Light and Love flowed through him, presenting him with the experience of the knowing, of the living, breathing Divine Energy Source that provides for the whole universe.

How could another human do that for us? How is that even possible? And why would we want someone else doing all of that for us?

Being able to transcend all that is transient and discover all that is True and Real, would be the most exciting Divine experience available; please sign me up! I am ready to make my own way down this path.

Have no fear, for the path has been made ready for all of us, for this man cannot do it for us. Yet He does stand at the ready to guide and assist all who ask.

This path is a gift from the Divine Oneness that we each get to travel, discovering and realizing the beauty and Divine nature that is our Creator; for ourselves. No matter how often we falter, we are always given the forgiveness and assistance to, once again, travel on this path that takes us home.

The inducements to get me to live a life of piousness were actually so outlandish that it made me wonder, what is the big fuss about being good? So many people are behaving so poorly. Why do I have to be the only good one?"

I felt doomed to go to hell right from the start because I believed I was born a sinner. An authority figure made the claim, and my society and culture confirmed; what was I supposed to do? The part of me that wanted to be good went to sleep and stayed that way until I reached my mid-twenties. When I began to question these assumptions, this is when my journey began. I discovered that peace was possible, but not with these beliefs.

I came to understand that beliefs are potent and compelling; beliefs determine your destiny... whatever you believe ultimately manifests in your life.

And consequently, the beliefs a society or a culture clings to also determines its future. So as I started to question these beliefs, I realized that only one Creative Force brought into being all that we see, feel, and experience. And every religion is just that culture's interpretation of their relationship to that same Creative Force. It doesn't make them right or wrong. It is just their living experience of what is for them, which is okay, but to claim one's religion is the only way to God negates the possibility of peace among people and nations.

Every being was given a gift... the opportunity to incarnate into a physical body in a physical realm in order to actually experience the significance and consequences of their choices. This gift included free will, or the ability to do and be as you please without the threat of eternal damnation after the completion of one life.

I found that I did not have to wait until my life was over to determine my fate as a good or bad person. Instead, it is much more immediate! Whenever I choose something, I notice a good or bad feeling about it. Preferring to feel good, I opted for behaviors like being kind, helpful, positive, and loving. During this realization, it became apparent there were competing forces vying for my allegiance. (Angel/devil syndrome)

My ego is always trying to get over on others and me, securing more for myself and judging everyone as a way to keep them separate and beneath me. This ego promised me more if I followed its dictates, and it sort of made sense. Fortunately for me, my ego was a tyrant. I felt more pain and suffering than peace, making me more willing to try anything to relieve the pain.

When I learned that this Creative Force is interested in developing a relationship with each and every being in order to help and guide, I decided to take a chance and go for the ride. I learned that every being has the same option to remain ego- or fear-based or embark on a journey with the Creative Force that lives inside each and every one of us. I learned some exciting things right away.

We are all One! At the center of every being is this Creative Force; we have all originated from the same place, with the same Creative Force DNA. This Creative Force made possible the incarnation into physical bodies, each with their own individual thoughts and sense of separateness. This occurred because the Divine Creative Force wanted to actually experience the drama of thoughts, good and bad behavior, consequences, turmoil, victory, defeat, pain, and suffering, providing a context with which to view love, peace, compassion, forgiveness, empathy, and fortitude.

Nonphysical realms are teeming with love, peace, compassion, forgiveness, empathy, and fortitude, and that is all there is there.

Physical realms provide the possibility to explore that which is not your Creative Energy Source, providing a better understanding of the beauty and blissful nature of your Creative Energy Source. Which is who and what you are.

It is a process and a path that every being is in the middle of traversing. Every being is slowly rediscovering and remembering the nature of their own Creative Force. Every individual eventually comes to understand the mystery fully and is rejoined with this Creative Force! There is no need for an eternal afterlife of hell to enforce this evolution. Running away from this Creative Force and joining with the ego feels like hell. It doesn't have to be forever; just until you feel like trying something new and you can follow your inner nature impulses and walk right out of hell.

Do you believe in a loving, kind, and benevolent God? For what purpose would this God have for hell? How would the eternal suffering of hell serve this God?

Do you believe in a vengeful, wrathful, and judgmental God? This God will certainly send you to hell!

Your ego is vengeful, wrathful, and judgmental, and you are free to align with this side of yourself for as long as you desire or until you determine that it no longer serves you.

When you decide to acknowledge your inborn desire to feel good and be a part of the whole that encourages your discovery of a God whose delight is the care, protection, and guidance of his Creations, then you are free to live in a state of love with a kind, benevolent, and loving God.

You only have to be willing to challenge the beliefs that bind you to the ego behaviors that will eventually send you to a hell of your own making.

Interested in challenging the beliefs that bind and constrict? An examination of the difference between fear based beliefs and beliefs connected to a benevolent, kind, and loving God, will show you the way home. Any belief that does not include Love or expand Love should be questioned.

When one encourages Light and Love to flow through their body, the ego corrupts that flow, making it subservient to itself. Without an understanding of the ego or how to defend against its dictates, the self-actualization that usually follows an influx of Light and Love is derailed, as planned, by the Creator. The awakening process is slow and intentional. Occasionally, one may stumble onto self-actualization, which can be a difficult road for the unaware individual. Essence intended for every individual to choose the awakening path; sincerity and devotion are key components.

Become willing to unsee the untrue, making room for the realization and recognition of the ultimate Truth. That Light and Love have carried us through this whole ordeal of being human. When we relax and allow ourselves to go with the flow of life living through us in the present moment, there is no need to worry, much to the chagrin of our delusional ego. We are Co-Creators whenever we desire to be and are willing to do the work to be afforded the grace of that mantle of Love from above.

The ego's purpose is to simulate separateness from the sublime immensity that is our Creator. Once we understand ego and its purpose, we can decide to spend the time to disassociate from it. Eventually, Light and Love will flow into our Hearts, providing for the complete undoing of what we thought was real and the ushering in of the very Truth of our Reality, and the knowing that everything alive has this same Creative Force emanating from inside it.

Allowing Love to flow through your Heart opens you up to the Love and guidance of this Divine Creative Force innate in all of us. Bringing forth, all of the Light and Love of the universe to assist you in all of your affairs and align you with your Soul Mission.

Once you embark upon this new path, remaining and persevering feels light, loving and natural. With this power of Light and Love coursing through your body, it now feels possible to traverse the density and confusing nature that is our physical world in an enlightened manner.

No longer forced to see the world through ego eyes, your way is made easy. In this physical realm, the benevolence of your whole existence becomes plain to see. The fear of God becomes another ancient relic that no longer has any meaning, for the Truth has been revealed, and the birth of a Full Expression Society becomes possible.

Transitioning will take time, and that is okay! We are here to enjoy the ride through evolving and expressing our inner nature.

What is the next step? Understanding the differences between a (Fear-Based Society) and a *Full Expression Society.*

So how would the beliefs differ from (Fear-Based) to a *Full Expression Society?*

(Be a good person or go to hell.)

There is no Hell, hence no fear of hell.
Being a good person becomes the go-to choice because of the joy associated with such a decision. Aligning oneself with the guidance of the Creative Force brings Light, Love, and Joy!

(Go to church or go to hell.)

There is no hell, hence no fear of hell.
Church would become a choice derived from how it felt to be involved instead of a guilt-ridden obligation.

(Follow the Ten Commandments or go to hell.)

There is no hell, hence no fear of hell.
Ten Commandments – a basic guideline that has stood the test of time. Maybe we should all take a look and see how many we remember.

(Believe in the Savior or go to hell.)

There is no hell, hence no fear of hell.
No longer forced to believe for fear of hell, one could investigate the teachings of the Savior to determine usefulness to oneself. (Hint: Many groups teach different things about this human, who was

fully Divine and fully human, as we all are.) Truly a Divine experience, developing a relationship with this human and learning about his journey, one we are all destined to travel.

(Go to the right church or go to hell.)

> *There is no hell, hence no fear of hell.*
> *No longer forced to believe for fear of hell, one could investigate the teachings of any church to determine the usefulness of each for oneself.*

(You were born a sinner; you probably go to hell anyway.)

> *There is no hell, hence no fear of hell.*
> *You are now free to develop a relationship with the Creative Force if you so desire and see for yourself how it feels when you make the Love flow through your heart. When you gain access to your heart, you will always be able, to tell the Truth about anything. Once activated, your heart will guide you through to the Truth of anything!*

(Pay for a university degree or end up jobless and homeless.)

> *In a Free Expression Society, joblessness and homelessness are something people are no longer forced to endure. Free job training and placement are readily available, as well as assistance to secure suitable housing. Education becomes a cornerstone of a Full Expression Society and becomes free. The desire for a university education becomes one of desire or interest in the subject matter and the desired position or job upon completion of the degree.*

(Keep your low-paying job or end up homeless.)

> *Opportunities are available for job training and placement. Homelessness has been eradicated and is no longer a primary fear in Full Expression Society.*

(Be a good husband or wife or end up divorced, jobless and homeless.)

> *Being a good husband or wife is simply an extension of being a good person, which is readily developed while in a relationship with the Creative Force.*

Of course, free training would be available on all of these subjects: being a good person, good wife, good husband, good employee, good employer, good mother, good father, good sister, good brother.

(Follow the rules of our society or go to jail.)

Most of the lawlessness now has to do with people who do not have their basic needs met, which will be alleviated in a Full Expression Society. Of course, education on how to get along in society will ease the number of interruptions to their peace. If someone is sentenced to confinement, it will be coupled with an intense educational and rehabilitation program; no need to keep people confined if they can learn to be a part of a society that embraces fundamental change at the heart level. Making mistakes and turning away from the dark side is one of the most liberating experiences in this planet's curriculum.

(Play it safe. Living life dangerously could cause early death.)

The reason for death becomes understood and no longer feared. Citizens are free to live as they please, provided they harm no one.

(Eat healthy food or die early.)

The reason for death becomes understood and no longer feared. The truth about food becomes clear once food lobbies are no longer allowed to lie or pay for votes.

(Be first, or you are a loser.)

Competition takes a backseat to inclusivity. Being first is no longer valued, but helping everyone to cross the finish line becomes the point of it all.

(Never give a sucker a break.)

In the context of this list, this item is so offensive for so many reasons. It would be unconscionable in a Full Expression Society!

(Be handsome or pretty, or no one will like you.)

Another false belief that is so harmful in so many ways and would not be entertained in a Full Expression Society!

(Maintain a large budget for military preparedness or lose a war.)

Hope for the best, prepare for the worst, is not a bad motto. Nor is peace through superior firepower. They seem to make sense when packing for a hunting trip. What everyone is failing to realize is the juvenile level of thinking that these statements force us to embrace as a country and our military obligations. When negotiations with another government fail, the fallback is, "We have bigger guns, and you have to do as we say or else." Surely we have diplomats serving our government who can negotiate without using this giant hammer of a negotiating tool. Embracing this thinking forces an arms race between all countries vying for supremacy, wasting vital resources and funding for a no-win situation!

It doesn't make sense, the level of preparedness of our military services. Do we really have to spend that much money? Does WTP have a choice in this matter? Could that money be better spent elsewhere? Perhaps educating our citizens, providing job training and housing assistance, and developing a Full Expression Society (FES)?

Considering the option to go to war becomes a thing of the past.

In an FES, nobody would be willing to detonate a nuclear bomb for any reason, so why have them? They cost money, and that money would be better spent on almost anything else! And worst of all, they can destroy the planet in one afternoon, forcing humans down a path from which they can never return. Can we just agree never to use them and take them off the table?

So there are the differences lined out next to one another. With the assumptions in a Full Expression Society, the citizen will invariably be much more relaxed and at peace with their situation, knowing that it is the desire of the whole to get each individual member better situated to enjoy life, liberty, and the pursuit of happiness. There is no longer any need to be self-righteous because they won't feel alone trying to figure it all out for themselves, nor will they have to defend their decisions. There is no longer any need to be hyper-focused on only their own needs because everyone in this society wants everyone to have enough so as to promote a feeling of generosity, trust, and goodwill towards others. There is no more violent competition, and nobody is trying to take their stuff away. There is also no longer any need to judge others to feel better. Everyone is encouraged to improve their lives. The ideology of an FES provides the encouragement, opportunity, and funding to make it all possible.

So maybe not everyone is ready for a "Full Expression Society." I understand that new ideas need to be rejected before they are embraced, and what I am proposing is an evolutionary change to the current system. So, while we are waiting for this FES idea to be fully embraced, let's discuss what we can do right now to get us moving forward in a direction that benefits and empowers WTP to take back control and lead the government down a path that serves WTP.

While working on this section, I received an idea for a poem. I would like to include that poem here:

Innermost Desires

What would it be like, if everyone was encouraged, to express their innermost desires

Encouraged to learn to connect to that peace-laden voice of Love within and live a life Co-Creating with that activated inner guidance

How would this affect the individual and society at large

The amount of love permeating this guidance would instantly reassure, embolden, and blossom

Unto the individual, strength, peace, and knowing with too which they could draw upon

During any situation too which they are called to and inspired to deliver themselves from

For their Co-Creator demands much and so much more is given unto which they shall surely deliver

Once fully engaged, the individual takes flight with this new-found Energy Source and becomes known

To themselves and to the world to which they unravel perpetually for the good of All

Forever changing our evolving evolution hence drawing us closer to the presence of the Now

For society, the disillusionment that now plagues the common mortal and Trillionaire alike

With so much fear, as if we were all locked away in a deep dank dungeon of our own making

Fear, like smoke, in a soft breeze, unknowingly drifting, swirling about our Being

Infiltrating the hollowed dismal abyss of this existence, threatening to suck dry all hope

Until we see the fear mechanism falsity on full display

And set our intent upon the Divine, Love rushing in, hearts pounding, pressure pulsing

All remnants of fear, abruptly consumed by the setting Sun God in a brilliant array of reds and oranges

Our collective inner knowing bursting forth, freeing us from the lurking fear standing heavy foot on our hearts

Relieved of the need to cower, we rise up to face the zenith

Unlike Sisyphus, we race to the top of the mountain, boulder held high to the sky, as it melts in our hands

Freed from the chains that bind us

We look to one another

Love drawing us together
The peace and unity provided for, by the Love, begins to emerge
Instantly, we all know the Truth

We are all One and we are All alright

Cradled in the Symphony of Sisterhood, the Bosom of Brotherhood, and open to the Oneness deep in the Heart of our Co-Creator

---

Chapter Four:
The American Dream

The American Dream is simply a desire for a better life, free from the strife and struggle of oppression of any sort. Throughout history, oppression has been responsible for the plight of most people's failings to adequately provide for themselves, forcing hunger and constant work to be a part of everyday life.

During the birth of this nation on newly conquered land, hard work and hunger were constant companions. The significant difference was the absence of a monarchy and an appointed nobility that owned and hoarded all the land, essentially making indentured servants of the bulk of the population.

Freed from that oppression, the opportunity to make more than just a meager wage was possible. The birth of the middle class became a reality sustained by the people, allowing for the development and personification of the American Dream. America became the place that rewarded hard work with a better life. The definition of a better life doesn't always mean the same thing to everyone. What does it mean to have a better life?

The one variable to everyone's definition of the American dream is perspective, where you are coming from, and where you want to go. So, improving your life may mean another $5 an hour, the opportunity to further your education, or in some cases, finally getting the corner office with a nice view.

Of course, being a trillionaire would ease a significant portion of people's problems and almost certainly bring on a few more.

Making life easier would mean having enough money to do as one pleases.

Without a higher goal, excess money would lend itself to placating one's vices. So having a moral idea of what constitutes the good life is in order here.

The ability to pursue one's goals while earning a sustaining wage, giving back to the whole, and developing nurturing, loving relationships with family, friends, and acquaintances, while being a vital part of the governing system that sustains us all, is an excellent start to a working definition of the good life!

If we are indeed a slice of the pure Energy Source, incarnate in a human body with a Soul Mission already agreed upon before we incarnate, it would make sense that we explore the Truth of our Being to reveal our Soul Mission. Upon that discovery, we plot our life course to carry out our Soul/Life Mission, unencumbered by the oppression that is so dominant in our world today. How many Soul Missions have been obliterated by the trauma of overt oppression?

What could be better than a life served accomplishing its Soul Mission? Imagine a society dedicated to fostering every individual's Soul Mission.

Now, it is time to refresh our idea of what it means to be living the American Dream. To discover the original meaning, let me refer you to an article by Sarah Churchill.

Source: https://www.bushcenter.org/catalyst/state-of-the-american-dream/churchwell-history-of-the-american-dream (Churchwell, S, 2021, Winter)

Winter 2021

A **Brief History** *of the* **American Dream**

An Essay by Sarah Churchwell, Professor at the University of London, and Author, **Behold, America: The Entangled History of 'America First' and 'the American Dream'**

Over time, the phrase "American dream" has come to be associated with upward mobility and enough economic success to lead a comfortable life. Historically, however, the phrase represented the idealism of the great American experiment.

If you ask most people around the world what they mean by the "American dream," nearly all will respond with some version of upward social mobility, the American success story, or the self-made man (rarely the self-made woman). Perhaps they will invoke the symbolic house with a white picket fence that suggests economic self-sufficiency and security; many will associate the phrase with the land of opportunity for immigrants. No less an authority than the *Oxford English Dictionary* defines the American dream as "the ideal that every citizen of the United States should have an equal opportunity to achieve success and prosperity through hard work, determination, and initiative."

If success and prosperity are the American dream, however, it's hard to understand why it was under assault by a mob of insurrectionists at the Capitol in January—but that is precisely what international commentators concluded. From Iran to Australia to Britain, global observers construed the Capitol riot as an assault on "the American dream," although it was not a mob driven by economic grievance, but rather an explicitly political assault on the democratic process.

No matter how often we talk about the American dream as a socioeconomic promise of material success, the truth is that most people—even people around the world—understand instinctively that the American dream is also a sociopolitical one, meaning something more profound and aspirational than simple material comfort. And indeed, that's what the phrase denoted to the Americans who first popularized it.

In 1931 a historian named James Truslow Adams set out to make sense of the crisis of the Great Depression, which in 1931 was both an economic crisis and a looming political crisis. Authoritarianism in Europe was on the rise, and many Americans were concerned that similar "despotic" energies would support the fabled "man on horseback" who might become an American tyrant. Adams concluded that America had lost its way by prizing material success above all other values: Indeed, it had started to treat money *as* a value, instead of merely as a means to produce or measure value.

For Adams, worshipping material success was not the definition of the American dream: It was, by contrast, the failure of "the American dream of a better, richer, and happier life for all our citizens of every rank." Adams did not mean "richer" materially, but spiritually; he distinguished the American dream from dreams of prosperity. It was, he declared, "not a dream of motor cars and high wages merely, but a dream of social order in which each man and each woman shall be able to attain to the fullest stature of which they are innately capable, and be recognized by others for what they are, regardless of the fortuitous circumstances of birth or position."

That repudiation is crucial, but almost always overlooked when this famous passage is quoted. Adams specifically gainsays the idea that the American dream is of material success. The American dream, according to Adams, was about collective moral character: It was a vision of "commonweal," common well-being, well-being that is held in common and therefore mutually supported.

It was, as Adams said, a "dream of social order," in which every citizen could attain the best of which they were capable. And it was that dream of social order that was so conspicuously under assault on January 6th. It was the same American dream that Martin Luther King Jr. would call to service in the civil rights struggle in 1963, when he told white America that Black Americans shared that dream:

I still have a dream. It is a dream deeply rooted in the American dream. I have a dream that one day this nation will rise up and live out the true meaning of its creed: "We hold these truths to be self-evident, that all men are created equal..."

I have a dream that my four little children will one day live in a nation where they will not be judged by the color of their skin but by the content of their character.

The idea of an American creed, now all but forgotten, was once a staple of American political discourse, a broad belief system comprising liberty, democratic equality, social justice, economic opportunity, and individual advancement. Before 1945, when it was replaced by the Pledge of Allegiance, the creed was recited by most American schoolchildren—including, presumably, a young Martin Luther King Jr.:

I believe in the United States of America as a government of the people, by the people, for the people, whose just powers are derived from the consent of the governed; a democracy in a republic and a sovereign nation of many sovereign States; a perfect Union, one and inseparable; established upon those principles of freedom, equality, justice and humanity for which American patriots sacrificed their lives and fortunes.

It was in that creed that the phrase the American dream was first used to articulate—not in 1931, when it was popularized, but when it first appeared in American political discourse, at the turn of the 20th century.

The American dream was rarely, if ever, used to describe the familiar idea of Horatio Alger individual upward social mobility until after the Second World War. Quite the opposite, in fact. In 1899, a Vermont doctor made the news when he built a house with 60 rooms on 4,000 acres, which was described as "the largest country place in America" at the time. It came as a shock to readers, and struck many of them as an "utterly un-American dream" in its inequality: "Until a few years ago the thought of such an estate as that would have seemed a wild and utterly un-American dream to any Vermonter," one article commented. "It was a state of almost ideally democratic equality, where everybody worked and nobody went hungry." We don't have to accept that Vermont was ever a utopian ideal to recognize that the comment overturns our received wisdoms about the American dream. Today, such an estate would seem the epitome of the American dream to most Americans.

In 1900, the *New York Post* warned its readers that the "greatest risk" to "every republic" was not from the so-called rabble, but "discontented multimillionaires." All previous republics, it noted, had been "overthrown by rich men" and this could happen too in America, where monopoly capitalists were "deriding the Constitution, unrebuked by the executive or by public opinion." If they had their way "it would be the end of the American dream," because the American dream was of democracy—of equality of opportunity, of justice for all. Again, today most Americans would clearly say that becoming a multimillionaire defines the American dream, but the fact is that the expression emerged to criticize, not endorse, the amassing of great personal wealth.

Although many now assume that the phrase American dream was first used to describe 19th century immigrants' archetypal dreams of finding a land where the streets were paved with gold, not until 1918 have I found any instance of the "American dream" being used to describe the immigrant experience—the same year that the language of the "American creed" was first published.

There were only a few passing mentions of the idea of an American dream before Adams popularized it in 1931, most notably in Walter Lippmann's 1914 *Drift and Mastery,* which described what Lippmann called America's "fear economy" of unbridled capitalism. Lippmann argued that the nation's "dream of endless progress" would need to be restrained, because it was fundamentally illusory: "It opens a chasm between fact and fancy, and the whole fine dream is detached from the living zone of the present." This dream of endless progress was indistinguishable, Lippmann wrote, "from those who dream of a glorious past." Both dreams were equally illusory.

For Lippmann, the American dream was the idea that the common man is inherently good and a moral barometer of the nation, the belief that "if only you let men alone, they'll be good." For Lippmann, the American dream was a delusion not because upward social mobility was a myth, but because undisciplined goodness is:

The past which men create for themselves is a place where thought is unnecessary and happiness inevitable. The American temperament leans generally to a kind of mystical anarchism, in which the "natural" humanity in each man is adored as the savior of society... "If only you let men alone, they'll be good," a typical American reformer said to me the other day. He believed, as most Americans do, in the

unsophisticated man, in his basic kindliness and his instinctive prac-
tical sense. A critical outlook seemed to the reformer an inhuman
one; he distrusted ... the appearance of the expert; he believed that
whatever faults the common man might show were due to some kind
of Machiavellian corruption. He had the American dream, which may
be summed up ... in the statement that the undisciplined man is the
salt of the earth.

The American faith in the individual taken to its inevitable extreme creates the monstrosity of a self with no consciousness of other standards
or perspectives, let alone a sense of principle.

James Truslow Adams ended *The Epic of America* with what he said
was the perfect symbol of the American dream in action. It was not
the example of an immigrant who made good, a self-made man who
bootstrapped his way from poverty to power, or the iconic house with a
white picket fence. For Adams, the American dream was embodied in
the Main Reading Room at the Library of Congress.

It was a room that the nation had gifted to itself, so that every American—"old and young, rich and poor, Black and white, the executive
and the laborer, the general and the private, the noted scholar and the
schoolboy"—could sit together, "reading at their own library provided by
their own democracy. It has always seemed to me," Adams continued,

to be a perfect working out in a concrete example of the American
dream—the means provided by the accumulated resources of the peo-
ple themselves, a public intelligent enough to use them, and men of
high distinction, themselves a part of the great democracy, devoting
themselves to the good of the whole, uncloistered.

It is an image of peaceful, collective, enlightened self-improvement.
That is the American dream, according to the man who bequeathed us
the phrase. It is an image that takes for granted the value of education,
of shared knowledge and curiosity, of historical inquiry and a commitment to the good of the whole.

That depiction of a group of Americans serenely reading together on
Capitol Hill serves as a deeply painful corrective for the nation we have
become, filled with people who put political partisanship above country, above democracy, above any principle of civic good or collective
well-being.

Writing in the midst of the Great Depression, Adams was neither naïve
nor especially sentimental about the America he was viewing in 1931.

His reflections on the Library of Congress as the American dream led him to conclude that its fundamental purpose was to keep democracy alive:

No ruling class has ever willingly abdicated. Democracy can never be saved, and would not be worth saving, unless it can save itself. The Library of Congress, however, has come straight from the heart of democracy, as it has been taken to it, and I here use it as a symbol of what democracy can accomplish on its own behalf.

That is the American dream: what democracy can accomplish on its own behalf for its citizens. The first voices to speak of the "American dream" used it not as a promise, or a guarantee, but as an exhortation, urging all Americans to do better, to be fairer, to combat bigotry and inequality, to keep striving for a republic of equals. That is the American dream we need to revive: the dream of a social order defined by the American creed, a belief in the United States of America as a government whose just powers are derived from the consent of the governed; a democracy in a republic.

When we have a road map, we at least can get to where we want to go. The governing documents for this country have been a reliable road map to creating a system that brings together all people from all walks of life, and all income levels, into one unifying system that allows for the continued evolution of each individual.

Knowing that we are all One, making space for each individual to discover their own way, with dignity and respect for themselves and others, is paramount to stimulating and empowering this experiment to continue.

Subverting the general wisdom of these documents for personal gain results in chaos, discontent, anarchy, malfeasance, homelessness, a decline in mental health, selfishness that disregards the safety of others, and a loss of unity and Oneness. In short, a complete breakdown and total disregard for the benchmarks that created and will propel this country forward! The American Dream only became possible when we all pulled together to throw off the oppression of the monarchy across the pond.

What are the lessons learned? Oppression cripples our ability to dream the American Dream of women and men, free to discover their true potential and the Truth of their Reality.

We are not here to toil our life away. Of course, taking care of our basic needs comes from working and making money, but when we are forced to spend all our time working to cover our basic needs, we are oppressed. Capitalism, the way it is now practiced, is our new oppressor. Obscene amounts of accumulated money, in the hands of a small percentage of our people, have buried the rest of the population under a mountain of lies and deceit that make it difficult to see the Truth. WTP are the designated ones who decide what kind of America we want to live in, not the few subverting our dream and governing documents to serve themselves.

Let's face it; human beings are not perfect. We have managed to muck things up in a colossal way from time to time, yet when we try to be our best selves, we have accomplished some pretty amazing feats! Knowing we are not perfect yet fully capable of being marvelous, it makes sense that our government reflects our diligence in being our best self as a nation and as a governing body charged with the care and protection of its citizens. Are we our best selves? Can we do better? How can we consistently be our best selves?

It seems to be a disease that people allow their worst selves to rise to the surface, leaving pain and suffering in their wake, only to discover the joy that is their birthright when they allow themselves to feel and express love. How many movies, books, and stories illustrate this scenario over and over, and yet this disease continues to be the norm in our society? People act unkindly for no apparent reason towards other people.

Perhaps we could change the focus and learn how to get along with one another, making possible the flow of love for all of us!

If only people knew and understood the power of love and how it could release them from the pain of their trauma, allowing them to generate and share the love instead of the pain and suffering.

For a deep dive into the Truth of our Reality and the power of love, here is an excerpt from a Gina Lake book:

Source: https://www.amazon.com/Ten-Teachings-One-World-Wisdom/dp/1492173452 (Lake, G., 2013)

Gina Lake, "I'm reading from a book given to me by Mother Mary": *Ten Teachings for One World: Wisdom from Mother Mary.*

Let Love Be Your Guide

That love is the highest value is indisputable. Only someone who has been deprived of love might dispute this out of his or her woundedness; and yet, love is the only thing that can heal such woundedness. Love is that powerful and pervasive a force. It is, in fact, the only force in the universe. And that is very good news.

Words are inadequate to describe this force. If you call it love, it becomes limited to the realm of human emotions. But the emotion of love is a poor reflection of the force I am speaking about. This force as it moves through the human being gets corrupted by self-interest and greed. Love becomes something you have to get from someone else and something you never have enough of, like everything the ego seeks. This is not love but a lack of love masquerading as love. Neediness is a better word for it.

Neediness is the opposite of love, for true love results in a natural outpouring of love to others, not in desiring anything from them. You can pretend to love others in hopes of getting what you want and you can love them because they give you what you want or because you imagine that they will, but this is the ego's version of love, and it stems from need.

When you are connected to the force that governs the universe, you are naturally loving, and this is its own reward. You need nothing from anyone. Love is a state of completion, not need. It is a state of giving, not taking. From this sense of completion flows an adoration of and generosity toward all life. When you feel complete and at peace, you are full of love, gratitude, and joy. This state is what everyone longs for.

The ego does not know how to achieve this state. The things the ego does to try to attain this state only take one deeper into egoic consciousness, which is a state of lack and fear in which love cannot flow and peace does not exist. You can only achieve a state of peace and love by seeing that nothing is lacking within you, within others, or within life, that everything is already good and as it is meant to be. All is well and unfolding as it needs to, and love is what is behind this unfolding. Love is all that exists.

To the ego, this sounds flowery and untrue. That love is behind all of life and that life is good is difficult for human beings to comprehend. It is not how the mind sees things, and the mind is what tries to comprehend this. But the mind will never be able to understand the nature of life or the nature of love. The truth about life is so far beyond the mind that the mind is inadequate to the task. But that does not change the truth.

Despite the difficulty of the mind to know the truth, the truth is known to you in your heart of hearts. You know the love that is at your core, and often you obey and honor it. When you are aligned with it, you are happy and at peace; when you are not, you are not happy and at peace. You know this much: Love is what you want, not a love that needs but a love that forgets itself in the presence of the beloved, which is all of life.

This self-forgetfulness is love. What is the self that is forgotten? It is the false self. When you move beyond all ideas of yourself, all images, and the sense of yourself as someone who is this or that, you fall in love with life. And you discover that you are life. No longer does anything separate you from life. You lose your boundaries, as the you that you thought you were falls away, and all that remains is the spaciousness of your being.

The being that you are is the same being that everyone is. Being-ness flows everywhere, without boundaries that distinguish you from everyone else. Your being and everyone else's being are the same, merged into one! What a surprise, when previously you felt such a distinct sense of self. When this sense of self dissolves, you are left with your true nature, which is deeply in love with life and sees itself in all life. The joy you feel in this dissolving is the joy you have been looking for, but it was not to be found in riches, popularity, or acclaim. Your very being is the source of the exquisite joy you have been searching for.

How do you arrive at this place of exquisite joy? Let love be your guide. This is the tenth teaching. For as long as the ego has been your guide, it has taken you away from love. It is time to recognize this now and shift your allegiance. Once you realize the falseness of the guide you have been following and that there is another, truer guide, you can be on your way Home.

If you have a false guide, then no matter where it takes you, even if some of those places are pleasant, you will not arrive at your intended destination. No matter how convincing that guide is, it still cannot take you there. That is the human condition: The guide is very convincing but also false. It does not know the way, although it acts like it knows and other people are following it. But that does not change a thing—it does not know the way.

When you are trying to get somewhere and you do not succeed, that is painful. But once you know you are on the right path and that you will get there, you find the strength to overcome any challenges along the way. You feel strong, supported, uplifted, and confident in your steps. Being aligned with your true nature feels good and right, and that is enough.

On the other hand, following a false guide is like being stuck in brambles. The path hurts, and it is difficult to summon the courage and strength to continue. When you are not aligned with your true nature, nothing ever feels like enough. You are never satisfied and you can never rest. But that is as it is meant to be. You are not meant to find the wrong path rewarding.

Let love be your guide means align with the divine force of love within you and let it move you in your life. When you were aligned with the false guide, it moved you by scaring you and telling you that you needed something else to be happy. It used a stick and a carrot to move you. With love as your guide, you act because it is intrinsically joyful to act. Acting, when that action is aligned with being, is its own reward.

Let love be your guide also means let love be your master, let it guide your actions and speech. Be the servant of love. Do your actions and speech come from love? If not, do not engage in them. Do your actions and speech lead to greater love between you and others? If not, do not engage in them. Will you be a force for love on this planet? One individual acting as a force for love can counteract hundreds, even thousands, acting otherwise. You are powerful. What you do matters. How you act and what you say matters. Be the loving force you can be. This is my final teaching.

Amazon description of the book, **Ten Teachings for One World: Wisdom from Mother Mary,** by Gina Lake

Ten Teachings for One World is a channeled message from Mother Mary to her beloved children on earth. The teachings are intended to bring us into closer contact with the peace and love that is our divine nature, which has the ability to transform our hearts and our world. Mother Mary's gentle wisdom will inspire and assist you in awakening to the magnificent being that you are.

On a glorious fall day in 2012, while sitting in a garden graced by a statue of Mother Mary, Gina Lake heard Mother Mary address her: "You are my beloved child." This began an ongoing relationship and communication with Mother Mary. Ten Teachings for One World is the little book of wisdom teachings that Mother Mary wished to share with the world. Here is a taste of this wisdom: "For this transformation to happen, you have to be willing to see yourself differently. You have to be willing to see yourself as the magnificent and loving being that you are and can be. Are you willing? What beliefs keep you from being willing to see yourself this way? How do you see yourself? Do you realize that that is an imagination? You made that up, possibly with the help of others who told you who and what you are. Why not imagine something grander, something much more true, and that will become your experience. This is how you awaken from the illusion of being limited, small, inadequate, less than. Be willing to see yourself as the divine being that you truly are—and you will be!"

Knowing this force is available to us all and that it can free us from the pain of allegiance to our ego gives hope.

Maybe one day, a majority of people will understand and apply this force of love to their lives, their livelihood, their families, and the world in general, producing a Golden Age to rival all Golden Ages!

Until then...

We will struggle with unity, equality, and goodwill towards all people, which will be reflected in our society, our citizens, and our government.

Currently, our government has failed in its duty to protect and care for all of its citizens...

Our government has been corrupted by ordinary human failings, greed, and the desire for power.

Our government suffers from the tyranny of a minority.
We can certainly do better; it is up to WTP to make this happen.

WTP are still the majority, and when we join together, we can create mountains of change.

WTP pushed back the oppression of the British monarchy in the Revolutionary War so many years ago.

WTP pushed back the oppression of two World Wars and experienced an expansion of the middle class after WWII, unparalleled in modern history.

We have the knowledge and capability to expand the middle class.

WTP must unite and demand this inalienable right for it to happen!

No ruling class has ever voluntarily surrendered its power in history.

Our situation is not as dire as a peasant revolt, farmers armed with pitchforks and rakes attempting to overthrow a heavily armed military. No!

We have a government accountable to a democratic constitution and WTP elect who serve this country. The election cycles are two, four, and six years. Within a decade, WTP can replace every single congressman, president, and senator who is not serving the needs of WTP as WTP see fit.

No bloodshed is required.

Anarchy destroys everything and never makes anything better.

Working together in a truly democratic fashion makes everything better for the majority of the people.

Knowledge, unity, and diligence are all we need to help us make the changes.

An overwhelming majority of WTP would welcome a revival of this original American Dream, mainly because this majority would benefit the most. When the bulk of society can afford to live comfortably, the metrics for happiness and satisfaction with life increase.

We have all heard the term "Middle Class," but how many people would claim this status level? How many would be satisfied with this status level? A careful consideration of the alternatives helps me to decide right away. I would be content to live a middle-class life if it wasn't such a struggle. And if life is just one struggle after another, then it is not a middle-class life – living to work is no life at all!

"Give me liberty or give me death!" Patrick Henry (one of the many Founding Fathers)

Working so you may have an abundant life full of love is absolutely attainable. I have dedicated my life to this end for all people.

There will always be people at either end of the wealth spectrum. Still, without a middle class, the stratification delineates into haves and have-nots. The have-nots become disposable and without value.

Obviously, this oppression has adverse effects on the whole of society. The poor and rich alike suffer, but just in different ways. The poor have nothing with which to soothe their pain, and the rich struggle to get richer; putting the love of money above all else; fearing they could lose it all; never knowing whom they can trust as a real friend.

Money is not necessarily a bad thing... I enjoy the options: money affords me! I enjoy spending money. I enjoy making money. What is it with money, and how it makes people act crazy?

We have all heard the saying that "Money is the root of all evil" ...

This quote vilifies money as the culprit of evil. Interesting because money is not alive; it is made of metal and paper and cannot choose good or evil.

"The love of money is the root of all evil." Is the original quote and produces quite a different meaning! When one's focus is solely upon the accumulation of money purely for the sake of having a lot of it, it can lead to many adverse decisions concerning how to get more of it. Many of these decisions include, but are not limited to, lying, cheating, and stealing.

I am not prejudiced against rich people or poor people. I do not approve of nor condone anyone's decision to lie, cheat or steal, be they rich or poor. Generally speaking, if poor people lie, cheat, or steal, it is because they are hungry. Anyone who hasn't eaten for three days would almost surely steal food if they could not purchase food. If rich people decide to lie, cheat, or steal, my guess is the disease known as "The Love of Money is the Root of All Evil!" Just like an alcoholic who cannot stop drinking, someone operating under an abnormal desire for accumulating cash needs help to modify that desire, and WTP have got to step in and help. People on the fringe of society, be they rich or poor, whenever it becomes obvious that they need help, WTP have got to be willing to step in and bring them back to the middle. It is lonely out on the edges, and bringing everyone closer to the center unites us all.

People with excesses of money must realize that they are not the sole factor in accumulating that money. They need someone to buy their products and services. A strong, vibrant middle class provides a consumer base to realize all successful businesses. When someone creates a product or service, they must be able to sell it. Selling involves other people. People only make money through interactions with other people. No one can make money in a void.

For the relationship to be reciprocal, the individual with the recently earned money must reintroduce the acquired money back into circulation, or the whole system locks up. Money is not something that you can own. Money is what makes a capitalist society move. Money comes in, and money goes out.

When money is hoarded, the system locks up. Fear permeates—facilitating more anxiety and the hoarding of more money, forcing everyone to scramble to make and collect more money, reducing the free flow of money, and transmitting the false idea that there is not enough money! It reminds me of a Fairytale myth from my youth:

Source: https://reenchantements.files.wordpress.com/2018/08/warm-fuzzy-tale.pdf (Steiner, C.M., 1969)

The Warm Fuzzy Tale

By Claude M. Steiner

Once upon a time, a long time ago, there lived two happy people called Tim and Maggie with their two children, John and Lucy. To understand how happy they were you have to understand how things were in those days. You see in those happy days everyone was given a small, soft Fuzzy Bag when born. Any time a person reached into this bag they were able to pull out a Warm Fuzzy. Warm Fuzzies were very much in demand because whenever someone was given a Warm Fuzzy it made them feel warm and fuzzy all over. In those days it was very easy to get Warm Fuzzies. Anytime that somebody felt like it, he might walk up to you and say, "I'd like to have a Warm Fuzzy." You would then reach into your bag and pull out a Fuzzy the size of a child's hand. As soon as the Fuzzy saw the light of day it would smile and blossom into a large, shaggy, Warm Fuzzy.

When you laid the Warm Fuzzy on the person's head, shoulder or lap it would snuggle up and melt right against their skin and make them feel good all over. People were always asking each other for Warm Fuzzies, and since they were always given freely, getting enough of them was never a problem. There were always plenty to go around, and so everyone was happy and felt warm and fuzzy most of the time.

One day a bad witch who made salves and potions for sick people became angry because everyone was so happy and feeling good and no one was buying potions and salves. The witch was very clever and devised a very wicked plan. One beautiful morning while Maggie was playing with her daughter the witch crept up to Tim and whispered in his ear, "See here, Tim, look at all the Fuzzies that Maggie is giving to Lucy. You know, if she keeps it up she is going to run out and then there won't be any left for you!"

Tim was astonished. He turned to the witch and asked, "Do you mean to tell me that there isn't a Warm Fuzzy in our bag every time we reach into it?" And the witch answered, "No, absolutely not, and once you run out, that's it. You don't have any more." With this the witch flew away on a broom, laughing and cackling all the way.

Tim took this to heart and began to notice every time Maggie gave away a Warm Fuzzy. He got very worried because he liked Maggie's Warm Fuzzies very much and did not want to give them up. He certainly did not think it was right for Maggie to be spending all her Warm Fuzzies on the children and other people. Tim began to complain or sulk when he saw Maggie giving Warm Fuzzies to somebody else, and because Maggie loved him very much, she stopped giving Warm Fuzzies to other people as often, and reserved most of them for him.

The children watched this and soon began to get the idea that it was wrong to give Warm Fuzzies any time you were asked or felt like it. They too became very careful. They would watch their parents closely and whenever they felt that one of their parents was giving too many Fuzzies to others, they felt jealous and complained and sometimes even had a tantrum. And even though they found a Warm Fuzzy every time they reached into their bag they began to feel guilty whenever they gave them away so they reached in less and less and became more and more stingy with them.

Before the witch, people used to gather in groups of three, four or five, never caring too much who was giving Warm Fuzzies to whom. After the coming of the witch, people began to pair off and to reserve all their Warm Fuzzies for each other, exclusively. When people forgot to be careful and gave a Warm Fuzzy to just anybody they worried because they knew that somebody would probably resent sharing their Warm Fuzzies.

People began to give less and less Warm Fuzzies, and felt less warm and less fuzzy. They began to shrivel up and, occasionally, people would even die from lack of Warm Fuzzies. People felt worse and worse and, more and more, people went to the witch to buy potions and salves even though they didn't really seem to work.

Well, the situation was getting very serious indeed. The bad witch who had been watching all of this didn't really want the people to die (since dead people couldn't buy his salves and potions), so a new plan was devised.

Everyone was given, free of charge, a bag that was very similar to the Fuzzy Bag except that this one was cold while the Fuzzy Bag was warm. Inside of the witch's bag were Cold Pricklies. These Cold Pricklies did not make people feel warm and fuzzy; in fact, they made them feel cold and prickly instead. But the Cold Pricklies were better than nothing and they did prevent peoples' backs from shriveling up. So, from then on, when somebody asked for a Warm Fuzzy, people who were worried about depleting their supply would say, "I can't give you a Warm Fuzzy, but would you like a Cold Prickly instead?" Sometimes, two people would walk up to each other, thinking they maybe they could get a Warm Fuzzy this time, but one of them would change his mind and they would wind up giving each other Cold Pricklies instead.

So, the end result was that people were not dying anymore but a lot of people were very unhappy and feeling very cold and prickly indeed. The situation got very complicated since the coming of the witch because there were fewer and fewer Warm Fuzzies around and Warm Fuzzies which used to be free as air, became extremely valuable. This caused people to do all sorts of things in order to get Warm Fuzzies. People who could not find a generous partner had to buy their Warm Fuzzies and had to work long hours to earn the money. Some people became "popular" and got a lot of Warm Fuzzies without having to give any back. These people would then sell their Warm Fuzzies to people who were "unpopular" and needed them to feel that life was worth living.

Another thing which happened was that some people would take Cold Pricklies--which were everywhere and freely available-and coated them white and fluffy so that they almost looked like Warm Fuzzies. These fake Warm Fuzzies were really Plastic Fuzzies, and they caused additional problems. For instance, two or more people would get together and freely give each other Plastic Fuzzies. They expected to feel good, but they came away feeling bad instead. People got

very confused never realizing that their cold, prickly feelings were because they had been given a lot of Plastic Fuzzies.

So the situation was very, very dismal and it all started because of the
coming of the witch who made people believe that someday, when least
expected, they might reach into their Warm Fuzzy Bag and find no more.

Not long ago, a young woman with big hips came to this unhappy land.
She seemed not to have heard about the bad witch and was not worried about running out of Warm Fuzzies. She gave them out freely,
even when not asked. They called her the Hip Woman and disapproved
of her because she was giving the children the idea that they should not
worry about running out of Warm Fuzzies. The children liked her very
much because they felt good around her and they began to follow her
example giving out Warm Fuzzies whenever they felt like it.

This made the grownups very worried. To protect the children from
depleting their supplies of Warm Fuzzies they passed a law. The law
made it a criminal offense to give out Warm Fuzzies in a reckless manner or without a license. Many children, however, seemed not to care;
and in spite of the law they continued to give each other Warm Fuzzies
whenever they felt like it and always when asked. Because they were
many, many children, almost as many as grownups, it began to look as
if maybe they would have their way.

As of now it is hard to say what will happen. Will the grownups' laws
stop the recklessness of the children? Are the grownups going to join
with the Hip Woman and the children in taking a chance that there will
always be as many Warm Fuzzies as needed? Will they remember the
days their children are trying to bring back when Warm Fuzzies were
abundant because people gave them away freely? The struggle spread
all over the land and is probably going on right where you live. If you
want to, and I hope you do, you can join by freely giving and asking for
Warm Fuzzies and being as loving and healthy as you can.

The free exchange of warm fuzzies is what makes life worth living! Just
ask your kids. Warm fuzzies are the best; they know they get it!

In a healthy middle-class society, people are friendly to one another, and there is a higher degree of trust. Everyone can afford their lifestyle
while maintaining their integrity, peace of mind, and ability to keep the

174

love flowing. For a thorough understanding of the merits of a strong and vibrant middle class, I would now like to share an article from:

Source: https://www.americanprogress.org/article/the-american-middle-class-income-inequality-and-the-strength-of-our-economy/ (CAP (Center for American Progress), 2012, 17 May)

Report May 17, 2012

The American Middle Class, Income Inequality, and the Strength of Our Economy

New Evidence in Economics

Heather Boushey and Adam S. Hersh discuss ways that the strength of the middle class and the level of societal inequality both affect economic growth and stability.

To say that the middle class is important to our economy may seem noncontroversial to most Americans. After all, most of us self-identify as middle class, and members of the middle class observe every day how their work contributes to the economy, hear weekly how their spending is a leading indicator for economic prognosticators, and see every month how jobs numbers, which primarily reflect middle-class jobs, are taken as the key measure of how the economy is faring. And as growing income inequality has risen in the nation's consciousness, the plight of the middle class has become a common topic in the press and policy circles.

For most economists, however, the concepts of "middle class" or even inequality have not had a prominent place in our thinking about how an economy grows. This, however, is beginning to change. One reason for the change is that the levels of inequality and the financial stress on the middle class have risen dramatically and have reached levels that motivate a closer investigation. The interaction and concurrence of rising inequality with the financial collapse and the Great Recession have, in particular, raised new issues about whether a weakened middle class and rising inequality should be part of our thinking about the drivers of economic growth.

Over the past several decades, the United States has undergone a remarkable transformation, with income growth stalling for the middle class while the incomes of those at the top continued to rise dramatically compared to the rest of the working population. Between 1979 and 2007, the last year before the Great Recession, median family income rose by 35 percent, while incomes for those at the 99th percentile rose by 278 percent. Families in the middle class have also pulled away from those at the bottom, but achieved these modest income gains only by working longer hours, increasing their labor supply—particularly among wives and mothers—and increasing household debts to maintain consumption as wages failed to keep pace with inflation.

In 1979 the middle three household income quintiles in the United States—that is, the population between the 21st and 80th percentiles on the income scale—earned 50 percent of all national income. But by 2007 the income share of those in the middle shrank to just 43 percent. Evolution of the Gini coefficient, which measures how much a distribution deviates from complete equality, also shows a similar pattern of rising inequality. Between 1979 and 2007 the Gini coefficient including capital gains, in the United States climbed from 48 to 59, ranking the United States in the top quarter of the most unequal countries in the world.

Theories of economic growth, however, do not typically include models for investigating the implications of changes in the strength of the middle class. If you ask an economist "what makes an economy grow?", they will almost certainly begin their answer by pointing to an economy's level of knowledge about how to produce goods and services (knowledge and technology), the skills of the potential labor force (human capital) and the number of workers, and the stock of physical capital (factories, office buildings, infrastructure). The economy grows when technological improvements or investments in human or physical capital boost productivity, when the labor force increases, or when investment in physical capital adds to the economy's productive stock—and thus total output expands.

But this begs the question: What boosts productivity or creates incentives to invest? Economists differ in their specific answers to these questions, but the different theories point to five primary factors:

- The **level of human capital** and whether talent is encouraged to boost the economy's productivity

- **Cost of and access to financial capital**, which allow firms and entrepreneurs to make real investments that create technological progress to use in the economy
- **Strong and stable demand**, which creates the market for goods and services and allows investors to plan for the future
- The **quality of political and economic institutions**, including the quality of corporate governance as well as political institutions and a legal structure that enforces contracts
- **Investment in public goods, education, health, and infrastructure**, which lays the foundation for private-sector investment

Strong empirical evidence in economics and other social sciences suggests that the strength of the middle class and the level of income inequality have an important role to play for each of these five factors boosting productivity and spurring investment.

The research for this project began with a series of interviews and a national conference with leading U.S. economists to learn their views about the mechanisms through which income inequality and the strength of the middle class affect economic growth and economic stability. This paper summarizes what we have learned from these conversations, alongside our analysis of the economic research in the academic arena. We have identified four areas where literature points to ways that the strength of the middle class and the level of inequality affect economic growth and stability:

- A strong middle class promotes the development of human capital and a well-educated population.
- A strong middle class creates a stable source of demand for goods and services.
- A strong middle class incubates the next generation of entrepreneurs.
- A strong middle class supports inclusive political and economic institutions, which underpin economic growth.

We detail the evidence for these four points in the main pages of our paper, but briefly we encapsulate the economic research here. As we will demonstrate, the ways in which a strong middle class is important for economic growth are both interrelated and mutually reinforcing.

A strong middle class promotes the development of human capital and a well-educated population

Economists agree that human capital—knowledge, skills, and the health to put those to work—is a key component of growth. To be most effective, opportunities to build human capital must be broadly available in the population. For the nation to make the most of its human potential, a child from a low- or moderate-income background needs his or her talents and abilities to be nurtured and matched to the most suitable occupation. The evidence is fairly clear that inequality and the strength of the middle class have direct effects on access and use of human capital:

- As the United States has grown more unequal in terms of income, there has been both a decrease in the rate of improvement in educational outcomes and these outcomes have become more unequal.
- The data point to the conclusion that human capital, and the higher incomes that go along with it, are increasingly passed from parents to offspring through social (not biological) channels. This means that individuals are being rewarded for privileges conveyed by their parents' socioeconomic status, not just their productivity characteristics, which will pull U.S. economic growth down.
- The contribution of human capital to growth is not only about access to education: Individuals also must be able to make use of their skills, matching talent to appropriate occupations. If inequality stands in the way of those matches, then it is having a pernicious effect on our nation's growth path.

A strong middle class creates a stable source of demand for goods and services

A strong middle class gives certainty to business investors that they will have a market for their goods and services. Supply-side thinkers argue that light tax and regulatory policies will lead to high investment, employment, and economic growth. But many economists acknowledge that an increase in supply does not automatically lead to an increase in aggregate demand. Rather, economies may have prolonged periods of unemployment and underutilized capital, which can be both the cause and the result of depressed and unstable demand.

If demand matters for economic growth, the question is then, how do high inequality and the strength of the middle class impact demand? Economists have developed a number of theories about how inequality affects demand:

- As more of the nation's economic gains go to those at the top of the income distribution—and if those families have a lower propensity to consume—then this will pull down demand from potentially higher levels given more equitable distribution.

- Heightened inequality and a squeezed middle class leads families to either consume less, lowering demand, or put in place short-term coping strategies, such as borrowing more, which has long-term implications for growth and stability.

A strong middle class incubates the next generation of entrepreneurs

Entrepreneurship is a matter of taking risks, and there are a variety of ways that a strong middle class and less inequality can create the kinds of conditions that reduce the risks of innovators and give them the skills to start up a business:

- Middle-class families can provide entrepreneurs with the financial security and access to credit so they have the time to nurture their ideas and take the risk to start a new business.
- An individual in a middle-class family is more likely than someone from a low-income background to have access to the kind of education that provides the training and skills necessary to start a business.
- As described in above, less inequality is associated with greater macroeconomic stability, which allows entrepreneurs to make informed investment decisions with greater confidence about economic conditions and the risks of starting a business.

A strong middle class supports inclusive political and economic institutions, which underpin economic growth

This dynamic of a strong middle class boosts efficient and honest governance of an economy's enterprises. In the U.S. context, less inequality and a stronger middle class support more inclusive political institutions and steer politics away from only responding to an economically powerful elite. This provides the foundation for more inclusive economic institutions, which, in turn, promote growth. This includes encouraging effective governance that supports broad-based economic growth through establishing secure property rights; investing in public goods and quasi-public goods, such as education, health, and infrastructure; and a level playing field, including transparent and accountable legal and regulatory structures. A strong middle class prevents the concentration and exploitation of power that led to entrenched privilege in aristocracies—the antithesis of dynamic societies throughout human history.

The evidence of the role of the middle class in economic growth

To be clear, we do not assert that the middle class is the only factor affecting economic growth. The price of capital, taxes, resource endowments, luck, chance, and other causes all have important roles to play. But after surveying the available theories and evidence, it is difficult to point to anything else so central to so many causes of economic growth as a strong middle class. This paper explains the most current, empirically grounded economic evidence showing how income distribution affects the efficient functioning and growth potential of our economy.

In this paper the concepts of "inequality" and "middle class" are broadly construed. When we say "middle class," we mean more than just families who are, broadly, in the middle of the income distribution. By middle class, we do not mean rich, but we do mean families with enough financial security to make ends meet, provide investments in the next generation's success, and have a little margin of safety to boot. A middle-class family has some economic security, be that a good job with health insurance and a retirement plan, or some savings in the bank to tide them over in an emergency, send a child to college, or even float a loan to a family member who wants to start up a business. This is consistent with individuals' perceptions: Surveys show that most Americans believe they are in the middle class, from those generally in the 20th or 30th percentile of the income distribution to the 80th and even above. Our conception of inequality is tied mostly to income, although there is a high degree of overlap between individuals with very high incomes and individuals with high net worth.

Throughout the paper we examine the ways that either category affects economic growth. There are distinct ways in which each can relate to the growth potential for an economy. The security that a middle-class family provides goes beyond wages to include a sense of a longer time horizon for economic decision making than a family hovering on the edge of poverty, or the way that a middle-class child may be able to pursue a field of study suited to their interests. Nevertheless, given the interrelationship and overlap between the two, it makes sense to include both in our thinking as we discuss causal relationships with macroeconomic performance.

Finally, we wish to make a note on our approach to the subject of the relationship of inequality and the strength of the middle class and U.S. economic growth. There is, of course, a rich literature on the relationship between inequality and growth. (see box on next page) Although there are many conflicting views, there is ample evidence that inequality can, in fact, hurt growth under many circumstances. But this literature focuses mostly on the experience of developing countries, and its applicability to the challenges currently facing the United States is not entirely clear.

The United States is a developed economy at the edge of the techno-logical frontier, with the highest levels of income inequality it has ever seen. Panel data studies analyzing how inequality affects growth across a range of countries are unlikely to tell us much about this unique sit-uation. Thus, we have taken a different approach in this investigation. Instead of looking broadly at analyses of inequality and growth in other countries, we have looked at the evidence regarding the specific ways in which inequality and the strength of the middle class might affect economic growth in the U.S. context. If, in fact, there are specific ways that growth is affected, then it is reasonable to assume that there is a relationship overall.

At the end of the day, the conclusions that economists come to about what makes an economy grow are important for how we understand the complexities of an economic system. Economists are often seen as the arbiters of credibility about what is good for the economy. Thus, sift-ing through how disparate pieces of the economic evidence fit together to tell a cohesive story about how inequality and the middle class affect economic growth is a critical and timely task. We turn now to examining in detail the leading channels through which the middle class impacts economic growth.

Heather Boushey is Senior Economist and Adam Hersh is an Econo-mist at the Center for American Progress.

A strong, vibrant middle class is evidence of a government that pro-tects and serves a majority of its people. A government that protects and serves a majority of its people has the luxury of a satisfied popu-lous supporting it. When the government and the governed are in sync, this is referred to as a Golden Age. When it swerves off the tracks, the governed are unaware until the oppression has begun to squeeze life and livelihood from them. The difficulty is finding your way back without wasting time finding blame, angered backlash, and wishing it never happened.

Once it becomes evident that something is amiss, renewed focus on what happened and the steps back to the Golden Age are in order.

So let's be honest! Something has gone wrong! Time to focus on what happened and how we can return to something resembling a Golden Age.

The following article brings us some uncommon knowledge from a man who started in a lower middle-class situation and now resides in the upper 1% of our society

Source: https://www.theatlantic.com/business/archive/2012/05/the-100-econ-omy-why-the-us-needs-a-strong-middle-class-to-thrive/257385/ (Tankersley, T., 2012, 18 May)

The 100% Economy: Why the U.S. Needs a Strong Middle Class to Thrive

By Jim Tankersley
May 18, 2012

SEATTLE--Nick Hanauer toddled through his early years in a cramped Greenwich Village apartment. His mother waited tables at the Bitter End. His father worked low-level jobs on Wall Street and as an editor at a publishing house. When Nick was 5, his folks left New York to join a family pillow-making business in the Pacific Northwest. They raised their three sons in a three-bedroom house in the suburbs and sent them to public schools. After Nick, the eldest, earned a philosophy degree at the University of Washington, he went to work for his father. In his 30s, he scraped together $45,000 to invest in a small start-up that sought to revolutionize American retail. It was called Amazon.com.

This is how Nick Hanauer has come to be standing in the owner's box at a Seattle Sounders FC professional soccer game, snacking on chicken fingers, and listing the very expensive things he owns.

"I told you about Mexico," he says, meaning the villa in Cabo San Lucas. "Did I tell you about the fly-fishing ranch?" Meaning the 170 acres in Montana.

Yes, he did. He also mentioned the ski chalet in Whistler, British Columbia, the hideaway in the San Juan Islands north of Seattle, and the private jet. "And," he added helpfully at one point, "we have a really big boat." Last year, his wife and some of her friends decided they would like to renew their wedding vows. So Hanauer and a few buddies invited nearly 80 couples to Las Vegas for a vow-renewal ceremony featuring three officiants, followed by a private after-party in the rooftop lounge of the Palms Casino Resort. All captured by a professional filmmaker.

Hanauer is 52 and worth several hundred million dollars. His brown hair is thick and mossy, with just a fleck or two of gray, and he is fond of wearing dark denim pants and shirts with open collars. An ace venture capitalist, he is the founder of several companies, including one called aQuantive that he sold to Microsoft for $6.4 billion. On the day of the sale he personally banked $270 million.

In 2011, Hanauer says he paid an effective federal tax rate of 11 percent. He occupies the upper echelon of an elite group of Americans, the top 1 percent of all earners, who have amassed the lion's share of the nation's wealth gains over the past several decades. Many economists expect he and his class of entrepreneurs to fuel the country's next great engine of growth.

Like a lot of self-made rich guys, Hanauer has developed a theory on how to fix the ailing economy. He preaches it in op-ed columns, television interviews, political gatherings, and casual conversations with Seattle's innovation royalty. He was invited to give a speech this spring by the organizers of TED, the nonprofit that has grown famous for commissioning "TED talks" on such diverse topics as the nature of innovation, the science of global warming, and the need to spread contraceptives throughout the developing world. Hanauer's pitch took five minutes at the TED University conference on March 1. Afterward, organizers seemed keen to post it on their website. Then in May, they abruptly told him his remarks were too controversial, too political for TED, and wouldn't be published online.

The disqualifying notion at the center of Hanauer's talk was that the innovators and businessmen are not, in fact, "job creators"--that the fate of the economy rests instead in the hands of the middle class. So Hanauer wants to tax rich guys like himself more, to pay for investments to nurture middle-class families.

"We've had it backward for the last 30 years," Hanauer said at the TED conference. "Rich businesspeople like me don't create jobs. Rather, they are a consequence of an ecosystemic feedback loop animated by middle-class consumers." When the middle class thrives, he said, "businesses grow and hire, and owners profit."

Emerging research from high-powered experts across the ideological spectrum backs that economic inversion. Their work shows how

America's long-term prosperity is in jeopardy because the middle class is struggling and the super-rich are pulling away.

Widening Income inequality helped drive us into the Great Recession and is holding back our recovery. It is tempting to view the stagnation of the middle class and the disappearance of middle-skill jobs as a problem for only some of us. That's simply untrue. Mounting economic evidence suggests strongly that Hanauer's argument is correct and is, in fact, fundamental to America's future. It's not a do-good argument. It is a selfish one, both for innovators and for every other American counting on the innovator class to power growth for decades to come.

The evidence suggests that the United States needs a vibrant middle class. Not for any of sentimental reasons, but because it's a very dangerous thing not to have.

As Hanauer is discovering, that's not something many American elites want to hear.

DOING LESS WITH MORE

Economists don't even broadly agree on who is in the middle class. Some say it's anyone within a 50-percentile ring around the U.S. median income. As good a general definition as you'll find comes in a new paper summarizing the economic case for how the middle class spurs economic growth from economists Heather Boushey and Adam Hersh of the liberal Center for American Progress. "A middle-class family has some economic security," they write, "be that a good job with health insurance and a retirement plan, or some savings in the bank to tide them over in an emergency or to send a child to college or even float a family member who wants to start up a business."

By any definition, the middle class is eroding. Real median household incomes basically flatlined over the past 30 years. Each of the last three recessions has vaporized huge numbers of the middle-skilled jobs that used to pay a good family wage, on factory assembly lines or in customer-service centers or, most recently, in classrooms and city halls. This has led to what the MIT economist David Autor calls the "hollowing out" of American jobs, with a few middle-skill workers finding training for high-skilled, higher-paying careers, and the rest shoved downward into low-wage, low-skilled jobs or onto the unemployment rolls.

If the decline continues, this is what research suggests the U.S. will look like in the years ahead: Roads and bridges will fall into disrepair. Public schools will struggle to graduate students prepared for the job market.

Consumer spending will tumble. Small businesses will close, and fewer and fewer new ones will spring up to take their place. Corporations like Amazon and Apple will scrounge the country to cope with chronic engineering shortages. Rich guys like Hanauer will find themselves with fewer customers, fewer potential employees, and many more worries about the swelling ranks of the have-nots breaking out their pitchforks.

The timing couldn't be worse. The United States was first a resource economy, then a production economy, then a full-fledged industrial economy. In the past two decades, globalization turned the nation into a consumption economy--we bought things from other countries and from one another, increasingly with borrowed money. That model collapsed in the financial crisis.

What comes next, economists often tell us, is the innovation economy. Our international trading partners will boast cheaper labor, laxer business regulation, lower taxes, more abundant resources, and, in the case of China and India, faster-growing flocks of new consumers.

We'll still have the best ideas. We'll keep coming up with the best new products before anyone else does, and everyone else will be forced to buy them from us. That's our comparative advantage.

Research suggests that this advantage flows directly from the strength of the American middle class, starting with its spending power. The super-rich don't pay enough people to do enough things for them, or at least not enough to drive the economy. Middle-class families do. That's the core of Hanauer's argument, and research from the Census Bureau and the Brookings Institution, among others, support it. Middle-class families have more disposable income than low-income families, who largely buy only necessities, and they're more likely to spend their disposable income than wealthy families are.

As Hanauer puts it, he and his rich friends, for all their lavish parties and jet-away vacations, don't buy enough shirts, cars, and restaurant meals to match the spending that would occur if, say, their wealth was divided up among thousands of poor families. Studies on what economists call "marginal propensity to consume" bear out this idea.

Hence Hanauer's claim that middle-class consumers, not innovators, create jobs. Amazon didn't create a new group of book buyers; it just peddled a more convenient way to buy books. Its success created lots of jobs in Seattle, Amazon's hometown, but it also killed lots of jobs in strip malls across the country. Increasing the number of book buyers would boost sales and jobs in the industry, with no downside.

Middle-class families buy more than books. They invest heavily in two of the most important drivers of economic growth: infrastructure and human capital. The middle class demands the highways and the schools that boost the overall functioning of the economy. Unlike the Hanauers, those families can't afford to bypass the nation's air-transit system with a private jet, or to send their children to elite private schools. (Hanauer raises this point with his 12-year-old son, Cole, after picking him up from just such a school in the family's Audi. Cole objects. "Cindy's kids go to public school," he says. Nick nods. Cindy Crawford, he explains. The model. Their neighbor in Cabo.)

Statistics suggest that Cole Hanauer won't grow up to be an entrepreneur. The risk-takers of tomorrow are growing up in today's middle-class families. Data from the nonprofit Ewing Marion Kauffman Foundation suggest that seven of 10 American entrepreneurs have come from the middle class. Only one in 100 was born very wealthy or very poor.

The middle class incubates entrepreneurs because it offers a good combination of time, resources, and motivation to invest in skills and climb the innovation ladder. Put it this way: The comforts that flowed from the Pacific Coast Feather Co., his then-modest family business, provided Nick Hanauer with a house full of books and days full of time to explore big ideas. Think of those comforts as an investment. The eventual return was Hanauer's venture-capital portfolio. Poor families just scraping by at the margins can't make those investments, so their children struggle to achieve in school and pursue higher education. Children from rich families may, thanks to their extreme childhood comforts, lack the desire to build wealth and climb the economic ladder, which the Kauffman study found to be a key motivation for would-be entrepreneurs.

The economy sags when kids who could have grown up to be physicists end up spending their lives brewing lattes at Starbucks. Or when a young woman born to be a teacher finds herself babysitting, for peanuts, while she waits for a classroom to open up.

LOSING GROUND

Courtney Carbone, wrapped in a scarf and a nervous smile on a cool spring morning, is a transplant to the Northwest. She grew up in northwestern Connecticut, daughter of a carpentry teacher and a waitress who went on to teach preschool. Her parents were not so different from Nick Hanauer's, actually.

From the age of 9, Carbone knew what she wanted to do with her life. She was bright and rebellious. At the prep school she attended on loans that her parents took out, she routinely skipped classes when she didn't respect the teacher's effort. "That just made me want to be a teacher even more," Carbone says. "I wanted to be the one who made students want to show up."

She got her wish after graduate school, landing a job teaching English at a Connecticut prep school. That was 2006. In 2009, the recession brought budget cuts crashing down on her school, and she lost her job. She drifted West in her teal 1997 Nissan Altima to live with a friend and look for a teaching job in Seattle.

She is still looking. Last year, she attended a regional job fair in Northern California, which she compared to speed dating. She got several interviews. No callbacks.

Carbone has nannied and babysat. She has applied for teaching jobs up and down the West Coast. She taught two composition classes at a community college for 11 weeks. She suffered from depression, lost her sense of identity, saw her relationship with her boyfriend dissolve. She moved briefly to Utah last winter to work in a child-care center at a ski resort, earning a season lift pass and less than $10 an hour. Now, back in Seattle, she is caring for a friend's two special-needs children, for $15 an hour, in cash.

Carbone happens to be looking for a teaching job at the worst possible time. Washington state has shed 6,500 local education positions since 2009, due to budget cuts. "I know that every time I apply for a job, I'm one of hundreds of people," she says. "But at the same time, knowing something and feeling something are different things. After a while [not getting a job] starts to eat away at your soul."

Carbone isn't spending money, isn't feeding that great middle-class consumption engine of growth. She's paying a very small amount in sales taxes, which largely fund the state's road-building and school budgets. She's not doing her part to support the institutions that help stabilize growth.

"I keep selling things and getting rid of stuff," Carbone says. "It's freeing, in a way. But I do keep dreaming of the apartment I had when I was a teacher, full of plants and beautiful things that were mine."

Carbone's struggles aren't rare, even in one of America's most innovative cities. Seattle hides its erosion better than a lot of other places, away from the rain-soaked microbrew pubs and the towering new Amazon buildings near downtown. "This feels idyllic," says Jake Rosenfeld, a sociologist at the University of Washington. "Seattle doesn't seem like a place I'd worry about."

Except, he does. State forecasters expect no net middle-class job growth in the next decade, The Seattle Times recently reported. The state Supreme Court has declared that Washington's schools are failing their constitutional mandate to educate all children ad-equately. Tuition at Rosenfeld's university now runs 20 percent of a median family income, up from 6 percent two decades ago. The Seattle-based real-estate data firm Zillow reports that middle- and lower-tier homes in the metro area lost an average of 38 percent of their value in the housing collapse, compared with 29 percent for top-tier homes.

ELEVATOR DOWN

Here, and across the country, the economy is suffering because peo-ple cannot fulfill their potential. Researchers at the University of Chi-cago and Stanford University published a paper this spring arguing that up to one-fifth of America's wage growth over the past 50 years can be attributed to the knocking down of social barriers that pre-vented women and minorities from doing their best--clearing the way for waitresses to become lawyers, or African-American orderlies to become doctors.

Now, the reverse appears to be happening. Workers who once pro-duced $100,000 a year of manufactured goods have been forced downward into jobs flipping $20,000 worth of burgers. Carbone, who once produced $40,000 in education services, now tends tod-dlers for half that value. That's an economy-wide output loss. If the slide continues, "growth would go down, no question," says Chang-Tai Hsieh, an economist at Chicago's Booth School of Business who was the study's lead author. True, a branch of economists and conservative politicians say that rising inequality isn't bad for growth and might even be good. Edward Conard, a former man-aging partner of private-equity firm Bain Capital, argues in a book out this month that the income gulf should be even wider because it's a sign that the economy is rewarding risk-takers. Conard con-tends that too many Americans today avoid risk-taking, settling into comfortable fields such as law. The only way to jar more smart peo-ple into the innovation game, he says, is to increase the rewards of success.

History contradicts that argument. For nearly all of the recorded economic past, rising national wealth went hand in hand with rising equality. A seminal 2000 study by World Bank economist William Easterly, "The Middle Class Consensus and Economic Development," found that countries with larger middle classes enjoy higher levels of growth and income, along with a variety of health benefits such as lower infant mortality rates and greater life expectancy.

In a 2011 paper, economists Andrew Berg and Jonathan Ostry of the International Monetary Fund studied nations' economic growth through history and concluded that "longer growth spells are robustly associated with more equality in the income distribution." The correlation was greater than for any other factor, including liberalizing trade and cracking down on corruption.

Widening inequality can throw the economy into crisis. Chicago Booth economists Marianne Bertrand and Adair Morse argue in a draft paper this spring that the rising income gap in the United States fueled a surge in recent years of what they dubbed "trickle-down consumption"--middle-class families drained their savings and maxed out their credit cards to keep up with the jet-set lifestyles of the Hanauers of the world.

Hanauer worries about the prospect of inequality expanding not contracting, in the years to come. If you extrapolate the trends over the past 30 years, he warns, in another 30 years, the richest 1 percent will take home 37 percent of U.S. income. The bottom 50 percent will earn a paltry 6 percent. "If you let that happen," he says, "very bad things happen."

Wide income inequality correlates to political unrest--the Arab Spring is a classic example--and just the threat of turmoil distorts the economy. Wealthy people who fear massive attempts to redistribute their wealth--we're talking huge tax increases here, not a few extra points tacked on the top marginal rate--do inefficient things with their money. They wall off their houses and install high-tech security systems. They park money in offshore bank accounts. They don't buy new equipment, or hire more workers, even if they see a chance to profit from those investments, because they worry that someone could come along at any moment, a mob or a cash-strapped government, or both, to take it all away.

We aren't there yet. Seattle was jostled by protests on May Day, when anarchists broke off from an Occupy march downtown and smashed store windows; by the next day, most people in town had shrugged off the damage as a small-group aberration. But Hanauer worries that the climate could change. Soon.

"Ultimately, taxes are a bribe rich people pay to poor people so they won't kill them," he says. "People understand that. We're an armed nation, you know. Things could get very fucking ugly."

BEHIND THESE WALLS

The Hanauers live 50 blocks north of Courtney Carbone, behind a guardhouse and down a narrow road that hugs the emerald fairways of the Seattle Golf Club and winds through ferns, cedars, and tall Douglas firs.

Hanauer is a mammoth political donor who has given hundreds of thousands of dollars to Democratic candidates and just as much to push state ballot measures that would have raised taxes to support schools, fund teaching jobs to build the state's human capital stock, and employ eager young educators like Carbone. (Lately, he has also picked a huge fight with the state teachers union over accountability, charter schools, and other components of education reform.)

On days when Hanauer and his wife host political events, a squad of valet parkers wait in their gravel courtyard driveway. Guests enter through a foyer into a library stocked with old books shedding their spines and tapestries on the walls. The back window opens onto a patio, a swimming pool, and, beyond a hedgerow, a sprawling garden.

The garden is one of Hanauer's favorite metaphors to describe a well-functioning economy. He developed it over 20 years of reading on complex systems, chaos theory, and evolutionary biology. Eventually, he says, he arrived at a place where "you realize that the economy is characterized by the same kind of circle-of-life, natural feedback loops that characterize natural ecosystems." The plants need the bugs need the birds need the predators. Throw off the balance, and everything wilts.

This is the argument that Hanauer and coauthor Eric Liu made in their recent book The Gardens of Democracy, and the one Hanauer made in his TED talk. It is an abandonment of a moral argument--the rich really should care about the middle class because it's the right thing to do--in favor of a self-centered one: Caring about the middle class is very good for business. The solution that Hanauer advocates, which jarred TED organizers, is to tax rich guys like him more and spend the money building up schools and other middle-class institutions.

190

That's an incomplete prescription, at best. Just as the middle-class is essential for more reasons than the ones Hanauer talks about, so is the fix for the declining middle class more complicated than taxing the top earners. After all, Europe has higher tax rates but has also experienced widening income inequality in recent years.

But Hanauer has his argument, which he loves--loves--to make, on any platform he's given. He penned a Bloomberg View op-ed in December in which he declared, "I've never been a 'job creator' " He celebrates that Bloomberg editors tell him the piece remains one of their most-viewed op-eds of all time. He has debated the theory on cable news with conservatives, and he and Liu defended it in an interview with Charlie Rose on PBS. He raises it with the members of Congress who call him to ask for money.

The day after May Day, Hanauer began extolling the middle class in his office at 3 p.m., starting with a profane tirade against Conard, the former Bain executive who argues that income inequality should widen even more to promote risk-taking. "What risk did Sergey Brin and Larry Page take?" Hanauer demands, invoking Google's founders. "They got fucking Ph.D.s in computer science at Stanford. They got a bunch of venture capitalists to back them."

He springs from a couch that backs up to a stunning view of Puget Sound and the Olympic Peninsula, with ferries chugging in between, and waves his arms.

"What's the worst thing that can happen to those guys?" Hanauer shouts. "Will they starve? Will they be executed? No!" He wheels around. "We have to find ways to get people to innovate. But the idea that lower taxes lead to more innovation--wrong."

And so it goes for two more hours in the office, and on the Audi ride to pick up Cole, and later in the owner's box at the soccer match. No one can duck hearing about inequality and its evils, not Cole and a school friend; not Nick's brother Adrian, who co-owns the Sounders FC; and not a handful of random visitors in the box, including a real-estate scion who may be in the market for a pro soccer team of his own. By the game's end, Hanauer has been making his case for six hours, nearly half of them in a stadium where 40,000 fans screamed lustily for their team to score a third goal, because it would have meant a free haircut for everyone in the crowd.

Hanauer has a lot more hectoring left, for politicians and peers alike. Friends say that his evangelism has stoked anger in his social circles and pushed some acquaintances to avoid him. Hanauer was so stung by the backlash from other innovator types to his Bloomberg piece that he wrote a follow-up op-ed, as yet unpublished, titled "If Not Job Creators, Then What Are We?" He is dismayed that President Obama talks about equality largely in terms of fairness (there's that moral imperative again), and not in terms of good business.

Flaunting his wealth is Hanauer's way of disarming critics of the guy who wants to raise taxes on the rich, but it also turns a lot of people off. "When Nick alienates people, it's generally because one of those lines about how much money he makes comes flying out of Nick's mouth," says J.D. Delafield, an investment banker who lives next door and vacations with him. "He uses that as a provocative contrast," adds Rich Barton, the executive chairman of Zillow and a cofounder of the travel site Expedia.com, who is another vacation companion. "Sometimes it makes me squirm. Like, geez, Nick, don't talk about your plane all the time." But on the question of who creates jobs, Delafield and Barton both say Hanauer has swayed them.

But within Hanauer's own investment portfolio, his record is spotty. Some companies he's backed, such as Amazon, have driven middle-class workers to unemployment. Pacific Feather Pillow, where Hanauer remains chairman of the board, recently closed plants in Illinois and Pennsylvania to cut costs. For all his money, Hanauer isn't going out of his way to overpay workers or to create a bunch of extraneous jobs just to prop up the middle class that holds his future earnings in its hands.

After all, he's not in it to lose. His fellow entrepreneurs and CEOs share this conflict, the tension between competitiveness today and sustainability long term.

Henry Ford famously paid his workers enough to be able to afford a Model T. But he wasn't competing against imports from Japan and South Korea and the onset of cheap labor from China. Today, Ford Motor pays new workers about half of what longer-tenured employees make, as part of a new union contract designed to boost competitiveness. No single business leader has the power to alter the trajectory of the middle class simply by sacrificing profits, Hanauer says. Which is why society needs to decide to do it, all at once, at the highest levels.

He pauses to reference a Business Insider column he read earlier this year that urged the heads of Wal-Mart Stores, McDonald's, and Starbucks to boost the middle class by paying their service employees more. "Here's the thing: I know Howard Schultz," the Starbucks CEO, Hanauer says. "He's a nice man. He's never going to do this on his own."

Nor, by extension, will Nick Hanauer. He's simply the alarm, the Lorax warning of the dangers that lie ahead.

Courtney Carbone, she's already navigating them. She sees the years without a teaching position piling up on her résumé. She knows the longer she looks for a job, the harder it will be to find one.

If she landed a teaching gig tomorrow, she'd return to boosting the economy in all the ways the middle class does. Carbone would maximize her talent and production, help cultivate the entrepreneurs of tomorrow, and pay more taxes for roads and schools. She'd buy more stuff, possibly from one of Hanauer's companies. Maybe even a new pillow.

Carbone knows that to beat the odds and find a position, she needs any extra advantage she can find. So, this summer, when her nannying stint ends, she will return to Connecticut to attend a nine-week certificate course that will help her teach in 42 states. She will also be $4,000 in debt. After three years of job-seeking, the only way she can come up with the $4,000 is to borrow it.

This, Carbone says, is probably her last shot before she's forced to give up her dream.

"I do see myself as a teacher still," she says. "There's nothing else I'd rather do."

She is 31 years old. Her whole future could depend on whether this works out.

In a way, all of ours could, too.

Jim Tankersley is an economics reporter for The New York Times in Washington and the author of The Riches of This Land: The Untold, True Story of America's Middle Class.

Peeling away at the layers of lies is the false notion that income inequality is a natural, sustainable feature of capitalism, and that is just not true. Some will indeed become insanely wealthy, but arguing that it is natural and suitable for everyone is not sustainable and completely untrue!

A strong, vibrant middle class is good for everyone, rich and poor alike. To keep our economic engine running on all eight cylinders, we need a high-octane middle class. Michael Ettinger discusses this point very eloquently in the article below:

Source: https://www.americanprogress.org/article/the-middle-class-and-economic-growth/ (Ettlinger, M., 2012, 1 August)

Article Aug 1, 2012

The Middle Class and Economic Growth

A Project of the Center for American Progress

CAP's Middle Class and Economic Growth project looks to provide a better understanding of the relationship between middle-class strength and the nation's economic health.

- Author, Michael Ettlinger

For our country to succeed going forward, we need to get back to the fundamental truth that our success hinges on the strength of the middle class.

Over the past 236 years, the United States has risen from a backward band of peripheral colonies to the greatest economic force in the history of the world. Why? Has it been because an elite handful of wealthy Americans made brilliant investments? Or has it been because hundreds of millions of Americans have worked hard, improved themselves, started businesses, invented new things, built communities, and constructed an economy that provides for the many and not just the few?

The Center for American Progress's Middle Class and Economic Growth project examines these two divergent views of how the economy works: one that embraces the supply-side, trickle-down dogma that has dominated policymaking for the past 35 years, and the other, which instead of attributing the success of our country to a scant few at the top, ascribes the nation's economic success to the role of the tens of millions of engines of growth who are the American middle class. The project does this through:

- Economic analysis from CAP and outside economists
- An event series featuring prominent economists, business leaders, journalists, and policymakers
- Multimedia presentations of the issues and the evidence
- Policy proposals to address the challenges faced by middle-class Americans

Our philosophy

The fundamental thesis of this project is that the middle class is the heartbeat of the American economy. The middle class is the indispensable workforce and the all-important consumer. The great American entrepreneurs and inventors who have been vital to our national success have come from the middle class. It is the education and skills of the middle class that have driven the rise in productivity that has underpinned our prosperity. And it is a stable middle class that has kept America free of the turmoil of much of the rest of the world and has made vital investments in education, roads, and other economically important infrastructure. The ascendency of America to being the richest nation in the history of the planet is fundamentally a middle-class achievement. For our country to succeed going forward, we need to get back to the fundamental truth that our success hinges on the strength of the middle class.

The proof of this can be found in:

- The clear failure of supply-side economics as an economic strategy[1]
- A growing economic literature as documented in our paper, "The American Middle Class, Income Inequality, and the Strength of Our Economy," [2] that shows how a strong middle class is vital, and how excessive income inequality is harmful to our national economic success
- A look back at our nation's economic history

The reason the middle class is so important isn't complicated:

- Businesses need middle-class customers. If you ask business owners what motivates them to make investments and create jobs, they'll tell you its customers. From where do the majority of customers come? The middle class.

- The economy depends on the skills of the middle class. If you look to what has been at the root of economic growth over time, it has been growth in worker productivity and the inventiveness of our people. Who among us has had the flexibility to postpone jumping directly into the workforce after a minimum level of education and instead avail themselves of the opportunity to enhance skills by pursing higher education? The children of those securely in the middle class.
- Innovators, inventors, and entrepreneurs come from the middle class. Why is this so? Unlike those with lower incomes— who, by necessity, are consumed with issues of day-to-day survival—middle-class individuals have the time and capacity to come up with innovative new business ideas, to invest in them, and to develop and foster them. Moreover, scary though it may be, middle-class Americans can afford to take the risk of leaving a job to start a business. If you look at the fortunes of the Forbes 400, they were mostly started with a risk, an invention, or an investment by someone from the middle class.
- The middle class creates stability and investment in the economy. It's also the middle class that has the biggest stake in seeing the U.S. economy succeed. The rich are largely immune from the success or failure of any particular country's economy—the question for them is the extent of their wealth, not whether they are going to be able to live lives of comfort or whether they can afford to send their children to college. The rest of us, however, are very dependent on the success of our country's economy. This doesn't mean that there aren't wealthy individuals who care deeply about the nation's economic well-being, but middle-class voters are those who form the backbone of support for public investments in education, infrastructure, and the other building blocks of a strong economy.

Our goal

The purpose of the CAP Middle Class and Economic Growth project is to provide a better understanding of the crucial relationship between a strong middle class and the nation's economic health. A strong and vibrant middle class isn't just good for the middle class. It's good for the poor, for whom joining the middle class is an aspiration. Just as important, a strong middle class is good for the wealthy, who reap the greatest benefits when the overall economy is healthy.

We hope that this project will establish a far better economic policy paradigm than the failed one that has dominated for too long—an approach that believes showering the rich with largess is what's best for the economic well-being of America. Instead, we seek to develop a more real, more believable, and more persuasive narrative of how 300 million Americans are far more important to the American economy than a few very wealthy individuals at the top, and that it is the large and dynamic middle class that should be the focus of our economic policymaking.

Michael Ettlinger is the Vice President for Economic Policy at the Center for American Progress.

The short-sightedness of squeezing the life out of the middle-class no longer makes any sense! A solid and robust middle-class is good for the economy, the rich and the poor, and our self-esteem as a country. It is time to grasp this truth's reality and make the necessary changes to bring about this advent, for an abundant life, in our country, for All.

Below is an example, of some middle-class relief, from Franklin Delano Roosevelt, the 32nd President of the United States. He delivered this message in his state of the Union address on January 11, 1944; from the website:

Source: https://www.ushistory.org/documents/economic_bill_of_rights.htm (USHistory.org, n.d.)

The Economic Bill of Rights

Excerpted from Franklin Delano Roosevelt's message to Congress on the State of the Union. This was proposed not to amend the Constitution, but rather as a political challenge, encouraging Congress to draft legislation to achieve these aspirations. It is sometimes referred to as the "Second Bill of Rights."

It is our duty now to begin to lay the plans and determine the strategy for the winning of a lasting peace and the establishment of an American standard of living higher than ever before known. We cannot be content, no matter how high that general standard of living may be, if some fraction of our people—whether it be one-third or one-fifth or one-tenth—is ill-fed, ill-clothed, ill-housed, and insecure.

This Republic had its beginning, and grew to its present strength, under the protection of certain inalienable political rights—among them the right of free speech, free press, free worship, trial by jury, freedom from unreasonable searches and seizures. They were our rights to life and liberty.

As our nation has grown in size and stature, however—as our industrial economy expanded—these political rights proved inadequate to assure us equality in the pursuit of happiness.

We have come to a clear realization of the fact that true individual freedom cannot exist without economic security and independence. "Necessitous men are not free men." People who are hungry and out of a job are the stuff of which dictatorships are made.

In our day these economic truths have become accepted as self-evident. We have accepted, so to speak, a second Bill of Rights under which a new basis of security and prosperity can be established for all—regardless of station, race, or creed.

Among these are:

- The right to a useful and remunerative job in the industries or shops or farms or mines of the nation;
- The right to earn enough to provide adequate food and clothing and recreation;
- The right of every farmer to raise and sell his products at a return which will give him and his family a decent living;
- The right of every businessman, large and small, to trade in an atmosphere of freedom from unfair competition and domination by monopolies at home or abroad;
- The right of every family to a decent home;
- The right to adequate medical care and the opportunity to achieve and enjoy good health;
- The right to adequate protection from the economic fears of old age, sickness, accident, and unemployment;
- The right to a good education.

All of these rights spell security. And after this war is won we must be prepared to move forward, in the implementation of these rights, to new goals of human happiness and well-being.

America's own rightful place in the world depends in large part upon how fully these and similar rights have been carried into practice for our citizens.

History is replete with examples of societies with only an upper and lower class. The upper class dictates the governing of the lower class, and opulence and oppression ensue. What drives men to pursue opulence? Nothing wrong with enjoying nice things! To do so at the expense of others, however, no longer makes any sense. How can anyone be so willing to oppress others to achieve their wanton opulent objectives? It is like a social disease, the willingness to oppress others to accumulate personal financial gain.

When a parasite kills its host, it has to find a new host. Kill the middle class, and what do you have left? A parasite left struggling to stay alive.

WTP are no longer respected or treated fairly, and the time for a reckoning is upon us.

After experiencing prosperity and overall satisfaction with life in a society with an expanding middle class, I believe WTP would be willing to fight for the opportunity to experience this phenomenon again.

There is a plan to reignite an expanding middle class, but first, we need to understand what happened to effectively make repairs and employ constructive steps back to a Golden Era of peace, tranquility, and the ability and freedom to enjoy life, liberty, and the pursuit of happiness.

Sometimes there is a tendency to ask why something happened, and while that may be an interesting question, it doesn't change the situation. It just slows down the way forward. Asking how we fix this situation is more functional and gets the job done.

So ask why if you must, but realize there is more to life than why. Now, I would love to share a poem of mine titled "Why."

Why

Why must I ask why

For that singular word is like a rejection of the gift, I am being offered

Everything in this life is either a gift or a curse

My freewill gives me the option to view my life anyway I deem proper
Continually asking why, condemns me to the view that life is a curse

Gratitude indicates the acknowledgement of the gift that life continually proffers

Pushing away the gift, nullifies the opportunity to prosper from the gift

I am here to expand, evolve, and grow exponentially

Gifts are like rungs on a ladder

At each rung, I intuit my situation, waiting for the gift that life is here to offer

Gifts are not always pots of gold

More often, I am challenged to see a new way to get to the next rung on the ladder

Usually by leaving behind, what no longer serves me,

Beliefs that bind and constrain

At each rung, I am born anew

Fresh and ready to see the Light and Love streaming down upon me

During quiet moments, like those just before sleep, I try to actually feel the Light and Love streaming through me

My desire now is to, feel fully, the experience of each rung

The question of why, now seems like a long time ago, back in the days, of my petulant aggression

The only why question I have now is; why did I wait so long

But this why question only tickles my insides as I reach for the next rung on the ladder

Smiling upon God as she smiles upon me

Chapter Five:
What Went Wrong

So what happened? How did our middle class shrink?

Below is an article from Robert Reich detailing how the shrinking of the middle class began with a memo encouraging the corporate takeover of American politics.

Robert Reich is an American professor, author, lawyer, and political commentator. He worked in the administrations of Presidents Gerald Ford and Jimmy Carter and served as Secretary of Labor from 1993 to 1997 in the cabinet of President Bill Clinton.

Source: https://www.youtube.com/watch?v=bbbgfnpJN9w (Reich, R. 2022, 13 December)

How the Corporate Takeover of American Politics Began?

The corporate takeover of American politics started with a man and a memo you've probably never heard of.

In 1971, the U.S. Chamber of Commerce asked Lewis Powell, a corporate attorney who would go on to become a Supreme Court justice, to draft a memo on the state of the country.

Powell's memo argued that the American economic system was "under broad attack" from consumer, labor, and environmental groups.

In reality, these groups were doing nothing more than enforcing the implicit social contract that had emerged at the end of the Second World War. They wanted to ensure corporations were responsive to all their stakeholders—workers, consumers, and the environment—not just their shareholders.

But Powell and the Chamber saw it differently. In his memo, Powell urged businesses to mobilize for political combat, and stressed that the critical ingredients for success were joint organizing and funding.

The Chamber distributed the memo to leading CEOs, large businesses, and trade associations—hoping to persuade them that Big Business could dominate American politics in ways not seen since the Gilded Age.

It worked.

The Chamber's call for a business crusade birthed a new corporate-political industry practically overnight. Tens of thousands of corporate lobbyists and political operatives descended on Washington and state capitals across the country.

I should know—I saw it happen with my own eyes.

In 1976, I worked at the Federal Trade Commission. Jimmy Carter had appointed consumer advocates to battle big corporations that for years had been deluding or injuring consumers.

Yet almost everything we initiated at the FTC was met by unexpectedly fierce political resistance from Congress. At one point, when we began examining advertising directed at children, Congress stopped funding the agency altogether, shutting it down for weeks.

I was dumbfounded. What had happened?

In three words, The Powell Memo.

Lobbyists and their allies in Congress, and eventually the Reagan administration, worked to defang agencies like the FTC—and to staff them with officials who would overlook corporate misbehavior.

Their influence led the FTC to stop seriously enforcing antitrust laws—among other things—allowing massive corporations to merge and concentrate their power even further.

Washington was transformed from a sleepy government town into a glittering center of corporate America—replete with elegant office buildings, fancy restaurants, and five-star hotels.

Meanwhile, Justice Lewis Powell used the Court to chip away at restrictions on corporate power in politics. His opinions in the 1970s and 80s laid the foundation for corporations to claim free speech rights in the form of financial contributions to political campaigns.

Put another way—without Lewis Powell, there would probably be no Citizens United—the case that threw out limits on corporate campaign spending as a violation of the "free speech" of corporations.

These actions have transformed our political system. Corporate money supports platoons of lawyers, often outgunning any state or federal attorneys who dare to stand in their way. Lobbying has become a $3.7 billion dollar industry.

Corporations regularly outspend labor unions and public interest groups during election years. And too many politicians in Washington represent the interests of corporations—not their constituents. As a result, corporate taxes have been cut, loopholes widened, and regulations gutted.

Corporate consolidation has also given companies unprecedented market power, allowing them to raise prices on everything from baby formula to gasoline. Their profits have jumped into the stratosphere— the highest in 70 years.

But despite the success of the Powell Memo, Big Business has not yet won. The people are beginning to fight back.

First, antitrust is making a comeback. Both at the Federal Trade Commission and the Justice Department we're seeing a new willingness to take on corporate power.

Second, working people are standing up. Across the country workers are unionizing at a faster rate than we've seen in decades—including at some of the biggest corporations in the world—and they're winning.

Third, campaign finance reform is within reach. Millions of Americans are intent on limiting corporate money in politics – and politicians are starting to listen.

All of these tell me that now is our best opportunity in decades to take on corporate power—at the ballot box, in the workplace, and in Washington.

Let's get it done.

Could this be true? What is lobbying? Has lobbying become a 3.7-billion-dollar industry?

Here is a definition from https://www.ncsl.org/ethics/how-states-define-lobbying-and-lobbyist (National Conference of State Legislatures, 2021, 3 September)

"Lobbying" means influencing or attempting to influence legislative action or non-action through oral or written communication or an attempt to obtain the goodwill of a member or employee of the Legislature.

Nothing inherently wrong with lobbying. It is how WTP communicates with the government. The problem arises when money is used to lobby, and government representatives accept that money.

So, 3.7 million dollars are being utilized to influence our government. From where does all of that lobby money originate?

Here is a report of Top lobby spenders from the website:

Source: https://www.opensecrets.org/federal-lobbying/top-spenders (Open Secrets, 2023, 16 February)

Top Spenders

Whether they do their own lobbying or hire it out to DC's infamous K Street firms (and often they do both), these organizations spend the most trying to influence government policy.

Select year:

2021

Top Spenders

	Total Spent
US Chamber of Commerce	$66,410,000
National Assn of Realtors	$44,004,025
Pharmaceutical Research & Manufacturers of America	$30,406,000
Business Roundtable	$29,120,000
American Hospital Assn	$25,255,934
Blue Cross/Blue Shield	$25,176,385
Meta	$20,070,000
American Medical Assn	$19,490,000
Amazon.com	$19,320,000
American Chemistry Council	$16,640,000
Raytheon Technologies	$15,390,000
National Assn of Manufacturers	$15,300,000
Lockheed Martin	$14,401,911
NCTA The Internet & Television Assn	$14,010,000
AARP	$13,680,000
Boeing Co	$13,450,000
Comcast Corp	$13,380,000
Biotechnology Innovation Organization	$13,290,000
Verizon Communications	$12,970,000
CTIA	$12,430,000

I know some of these entities, and now I understand why they charge me so much for their products. Just look at how much they spend on their lobby efforts. All this money is added to the sticker price of their products that you and I must pay. The other entities I do not recognize make me wonder who they are and what they want so badly that they are willing to pay that much. And would the rest of WTP want what they want?

Interesting that the US Chamber of Commerce is at the top of the list. The same entity that, in 1971, asked Lewis Powell, a corporate attorney who would go on to become a Supreme Court justice, to draft a memo on the state of the country.

Source: https://www.opensecrets.org/federal-lobbying/top-spenders (Open Secrets, 2023, 16 February)

Here is a list of The US Chamber of Commerce total money spent on Lobbying per year and their ranking for that year.

Year	Total Money spent	Ranking
2021	$66,410,000	1st
2020	$81,940,000	2nd
2019	$77,245,000	1st
2018	$94,800,000	1st
2017	$82,260,000	1st
2016	$103,950,000	1st
2015	$84,730,000	1st
2014	$124,080,000	1st
2013	$74,470,000	1st
2012	$136,300,000	1st
2011	$66,370,000	1st
2010	$132,067,500	1st
2009	$144,606,000	1st
2008	$91,955,000	1st
2007	$53,082,500	1st
2006	$72,995,000	1st
2005	$39,805,000	1st
2004	$53,380,000	1st
2003	$34,602,640	1st
2002	$41,560,000	1st
2001	$20,662,880	1st
2000	$18,689,160	2nd
1999	$18,760,000	1st
1998	$17,000,000	4th

As you can see, the US Chamber of Commerce ranked number one in all but three years of available data.

Money equals power and influence, and the US Chamber of Commerce is spending the most money and influencing the government the most; that is why the middle class has shrunk!

All of the reforms and actions spurred by the Powell memo have effectively taken control of the government, putting corporations and their goals at the forefront of our society. This tyranny from a minority has corrupted the government, and the government no longer serves WTP.

Now, we know that our government was created at the consent of the governed (We The People!), and its sole purpose is to serve those who they govern (We The People!), so it must follow that corporations, being government authorized entities, must also serve, We The People!

This fight for power between the government and corporations is not new. Below is an example of this balancing act.

Source: https://www.sparknotes.com/biography/troosevelt/section10/ (Spark-Notes, n.d.)

Theodore Roosevelt 26ᵗʰ President – 1901-1909: Domestic Policies

On the domestic front, President Roosevelt was one of the most visible Progressives of his time. Many of his domestic policies involved fighting big industry and corruption in an attempt to help the common man. He offered the American people a Square Deal to improve their standard of living and exert more control over large domineering corporations or trusts. Trusts, which were technically illegal under the 1890 Sherman Act, attempted to consolidate business interests to create a monopoly on specific products and eliminate competition. Many businesses attacked Roosevelt as a socialist, but he ardently refuted these accusations and refuted the principles of Marxism. In truth, Roosevelt did not despise big business, and in fact realized that the trusts had indirectly increased the standard of living for nearly every American in the latter half of the nineteenth century. Roosevelt did, however, dislike the power of the trusts and the fact that the American public had little control of them. On the other hand, however, he also feared giving too much power to labor. His Square Deal policies attempted to strike a balance between the two.

Roosevelt's first major domestic test as President came when 140,000 miners in eastern Pennsylvania went on strike in the 1902 Coal Strike. Coal was a vital energy source for almost all Americans during this era, and the nation panicked during the strike. Represented by John Mitchell, the miners formed the United Mine Workers Union to demand higher wages and better working conditions. The president of the Philadelphia and Reading Railroad Company and owner of the mine, George Baer, would not concede to the strikers' demands. Mitchell approached Roosevelt and asked him to establish an independent arbitration council. Baer—and, ironically, even the miners themselves—refused arbitration. Roosevelt, under pressure from Republicans and the American citizenry and not even considering the legality of his actions, planned to replace the strikers by force with ten thousand Army troops and begin mining coal again if a settlement could not be reached. Fortunately, Secretary of War Elihu Root was able to avert a disaster. Working with banker J.P. Morgan, Root was able to convince the miners to accept independent arbitration. Roosevelt won the American people's approval of the way he handled the situation.

Also in 1902, President Roosevelt shocked financiers on Wall Street with his decision to approve the government's lawsuit against Northern Securities, a large and recently merged western railroad company, for violating the Sherman Anti-Trust Act. J.P. Morgan, the financier who had arranged the merger and who had significant amounts of money invested in Northern Securities, took Roosevelt's decision as a personal insult. Many conservative Republicans in Congress and bankers on Wall Street attacked the President and Attorney General Philander Knox for the decision. The American people, one the other hand, loved Roosevelt for his boldness in the face of the trusts. To ensure the government's victory, Roosevelt also nominated Oliver Wendell Holmes, Jr., to replace Justice Horace Gray on the Supreme Court. As Chief Justice of the Massachusetts Supreme Court, Holmes had voted against industry and railroads in similar suits, making him the perfect choice from Roosevelt's perspective. In the end, the U.S. government won the suit, Northern Securities was dismantled into smaller companies, and President Roosevelt came to be known as the "Trustbuster."

As the Sherman Act had never been truly enforced until this time, the breakup of Northern Securities opened the floodgate for suits against other major trusts. Famous among these was Roosevelt's "busting" of the Standard Oil trust. Muckraker Ida Tarbell's *History of Standard Oil,* which was published in *McClure* magazine, detailed the business practices of Rockefeller's oil machine. Tarbell accused Standard Oil of issuing rebates in total of one million dollars to its customers to effectively eliminate competition. In 1906, Roosevelt had the Hepburn Bill drafted and passed through Congress to reform rate evaluations and outlaw excessive rebates designed to thwart competitors. The bill also stipulated that all companies engaged in interstate commerce were under the supervision of the federal government. The bill hurt not only Standard Oil but the powerful rebate-issuing railroads as well. In all, Roosevelt brought lawsuits against forty-three other trusts during his Presidency.

In 1907, financial troubles hit the United States when the Knickerbocker Trust Company in New York failed, leading to a cascade effect that caused many other banks to totter as well. Conservative Republicans blamed Roosevelt for the economic distress, claiming that his actions had undermined stability and shattered consumer confidence. Roosevelt shot back that it was the plutocracy that caused the troubles. Although it was impossible to discern at the time, the rest of the world was suffering as well, and the Panic of 1907 was neither the result of Roosevelt's policies or the plutocrats' business practices. When the large brokerage of Moore and Schley nearly collapsed, J.P. Morgan once again met with the President. Moore and Schley held five million dollars of stock in the Tennessee Coal and Iron Company that it could not convert to cash to pay its investors. Morgan suggested that financially sound U.S. Steel Company purchase the Tennessee Coal and Iron Company, validating its stock, and thus stabilize Moore and Schley. This plan would work so long as Roosevelt approved the merger and promised not to declare it a violation of the Sherman Act. Roosevelt consented, U.S. Steel purchased Tennessee Coal and Iron, and as a result the stock market did not collapse. Together, Roosevelt and Morgan successfully avoided a widespread economic depression.

Upton Sinclair's 1906 novel *The Jungle,* which graphically depicted the horrible working conditions of the Chicago stockyards and meatpacking industry, spurred Roosevelt to make other reforms. The President was especially disgusted by Sinclair's apparently fact-based account of a machinist who fell into a meat grinder and emerged as canned meat to be sold and eaten. Roosevelt called for immediate action and organized an investigation into the packinghouses in Chicago and other cities. The details of the report turned out to be not far from Sinclair's fictional account. An outraged public cry for action quickly produced the Meat Inspection Bill and later the creation of the Food and Drug Administration.

Another major component of Roosevelt's domestic policy was conservation, stemming from his great love of the outdoors. After having toured the nation on several campaign trips, including stints in California, the Pacific Northwest, and the Southwest, the president determined to conserve as much land as possible. Roosevelt's idea of conservation was groundbreaking—at the time, the idea of conserving the land primarily meant not preservation, but merely saving the land for future generations to use later. For this reason, most of the conserved land at that point was forest that provided valuable timber. During his administrations, Roosevelt purchased 150 acres of land to conserve. Roosevelt also consorted with many prominent conservationists of the time, such as Gifford Pinchot and John Muir, and established many wildlife preservations along with them. The National Forest Service was organized and additional National Parks were set aside throughout the U.S. for recreation and conservation purposes. Such acts faced opposition from many members of Congress and Western settlers who had plans to use the land that was being set aside. Settlers were, however, pleased with the 1902 Reclamation Act that set aside money to irrigate previously dry and unlivable tracts of land.

And the fight goes on! Here is another example of corporate power threatening to overtake Democracy.

Source: https://www.americanprogress.org/article/corporate-capture-threatens-democratic-government/ (Kennedy, L., 2017, 29 March)

Liz Kennedy is Director of Democracy and Government Reform at the Center for American Progress

Article Mar 29, 2017

Corporate Capture Threatens Democratic Government

Americans have always fought to expand democratic freedoms and protect democratic society from being corrupted through unchecked private greed and undermined through grotesque inequality.

America faces a crisis of corporate capture of democratic government, where the economic power of corporations has been translated into political power with disastrous effects for people's lives. In his new book, Captured: *The Corporate Infiltration of American Democracy*, Sen. Sheldon Whitehouse (D-RI) warns that "corporations of vast wealth and remorseless staying power have moved into our politics to seize for themselves advantages that can be seized only by control over government." The book illustrates what he calls, the "immense pressure deployed by the corporate sector in our government." We must rebalance our democracy by changing the rules to limit the power of money over government and empower people to engage politically as a countervailing force.

Currently, the domination of big money over our public institutions prevents government from being responsive to Americans. This certainly is not a new phenomenon—but it is growing. Even in 2009, before the *Citizens United v. FEC* ruling removed constraints on corporate political spending, 80 percent of Americans agreed with the following statement:

I am worried that large political contributions will prevent Congress from tackling the important issues facing American today, like the economic crisis, rising energy costs, reforming health care, and global warming.

In the first presidential contest after the *Citizens United* decision, 84 percent of Americans agreed that corporate political spending drowns out the voices of average Americans, and 83 percent believed that corporations and corporate CEOs have too much political power and influence. This aligns with more recent research showing that 84 percent of people think government is benefitting special interests, and 83 percent think government is benefitting big corporations and the wealthy.

As already noted, the undue influence of corporate interests on the functions of government is not new, and Sen. Whitehouse's book explains how Americans have faced and overcome this threat before. America's founders recognized the danger of corporate capture: In 1816, Thomas Jefferson warned the new republic to "crush in its birth the aristocracy of our monied corporations which dare already to challenge our government to a trial of strength, and bid defiance to the laws of their country." Almost a century later, President Theodore Roosevelt, in his annual address to Congress in 1907, said:

The fortunes amassed through corporate organization are now so large, and vest such power in those that wield them, as to make it a matter of necessity to give to the sovereign—that is, to the Government, which represents the people as a whole—some effective power of supervision over their corporate use.

President Roosevelt was responsible for the first federal ban on corporate political contributions. But now America's rules for using money in politics are out of date, and our system of government is out of balance. The Supreme Court's conservative majority has turned its back on reasonable limits for how concentrated wealth can be used to shape government and public choices. In 2010, *Citizens United* allowed corporate money to be used to support or attack candidates and influence American elections. Previously, in a case overruled by *Citizens United*, the Court upheld corporate political spending rules, decrying "the corrosive and distorting effects of immense aggregations of wealth that are accumulated with the help of the corporate form and that have little or no correlation to the public's support for the corporation's political ideas." In his book, Sen. Whitehouse calls out the Supreme Court's conservative majority, which has "obediently repaid the corporate powers by changing the basic operating systems of our democracy in ways that consistently give big corporate powers even more power in our process of government, rewiring our democracy to corporate advantage."

Corporate interests can vastly outspend labor or public interest groups on elections. For example, in 2014, business interests spent $1.1 billion on state candidates and committees compared to the $215 million that labor groups spent. That same year, business political action committees, or PACs, spent nearly $380 million in federal elections, while labor union PACs gave close to $60 million. In 2016, it is estimated that $1 out of every $8 that went to super PACs came from corporate sources. Super PACs—which didn't exist before 2010—raised almost $1.8 billion for the 2016 elections. Recently developed dark money channels have exploded, and more than $800 million dollars of political spending with no disclosure of donors has occurred since 2010. This denies voters information and blocks accountability by hiding the identity of political spenders who want to push their agendas and points of view without leaving fingerprints. Dark money has led to an increase in negative campaigning and deceptive statements in political advertisements, feeding the politics of destruction.

Moreover, the anti-democratic influence of money in politics doesn't end on election day. The dominance of corporations and business interests exists not just in election spending but also in lobbying elected officials and decision-makers. In 2012, an important study of political influence, Unheavenly Chorus, looked at organized-interest activity aimed at influencing policymaking in Washington, D.C.. According to the study, social welfare and labor organization made up just 2 percent of all organized-interest activity—corporations, trade associations, and business groups accounted for 48 percent. Corporations and business groups spend much more on lobbying than organizations that represent large constituencies of Americans. For example, between 1998 and 2016, OpenSecrets.org reports that the U.S. Chamber of Commerce—just one of many groups advocating for the interests of big business—spent $1.3 billion on lobbying the federal government compared to $720 million spent by all labor unions.

Corporate influence over government does not end with the passing of a law. Corporate entities with no natural limits and endless resources can wage a long-term, sustained attack across policymaking pressure points. For example, if a law is passed that corporate interests oppose, relentless industry pressure can be brought to bear on the agencies charged with enforcing that legislation. Again, in his book, Sen. Whitehouse describes "heavy lawyering of the rulemaking and enforcement processes, often as simple brute pressure to cause delay and cost" on the part of corporate interests. Furthermore, any final rule may be challenged in courts that are increasingly friendly to corporate forces at the expense of people.

In the short time that President Donald Trump has been in office, the revolving door between industry and the federal agencies regulating them is back in full swing thanks to the administration loosening restrictions on lobbyists taking posts at agencies they previously sought to influence on behalf corporate clients. The independent nonprofit newsroom ProPublica discovered dozens of federally registered lobbyists who were among the first Trump appointees to take positions in federal agencies. For example, lobbyists for the pharmaceutical industry and health insurance companies are now in key posts at the U.S. Department of Health and Human Services; a lobbyist for the construction industry who fought wage and worker safety standards now works for the U.S. Department of Labor; a lobbyist for the extractive resources industry is now at the U.S. Department of Energy; and a for-profit college lobbyist who sought to weaken protections for students worked at the U.S. Department of Education.

In the Trump administration, as noted by Eric Lipton at *The New York Times*, we continue to see "the merging of private business interest with government affairs." In just one example, billionaire investor Carl Icahn has been named "special adviser to the president," but because he is not officially a government employee, he is not subject to the same conflict of interest divestment requirements. As a consequence, Icahn maintains his majority holdings in an oil refinery while zealously advocating for a rule change that would have saved his refinery more than $200 million the previous year. We have reached an apotheosis of concentrated wealth running government for their interests—Trump's cabinet has more wealth than one-third of American households, and Icahn is wealthier than all of them combined.

Captured: *The Corporate Infiltration of American Democracy* tells hard truths about the central threat posed by the rule of the rich—plutocracy—and how it is overwhelming American democracy. Sen. Whitehouse writes, "Corporate money is calling the tune in Congress; Congress is unwilling or unable to stand up to corporate power (indeed, Congress is often its agent)." These are truths that must be faced to be fixed.

Our democratic society must demonstrate its resilience and return to core American principles and values of government that serve the people. We have the power to demand that Congress break the nexus between Wall Street and Washington that keeps the rules of our economy rigged to benefit the wealthiest few at the expense of the many. Americans can resist the slide to secret political spending and require disclosure for the big money interests behind our toxic politics of personal destruction. We can demand that lobbyists be prohibited from acting as fundraisers. And, amidst the shocking scandal of Russian interference in America's democracy, we can insist that Congress ban foreign corporate money in elections.

Let us harbor no illusions—this battle won't be easy, but that doesn't mean it is impossible. Ever since our founding as a republic, Americans have fought to expand democratic freedoms and protect democratic society from being corrupted through unchecked private greed and undermined through grotesque inequality. One can clearly see the result of corporate power over policy in the present levels of wealth inequality—unmatched since the Great Depression—where all the economic gains in the past several years accrued to the wealthiest 1 percent. But as Economist Thomas Piketty concluded his study of economic inequality in *Capital in the Twenty-First Century* by writing, "If we are to regain control of capitalism, we must bet everything on democracy."

For democracy to work, the rules must be rewritten to prevent corporate capture of government and to create a system that supports fair representation for all Americans. Whether we fight to preserve our free

system of self-government for ourselves and posterity is not a choice—
it is a moral obligation.

At the risk of being a bore, here is another article admonishing the separation of corporate money and elections.

Source: https://www.nytimes.com/2009/08/11/opinion/11tue4.html (Cohen, A.,
2009, 10 August)

A Century-Old Principle: Keep Corporate Money Out of Elections

By Adam Cohen

Aug. 10, 2009

The founders were wary of corporate influence on politics—and
their rhetoric sometimes got pretty heated. In an 1816 letter, Thomas Jefferson declared his hope to "crush in its birth the aristocracy
of our moneyed corporations, which dare already to challenge our
government to a trial of strength and bid defiance to the laws of
our country."

This skepticism was enshrined in law in the early 20th century when
the nation adopted strict rules banning corporations from contributing
to political campaigns. Today that ban is in danger from the Supreme
Court, which hears arguments next month in a little-noticed case that
could open the floodgates to corporate money in politics.

The court has gone to extraordinary lengths to hear the case. And there
are worrying signs that there may well be five votes to rule that the ban
on corporate contributions violates the First Amendment.

The origins of the ban lie in the 1896 presidential race, which pit-
ted the Republican William McKinley against William Jennings Bryan,
the farm-belt populist. Bryan was a peerless orator, but McKinley had
Mark Hanna—the premier political operative of his day—extracting

so-called assessments from the nation's biggest corporations and funneling them into a vast marketing campaign.

McKinley, who outspent Bryan by an estimated 10 to 1, won handily, proving Hanna's famous dictum: "There are two things that are important in politics. The first is money, and I can't remember what the second one is."

Popular outrage over corporate contributions reached a high point in the 1904 election.

The defeated candidate, the Democrat Alton Parker, charged—accurately, it turned out—that his opponent had been bankrolled by large life insurance companies. "The greatest moral question which now confronts us is," Parker insisted, "shall the trusts and corporations be prevented from contributing money to control or aid in controlling elections?"

In 1907, Congress passed the Tillman Act, the first federal law barring corporate campaign contributions. States adopted similar laws.

Since then, Congress has repeatedly ratified the federal ban. In 1925, it folded the Tillman Act into the Federal Corrupt Practices Act. In 1947, it made clear that the ban included not just corporate contributions, but corporate expenditures on campaigns—and that it also applied to labor unions. In the 2002 McCain-Feingold law, Congress once again underscored that corporations cannot contribute to campaigns.

It is inconceivable that Congress would now try to lift the ban. Americans are far too angry at Wall Street and the obvious failure of government regulations. But the Supreme Court has decided to force the question: It took a case, Citizens United v. Federal Election Commission, in which the ban on corporate contributions was not a central issue; told the parties to prepare legal briefs on the ban's constitutionality; and rushed to put oral arguments on the calendar in September before the new term even starts.

The court's conservative majority has been aggressively championing the rights of corporations, but overturning the contributions ban would take it to a new level. Corporations have enormous treasuries, and there are a lot of things they want from government, many of which clash with the public interest.

If the ban is struck down, corporations may soon be writing large checks to the same elected officials whom they are asking to give them bailouts or to remove health-and-safety regulations from their factories or to insert customized loopholes into the tax code.

If the conservative justices strike down the ban, they would be doing many things they disavow. They would be substituting their own views for the will of the people, expressed through Congress. They would be reading rights into the Constitution that are not expressly there, since the Constitution never mentions corporations or their right to speak. And they would be overturning the court's own precedents.

The only hope is that the court is listening to Americans. As it weighs the constitutional issues, it should be mindful that this is another historical moment in which the public is committed to strengthening the wall between government and big business, not tearing it down.

Allowing corporations to use money to influence our government can result in only one thing.

The government is going along with whoever has the most money.

Spoiler alert: Citizens United v. Federal Election Commission.

The Court ruled, 5-4, that the First Amendment prohibits limits on corporate funding of independent broadcasts in candidate elections. We are opening the floodgates of corporate money into politics and elections, going against over 100 years of precedence of keeping corporate money out of politics.

The government is caught in this tug-of-war between corporate money, power, greed, and "We the People."

Right now, it seems the corporations are quickly collecting all the power needed to completely do away with a democracy that has endured for over 230 years.

I cannot say it has been a perfect ride for all those years. Whenever there are issues that negatively affect WTP, it comes down to men who think they are separate from the whole of humanity.

They act as if their interests are more important than the rest of the people they are affecting, which is just not true! When anyone denies the unity of humanity, it forces them to live their life, experiencing their worst self. For living a lie shall not be comfortable. Knowing the Truth and living the Truth shall set you free and bring you everlasting peace.

Do you want to be free? Do you want to be the cause of oppression in your corner of the world? The choice is yours. I say, free yourself before it is too late!

We all know the story of Ebenezer Scrooge. He is the poster boy for this type of thinking, and he was suffering because of it; that is, until he saw the Light!

From Wikipedia, I bring you a short synopsis:

Ebenezer Scrooge is the protagonist of Charles Dickens's 1843 novella A Christmas Carol. At the beginning of the novella, Scrooge is a cold-hearted miser who despises Christmas.

Charles Dickens describes Scrooge as "a squeezing, wrenching, grasping, scraping, clutching, covetous, old sinner! Hard and sharp as flint... secret, self-contained, and solitary as an oyster." He does business from a Cornhill warehouse and is known among the merchants of the Royal Exchange as a man of good credit. Despite having considerable personal wealth, he underpays his clerk Bob Cratchit. He hounds his debtors relentlessly while living cheaply and joylessly in the chambers of his deceased business partner, Jacob Marley. Most of all, he detests Christmas, which he associates with reckless spending. When two men approach him on Christmas Eve for a donation to charity, he sneers that the poor should avail themselves of the treadmill or the workhouses or die to reduce the surplus population. He also refuses his nephew Fred's invitation to Christmas dinner and denounces him as a fool for celebrating Christmas.

Dickens describes Scrooge thus early in the story: "The cold within him froze his old features, nipped his pointed nose, shriveled his cheek, stiffened his gait; made his eyes red, his thin lips blue, and spoke out shrewdly in his grating voice." Towards the end of the novella, the three spirits show Scrooge the errors of his ways, and he becomes a better, more generous man.

My favorite part of this story is when Ebenezer wakes up from the last dream and changes his mind about everything. He is running around, so full of energy, screaming and shouting, all of the changes for the day. I didn't know it then, but I know it now, the energy that has taken over Ebenezer is the power of Love surging through his heart. We talked about the power of Love earlier in the book. This is an example of the power of Love in real-time.

Corporations and government need a wake-up call – exactly the same way Ebenezer was jolted out of his negativity and hateful demeanor. Before moving on to the next section, I would like to share a poem I wrote about negativity.

My Own Personal Negativity

Entertaining a lot of negativity in your life has a detrimental effect on the rest of your life

For no matter how good it gets, it is always going to feel amiss

For that is the way you live your life

And it won't stop just because you win the lotto

You have to stop it now or from here on out your life is always going to feel amiss

To the degree that you determine, by your focus

How much negativity are you willing to entertain today

How do you get to a positive state of existence

It's not that hard, just accept everything, just as it is (Obviously, I am not asking you to accept abuse!)

You need not do anything, extra, to accept everything, just as it is

Actually, in order to accept everything, just as it is, you get to stop doing something

You get to stop complaining, about how terrible, everything is

Just look and experience everything, just as it is

No complaining, no storytelling, no blaming, no excuses

Just let everything, be as it is, and know that everything is okay

Even though it may seem as if it isn't

You know that part of you, the part of you that is certain that everything is not okay

You know that part of you very well, for it seems as if that part of you, is you

Well, that is just a lie

That part of you is intentional programming feeding you false information

You can listen and obey, if you so desire, for that is your choice

You have freewill and may choose to align with this voice that you think is you

And for a time it will seem as if it is the right thing to do, for that voice is so insistent

One day you will realize the truth

One day you will realize that you are the Light and Love pervading, creating, and sustaining this entire Universe

And that Truth shall set you free

I am Light and Love and so are you and so are we all

Allowing yourself to accept everything just the way it is, resembles a vacation from the pressure of your ego. When your ego is quiet, and you allow everything just to be, that moment can expand, deepen, and feel more vivid. That is because you have made room for the One Singular power of the universe to flow into the moment you are sharing with your Creator; that is the power of Love.

Love is continuously flowing to each and every one of us, and we only notice when we create the space for it to flow in. The more time we allow for the flow, the easier it becomes, and more and more love flows. Love begets more love!

You have heard the old saying, "Take time to stop and smell the roses." Now we know why, on an energetic level, the meaning of this saying.

Chapter Six:
Seeing the Problem with a Clear Focus

I am the first to admit that I was unaware of the deviant nature of corporations and government entities. After doing the research, the problems are glaringly obvious!

Corporations are riding on the backs of the American people, skimming money, just like a leach drawing a steady supply of blood, with the government turning a blind eye to the situation.

Plenty of books and websites will detail corporations' misdeeds, so I don't feel compelled to justify that point with examples.

I know this government was created with the consent of the governed (WTP), and its sole purpose is to serve "We The People"!

I also know that corporations are entities allowed to exist and regulated with the government's consent. Why are the corporations running our government? The whole system is set up for the government to oversee the corporations and to ensure their operations comply with the goals of WTP.

The answer is simple: Money! Money from the corporations is used to bribe Government officials. How do we turn this around?

First things first, we need an impenetrable firewall between government and corporations through which no money can flow. The ability to influence our government with bribes is no longer an option. Government officials who accept bribes are removed from office and subjected to arrest and incarceration. Corporations caught attempting to bribe government officials lose their ability to operate as a legal entity, in the eyes of the government and WTP, plain and simple!

Second, corporations must match the goals of WTP or the corporations, lose their license to operate, and are shut down, never to open their doors again.

Currently, most corporations' goals are the bottom line comes first. The short-term goals are to maximize profits, and the long-term goals are to maximize profits, even at the expense of WTP, our environment, and anything else that stands in the way.

In no way does this line up with the goals of WTP. Granted, the goals of WTP may change from time to time, but that is their prerogative, and the government and corporations need to get on board and keep up.

What are the goals of WTP? I have an excellent article that discusses when and how business parameters became more important than the quality of life for WTP.

How Money Became the Measure of Everything

Two centuries ago, America pioneered a way of thinking that puts human well-being in economic terms.

The Atlantic

- *Eli Cook*

Money and markets have been around for thousands of years. Yet as central as currency has been to so many civilizations, people in societies as different as ancient Greece, imperial China, medieval Europe, and colonial America did not measure residents' well-being in terms of monetary earnings or economic output.

In the mid-19th century, the United States—and to a lesser extent other industrializing nations such as England and Germany—departed from this historical pattern. It was then that American businesspeople and policymakers started to measure progress in dollar amounts, tabulating social welfare based on people's capacity to generate income. This fundamental shift, in time, transformed the way Americans appraised not only investments and businesses but also their communities, their environment, and even themselves.

Today, well-being may seem hard to quantify in a nonmonetary way, but indeed other metrics—from incarceration rates to life expectancy—have held sway in the course of the country's history. The turn away from these statistics, and toward financial ones, means that rather than considering how economic developments could meet Americans' needs, the default stance—in policy, business, and everyday life—is to assess whether individuals are meeting the exigencies of the economy.

At the turn of the 19th century, it did not appear that financial metrics were going to define Americans' concept of progress. In 1791, then-Secretary of the Treasury Alexander Hamilton wrote to various Americans across the country, asking them to calculate the money-making capacities of their farms, workshops, and families so that he could use that data to create economic indicators for his famous Report on Manufactures. Hamilton was greatly disappointed by the paltry responses he received and had to give up on adding price statistics to his report. Apparently, most Americans in the early republic did not see, count, or put a price on the world as he did.

Until the 1850s, in fact, by far the most popular and dominant form of social measurement in 19th-century America (as in Europe) were a collection of social indicators known then as "moral statistics," which quantified such phenomena as prostitution, incarceration, literacy, crime, education, insanity, pauperism, life expectancy, and disease. While these moral statistics were laden with paternalism, they nevertheless focused squarely on the physical, social, spiritual, and mental condition of the American people. For better or for worse, they placed human beings at the center of their calculating vision. Their unit of measure was bodies and minds, never dollars and cents.

Yet around the middle of the century, money-based economic indicators began to gain prominence, eventually supplanting moral statistics as the leading benchmarks of American prosperity. This epochal shift can be seen in the national debates over slavery. In the earlier parts of the 19th century, Americans in the North and South wielded moral statistics in order to prove that their society was the more advanced and successful one. In the North, abolitionist newspapers like the *Liberty Almanac* pointed to the fact that the North had far more students, scholars, libraries, and colleges. In the South, politicians like John Calhoun used dubious data to argue that freedom was bad for black people. The proportion of Northern blacks "who are deaf and dumb, blind, idiots, insane, paupers and in prison," Calhoun claimed in 1844, was "one out of every six," while in the South it was "one of every one hundred and fifty-four."

By the late 1850s, however, most Northern and Southern politicians and businessmen had abandoned such moral statistics in favor of economic metrics. In the opening chapter of his best-selling 1857 book against slavery, the author Hinton Helper measured the "progress and prosperity" of the North and the South by tabulating the cash value of agricultural produce that both regions had extracted from the earth. In so doing, he calculated that in 1850 the North was clearly the more advanced society, for it had produced $351,709,703 of goods and the

South only $306,927,067. Speaking the language of productivity, Helper's book became a hit with Northern businessmen, turning many men of capital to the antislavery cause.

The Southern planter class, meanwhile, underwent a similar shift. When South Carolina's governor, the planter and enslaver James Henry Hammond, sought to legitimize slavery in his famous 1858 "Cotton Is King" speech, he did so in part by declaring that "there is not a nation on the face of the earth, with any numerous population, that can compete with us in produce per capita ... It amounts to $16.66 per head."

What happened in the mid-19th century that led to this historically unprecedented pricing of progress? The short answer is straightforward enough: Capitalism happened. In the first few decades of the Republic, the United States developed into a commercial society, but not yet a fully capitalist one. One of the main elements that distinguishes capitalism from other forms of social and cultural organization is not just the existence of markets but also of capitalized investment, the act through which basic elements of society and life—including natural resources, technological discoveries, works of art, urban spaces, educational institutions, human beings, and nations—are transformed (or "capitalized") into income-generating assets that are valued and allocated in accordance with their capacity to make money and yield future returns. Save for a smattering of government-issued bonds and insurance companies, such a capitalization of everyday life was mostly absent until the mid-19th century. There existed few assets in early America through which one could invest wealth and earn an annual return.

Capitalization, then, was crucial to the rise of economic indicators. As upper-class Americans in both the North and South began to plow their wealth into novel financial assets, they began to imagine not only their portfolio but their entire society as a capitalized investment and its inhabitants (free or enslaved) as inputs of human capital that could be plugged into output-maximizing equations of monetized growth.

In the North, such investments mostly took the form of urban real estate and companies that were building railroads. As capital flowed into these new channels, investors were putting money—via loans, bonds, stocks, banks, trusts, mortgages, and other financial instruments—into communities they might never even set foot in. As local businesspeople and producers lost significant power to these distant East Coast investors, a national business class came into being that cared less about moral statistics—say, the number of prostitutes in Peoria or drunks in Detroit—than about a town's industrial output, population growth, real-estate prices, labor costs, railway traffic, and per-capita productivity.

Capitalization was also behind the statistical shift in the South, only there it was less about investment in railroad stocks or urban real estate than in human bodies. Enslaved people had long been seen as pieces of property in the United States, but only in the antebellum Deep South did they truly become pieces of capital that could be mortgaged, rented, insured, and sold in highly liquid markets. Viewing enslaved people first and foremost as income-yielding investments, planters began to keep careful track of their market output and value. Hammond, in his speech, had chosen to measure American prosperity in the same way that he valued, monitored, and disciplined those forced to work on his own cotton plantation.

As corporate consolidation and factories' technological capabilities ramped up in the Gilded Age and Progressive Era, additional techniques of capitalist quantification seeped from the business world into other facets of American society. By the Progressive Era, the logic of money could be found everywhere. "An eight-pound baby is worth, at birth, $362 a pound," declared *The New York Times* on January 30th, 1910. "That is a child's value as a potential wealth-producer. If he lives out the normal term of years, he can produce $2900 more wealth than it costs to rear him and maintain him as an adult." The title of this article was "What the Baby Is Worth as a National Asset: Last Year's Crop Reached a Value Estimated at $6,960,000,000." During this era, an array of Progressive reformers priced not only babies but the annual social cost of everything from intemperance ($2 billion), the common cold ($21 a month per employee), typhoid ($271 million), and housewife labor ($7.5 billion), as well as the annual social benefit of skunks ($3 million), Niagara Falls ($122.5 million), and government health insurance ($3 billion).

This particular way of thinking is still around, and hard to miss today in reports from the government, research organizations, and the media. For instance, researchers in this century have calculated the annual cost of excessive alcohol consumption ($223.5 billion) and of mental disorders ($467 billion), as well as the value of the average American life ($9.1 million according to one Obama-era government estimate, up from $6.8 million at one point during George W. Bush's presidency).

A century ago, money-based ideas of progress resonated most with business executives, most of whom were well-to-do white men. Measuring prosperity according to the Dow Jones Industrial Average (invented in 1896), manufacturing output, or per-capita wealth made a good deal of sense for America's upper classes, since they were usually the ones who possessed the stocks, owned the factories, and held the wealth. As recognized by the Yale economist Irving Fisher, a man who rarely met a social problem he did not put a price on, economic statistics could be potent in early-20th-century political debates. In arguing for why people needed to be treated as "money-making machines," Fisher explained how "newspapers showed a strong aversion to the harrowing side of the tuberculosis campaign but were always ready to 'sit up and take notice' when the cost of tuberculosis in dollars and cents was mentioned."

John Rockefeller Jr., J.P. Morgan, and other millionaire capitalists also came to recognize the power of financial metrics in their era. They began to plan for a private research bureau that would focus on the pricing of everyday life. Those plans came to fruition in the 1920s with the formation of the corporate-funded National Bureau of Economic Research. The private institution would go on to play a major role in the invention of Gross Net Product in the 1930s (and continues to operate today).

Many working-class Americans, though, were not as enthusiastic about the rise of economic indicators. This was largely because they believed the human experience to be "priceless" (a word that took off just as progress became conceptualized in terms of money) and because they (astutely) viewed such figures as tools that could be used to justify increased production quotas, more control over workers, or reduced wages. Massachusetts labor activists fighting for the eight-hour workday spoke for many American workers when they said, in 1870, that "the true prosperity and abiding good of the commonwealth can only be learned, by placing money [on] one scale, and man [on another]."

The assignment of prices to features of daily life, therefore, was never a foregone conclusion but rather a highly contested development. In the Gilded Age, some labor unions and Populist farmers succeeded in pushing state bureaus of labor statistics to offer up a series of alternative metrics that measured not economic growth or market output, but rather urban poverty, gender discrimination, leisure time, indebtedness, class mobility, rent-seeking behavior, and exploitation of workers. The interests of businessmen, though, won the day more often than not, and by the mid-20th century economic indicators that focused on monetary output came to be seen as apolitical and objective.

That shift carried tremendous social ramifications: The necessary conditions for economic growth were frequently placed before the necessary conditions for individuals' well-being. In 1911, Frederick Winslow Taylor, the efficiency expert who dreamed of measuring every human movement in terms of its cost to employers, bluntly articulated this reversal of ends and means: "In the past the man has been first; in the future the system must be first."

In the end, men like Taylor got their wish. Since the mid-20th century—whether in the Keynesian 1950s or the neoliberal 1980s—economic indicators have promoted an idea of American society as a capital investment whose main goal, like that of any investment, is ever-increasing monetary growth. Americans have surely benefited materially from the remarkable economic growth over this period of time, an expansion wholly unique to capitalist societies. Nevertheless, by making capital accumulation synonymous with progress, money-based metrics have turned human betterment into a secondary concern. By the early 21st century, American society's top priority became its bottom line, net worth became synonymous with self-worth, and a billionaire businessman who repeatedly pointed to his own wealth as proof of his fitness for office was elected president.

Eli Cook is an assistant professor of history at the University of Haifa. He is the author of The Pricing of Progress: Economic Indicators and the Capitalization of American Life.

Assuming that quality of life is uppermost in the minds of WTP, then the simple fix is for government to rewire the goals of corporations to meet those of WTP, and their compliance allows them to retain their license to operate and make money.

Currently, I believe many citizens are feeling underserved and have felt this way for a very long time. Individually many have asked for redress many times and in many different ways, to no avail. Citizens of our country are willing to work and make a better life for themselves, but their government no longer protects nor serves them. The tension is overwhelming... something must give way!

It is time for "We The People" to come together. To unite our voices and speak as One! When WTP act and vote in unity as a majority, the government must follow our lead. Our message shall be clear, resolute, from the heart, and spoken as One people. It is time to declare our unity, to implore our government to protect us once again from the nefarious forces debilitating and obliterating our ability to enjoy our inalienable rights. Our Founding documents enumerate these inalienable rights; it is time to reclaim them!

To that end, I believe it is time for a Declaration, not of Independence, but a Declaration of Delinquent Behavior by our government. I don't want independence from our government – that would be a messy, bloody long haul and only worth it if the government is unwilling to serve WTP again.

So the intermediate step is to produce a Declaration of Delinquent Behavior. I don't want to fight with our oppressors. I want our oppressors to, once again, become our tutelary, our protector defender, and most ardent advocate. I want to consent to their existence again, and together we can build a solid middle class that provides opportunities for all our citizens.

I will not pretend to know how to change what has happened to our government over the last fifty years. I know that when a change is made at the heart level, the rest is forthcoming and will provide for itself.

I believe deeply in my Heart of Hearts that the American people are willing to come together, sit at the same lunch counter and come to an agreement about what it is they want most of all, as human beings and for all human beings that they are willing to work together and sacrifice their petty differences to accomplish something great; something that will affect and greatly enhance their children's and grandchildren's lives for many generations to come.

We need to give WTP something they can believe in, and they will step it up and make it happen... WTP have done it before, and I know they can do it again!

Here is the first draft of Our *Declaration of Delinquent Behavior*. I say the first draft because WTP is in charge of this project. Your input is important! This first draft is to get us started.

I used the format of the original Declaration of Independence. Then I added the current grievances as the issues that most affect WTP.

The original Declaration of Independence is in an Arial font for easy understanding.

My first draft edits are in: *(Arial font, bold, italicized within brackets.)*

(The Declaration of Delinquent Behavior of these 50 United States of America!)

When in the Course of human events, it becomes necessary for one people to dissolve the political bands which have connected them with another, and to assume among the powers of the earth, the separate and equal station to which the Laws of Nature and of Nature's God entitle them, a decent respect to the opinions of mankind requires that they should declare the causes which impel them to the separation *or (reorganization and modernization of their relationship.)*

We hold these truths to be self-evident, that all men are created equal, that they are endowed by their Creator with certain unalienable Rights, that among these are Life, Liberty and the pursuit of Happiness.—That to secure these rights, Governments are instituted among Men, deriving their just powers from the consent of the governed, --That whenever any Form of Government becomes destructive of these ends, it is the Right of the People to alter or to abolish it, and to institute new Government, laying its foundation on such principles and organizing its powers in such form, as to them shall seem most likely to effect their Safety and Happiness. *(We intend to alter our current state of Government utilizing the unity of our majority to bring about the desired change.)* Prudence, indeed, will dictate that Governments long established should not be changed for light and transient causes; and accordingly all experience hath shewn, that mankind are more disposed to suffer, while evils are sufferable, than to right themselves by abolishing the forms to which they are accustomed. But when a long train of abuses and usurpations, pursuing invariably the same Object evinces a design to reduce them under absolute Despotism, it is their right, it is their duty, to throw off such Government, and to provide new Guards for their future security. —Such has been the patient sufferance of these *(50 United States ever since the Heyday of the 1960s, and such is now the necessity that constrains them to alter their former Systems of Government. The history of the current ruling Elite, our complicit Government, and the Titans of Corporate Power)* is a history of repeated injuries and usurpations, all having in direct object the establishment of an absolute Tyranny over these States. To prove this, let Facts be submitted to a candid world.

(They have) refused *(their)* Assent to Laws, the most wholesome and necessary for the public good.

(They have) obstructed the Administration of Justice, by refusing *(their)* Assent to Laws for establishing Judiciary powers *(that reflect the Will of the Majority of the People.)*

(They have made Judges dependent on their Will alone to render decisions that go against 200 years of precedence.)

(They have) erected a multitude of New Offices, and sent hither swarms of *(Lobbyists)* to harass our people, and eat out their substance.

(They have) kept among us, in times of peace, Standing Armies *(of Lobbyists)* without the Consent of our legislatures.

(They have) affected to render the Military independent of and superior to the Civil power *(and not beholden to the Majority of Americans.)*

(They have) combined with others to subject us to a jurisdiction foreign to our constitution, and unacknowledged by our laws; giving *(their)* Assent to their Acts of pretended Legislation:

For cutting off our *(mutual beneficial)* Trade with all parts of the world:

For imposing Taxes on us without our Consent:

For depriving us in many cases, of the benefits of Trial by Jury:

For taking away our *(Freedoms),* abolishing our most valuable Laws, and altering fundamentally the Forms of our Governments:

For suspending our own Legislatures, and declaring themselves invested with power to legislate for us in all cases whatsoever.

(They have) abdicated Government here, by declaring us out of his Protection and waging War against us.

(They have) plundered our seas, ravaged our Coasts, and destroyed the lives of our people.

(They are) at this time transporting large Armies of foreign Mercenaries *{Lobbyists}* to compleat the works of death, desolation and tyranny, already begun with circumstances of Cruelty & perfidy scarcely paralleled in the most barbarous ages, and totally unworthy the Head of a civilized nation.

In every stage of these Oppressions We have Petitioned for Redress in the most humble terms: Our repeated Petitions have been answered only by repeated injury. *(A Corporate Elite)* whose character is thus marked by every act which may define a Tyrant, is unfit *(to live free in a nation of free people devoted to one another's well-being and continued Unity.)*

Nor have We been wanting in attentions to our *(Elite)* brethren. We have warned them from time to time of attempts by their *(Lobbyists)* to extend an unwarrantable jurisdiction over us. We have reminded them of the circumstances of our emigration and settlement here. We have appealed to their native justice and magnanimity, and we have conjured them by the ties of our common kindred to disavow these usurpations, which, would inevitably interrupt our connections and correspondence. They too have been deaf to the voice of justice and of consanguinity. We must, therefore, acquiesce in the necessity, which denounces our Separation, and hold them, as we hold the rest of mankind, Enemies in War, in Peace Friends.

We, therefore, the Representatives of the united States of America, in General Congress, Assembled, appealing to the Supreme Judge of the world for the rectitude of our intentions, do, in the Name, and by Authority of the good People of these United States, solemnly publish and declare, That these *(50)* United States are, and of Right ought to be Free and Independent States; that they are Absolved from all Allegiance to *(Underhanded Political Tyranny. Rein down upon us by the Moneyed Elites and Conglomerated Corporations, doing as they will to garner short-term profits and leave the spoiled remains for the 99% of us to clean up. All of the political coercion between our Government and corporate bribery is and ought to be totally dissolved and made illegal now and forever more.)* And as Free and Independent States, *(we)* have full Power to, *(expand the middle class),* conclude Peace, contract Alliances, establish Commerce, and to do all other Acts and Things which Independent States may of right do. And for the support of this Declaration, with a firm reliance on the protection of divine Providence, we mutually pledge to each other our Lives, our Fortunes and our sacred Honor.

We The People are particularly disappointed in the delinquent behavior of our Government officials; not only did they relinquish their duty to protect us, but they exposed us to a myriad of scammers, hackers, charlatans, and dirty dealing corporate mobsters in the following areas:

Health care

Health care insurance

Pharmaceutical drug companies

Life insurance

Home insurance

Auto insurance

Neglect of our Veterans

Education K-12 inequality

Education advance degree exorbitant cost

Prison confinement to appease public fears

Prison is about rehabilitation and if it is about anything else it is a crime

Police brutality and ineffectual training programs for officers

Inability to balance the budget

Inability or unwillingness to payoff national debt

Corporations that pollute our environment

Corporations allowed to make and sell food that is unhealthy for Humans

Corporations that dump toxic chemicals into our natural waterways

Corporations that contribute to climate change

Corporations allowed to make false claims in advertising

Corporations allowed to submit falsifying information on financial statements

Corporations allowed to manipulate the stock market for their own gain

Corporations allowed to bribe public officials

Insider trading that is illegal and not prosecuted

Insider trading that is legal for US Congress people

Free trade agreements and American workers lose more jobs

Not having a unified regulated industry to help working parents with childcare

Unemployment insurance that does not cover the cost of living

Lack of job training programs to put American workers back to work

Predatory credit card companies

Predatory home mortgage lending companies

Subsidizing philanthropic endeavors of the super-rich

Tax breaks that only line the pockets of the super-rich

Tax evasion by the super-rich

A military spending budget that is proportionally too large

Many different kinds of subsidies that only line the pockets of the super-rich

Allowing financial markets to expose the American public to financial ruin

And when a collapse happens, the only people that get bailed out are the super-rich

Allowing a banking system that only supports the super-rich and feeds off of the rest of the American public

Not enforcing antitrust laws

Not enforcing anti-monopoly laws

Not having meaningful penalties in place for companies that break the law

Deregulation – corporations are regulated for a reason... to keep the crooks from ripping off the American public!

Campaign finance reform

Your inability to keep corporate and elite money out of politics

Allowing the judiciary system to rule for Citizen United v FEC

Allowing corporations and the super-rich to avoid having to pay a proper percentage in taxes to support our Republic

Allowing Corporations and the super-rich to gain control of you and change the laws making it harder for WTP to live a middle-class life that is fulfilling, and able to afford a family, family vacations, and allows one to have a life with integrity!

Basically, you had one job! And that was to protect, promote, and preserve our inalienable rights, and you didn't do it!

And there you have it! The first draft of the Declaration of Delinquent Behavior. What do you think? Can our government improve? Are WTP willing to follow through to ensure our government protects and provides for us, our children, and our grandchildren? It will take some mighty dedicated women and men to perform many Herculean tasks. History will be made. We need everyone to participate! This will be an "All Hands On Deck Maneuver," and everyone will have an opportunity to contribute. We are all in this together!

I would love to close out this chapter with a poem of mine.

What Do the Great Ones Know That We Don't Know?

First of all, that they are no greater than thee

That they are made of flesh and blood just the same as thee

They know that their flesh and blood is animated by the same force that has created everything we see

And continues to create everything we can see and sense

They have opened a door, to allow this specious force, entry, into their knowing

They have come to know that their sense of isolation and separateness is an illusion

234

They have refocused their sense of self solely on this benevolent loving force

Allowing it to wash over them, enveloping them and transform them

They know that the very same universal force lives within each and every one of us

Our freewill allows us to embrace or ignore this benevolent animating force

They also know that eventually, we will tire of the pain and suffering, that our life

And our life choices, bring to us

And we will search for an end to this pain

And our sincerity will invite this specious force into our lives too

This loving benevolent force is always at the ready to seamlessly flow into our lives

Enveloping and transforming our flesh and blood lives to one of Light and Love

This force is always available, to all of us, anytime we are ready

---

So without further ado... Let's march down Main street and let everyone know that we are going to make some changes!

Chapter Seven:
Time to Become One

After reading this book, do you feel pumped, primed and prepared to take action? Are you ready to step up and play your part? We will need a lot of players, so that means a lot of roles for you to choose from. You can pick the position you want to play.

First things first, tell everyone you know about this book, what it says, what we can do to create change and make our lives, society, and country more functional. I want to live in a country where I can afford to live... is that too much to ask?

Education is the first step! Once everyone understands what we are trying to do, it will be easy for them to get on board and help. So getting the word out is first.

Once the momentum of this new information enlivens people to enlist themselves in the cause, we can focus on objectives that point the way to our overall goal.

Our first objective is a huge undertaking, never before attempted in the history of this country. The Constitution was written this way to allow for this to happen. When the government has found itself treading a path towards its own destruction, there had to be a mechanism to reverse that trend quickly—getting us back on course to a place of sustainability, inclusion, with freedom, and justice for all.

A supermajority of citizens is required for this action to be successful. After writing this book and talking to other citizens, the perfect storm for this change has arrived.

Here is the Solution that I promised at the beginning of this book.

Have you ever heard the phrase, "Vote the Bastards Out?" Well, that is precisely what we are going to do. Any politician who has accepted money from a lobbyist attempting to oppress "We The People" in any way, shape, or form; will be voted out. I am guessing the percentage to be about 98% of our current representatives. So, "Vote The Bastards Out" seems appropriate.

How do we do this?

Let us refer to the Constitution:

Congressional elections happen every two years. Voters choose one-third of senators and every member of the House of Representatives.

Members of the U.S. House of Representatives serve two-year terms. All 435 members get elected every midterm and presidential election year. A representative must be at least 25, a U.S. citizen for at least seven years, and live in the state they represent. The number of representatives a state has depends on its population. Each representative serves a specific congressional district.

Senators serve six-year terms. One-third of senators get elected during each midterm and each presidential election year. A senator must be at least 30, a U.S. citizen for at least nine years, and live in the state they represent. There are 100 U.S. senators, two from each state.

Tuesday, November 5, 2024, is the next election day for Federal offices, including the President, Vice President, and all members of The House of Representatives and one-third of Senators. Which Senators are up for re-election?

Class I – Senators Whose Term of Service Expire in 2025

Class I terms run from the beginning of the 116th Congress on January 3, 2019, to the end of the 118th Congress on January 3, 2025. Senators in Class I were elected to office in the November 2018 general election, unless they took their seat through appointment or special election.

Democrats

Baldwin, Tammy (D-WI)

Brown, Sherrod (D-OH)

Cantwell, Maria (D-WA)

Cardin, Benjamin L. (D-MD)

Carper, Thomas R. (D-DE)

Casey, Robert P., Jr. (D-PA)

Feinstein, Dianne (D-CA)

Gillibrand, Kirsten E. (D-NY)

Heinrich, Martin (D-NM)

Hirono, Mazie K. (D-HI)

Kaine, Tim (D-VA)

Klobuchar, Amy (D-MN)

Manchin, Joe, III (D-WV)

Menendez, Robert (D-NJ)

Murphy, Christopher (D-CT)

Rosen, Jacky (D-NV)

Sinema, Kyrsten (D-AZ)

Stabenow, Debbie (D-MI)

Tester, Jon (D-MT)

Warren, Elizabeth (D-MA)

Whitehouse, Sheldon (D-RI)

Republicans
Barrasso, John (R-WY)

Blackburn, Marsha (R-TN)

Braun, Mike (R-IN)

Cramer, Kevin (R-ND)

Cruz, Ted (R-TX)

Fischer, Deb (R-NE)

Hawley, Josh (R-MO)

Romney, Mitt (R-UT)

Scott, Rick (R-FL)

Wicker, Roger F. (R-MS)

Independents
King, Angus S., Jr. (I-ME)

Sanders, Bernard (I-VT)

How many volunteers do we need to become candidates for Federal offices?

Let's tally the numbers.

One for the office of President and one for the office of Vice President	2 people
435 volunteers for the office of the House of Representatives	435 people
33 volunteers for the office of the Senate	33 people
Total number of volunteers we need to become candidates for Federal offices	470
Total number of Senators left over from the old regime	67

That my friends is a majority! WTP 470 vs. 67 Crony Capitalists.

"We The People" only need 470 new Representatives to help enact the will of "We The People," which will change the course of history in our lifetimes. We only need one federal election cycle to turn this around.

Are we ready for this? Are we willing to come together and make this happen?

Do you want to be a candidate? Pretty scary, I know, but I am willing! Are you?

How do we know who is sympathetic to our cause?

We need to create and support a watchdog group to help identify candidates sympathetic to our cause and get that info published.

Hence, every voter knows who to vote for come election day. We also need volunteers to help with campaigning, fundraising, and getting the word out.

This is so exciting! I have never been a part of anything like this before.

Should we create a third party?? We could call it the "We The People Party."
I love the sound of that!

We should have a platform or a vision for change. Hmmm… So many things need to be changed! Let's work on the most significant and problematic issues first. Then the minor issue will be an easy mop-up job after we have cleared a path through all the big obstacles in our first pass through.

Significant Issues that need to be re-evaluated:

Get the dark money out of politics! Politicians may no longer accept money for preferential treatment. Corporations may no longer give money to politicians for preferential treatment. This will allow the government to serve the American public. Once the government renews its commitment as a protector of WTP and corporations accept their new role of engendering the strength of the middle class, the rest of the issues should be easy to resolve.

Next issue:

Should health care be a living right in this country, and should every citizen receive free care? Many would argue that a national form of health care is Socialism.

When I was growing up, Socialism and Communism were considered the same concept; both horrible and responsible for all the world's evil.

Now that I am an adult, I would like to investigate the truth or falseness of these ideas that turned into beliefs and now drive our collective behavior away from anything resembling Socialism or Communism.

So, if we have a national health care program funded by every person's taxes, when a person got sick, they would go to their doctor and get treated. They would get a statement outlining the treatment and the amount paid to the doctor, but it would not be a bill. And that person would go back to work when they felt better, and life would go on seamlessly regarding that person's finances; textbook Socialism.

For comparison, let's look at fire departments and how they operate. When you wake up in the middle of the night and smell smoke and see fire, you dial 911. You tell them there is a fire, they drive to your house and do their best to put out the fire, saving lives and property, and you never get a bill from the fire department. Can you imagine, for just a moment, in the middle of the night, you smell smoke, see fire, dial 911, and their response is, "Sorry, you are not up to date on your fire insurance. We will not be coming out to your house. Have a nice evening." Textbook Capitalism.

So we have a national fire response protocol that is paid for by our taxes and is accessible to whoever needs to use this service. This response protocol seems like Socialism to me, but in this case, it is good.

Remember the 2008 financial meltdown? Banks that had initiated and facilitated the meltdown were now in danger of going bankrupt, and they cried, "We are too big to fail! Somebody, please help us!" And the government bailed them out with enough cash to keep them solvent until the economy could stabilize. This bailout seems like Socialism to me too. And in this instance, the government deemed it proper.

When it came to all the homeowners who lost their homes due to negligent banking practices and mostly no fault of their own, the government decided that bailing out all of the homeowners would be too socialistic. The homeowners had to fend for themselves. Socialism is good for banking corporations and not suitable for WTP. Hmm...

Now, we know that this government was created to serve WTP. And in this case, it only provided for banking corporations that created the problem in the first place. Proof that our current government is bought and paid for by at least the corporate banking industry.

So what I am hearing is that Socialism is good sometimes. What makes it good sometimes and not good other times? In the fire department's case, fire is a terrifying ordeal. It can affect the rich and poor equally, and having a standing force of people ready to put out fires is comforting to the general public. So we consent, to the socialistic nature of our collective fire departments.

In the case of the 2008 financial meltdown, the Socialistic response to care for people in dire need only extended to the banking corporations. Homeowners were hung out to dry, and the banks were saved and enabled to continue to prey upon the American public. The banks only care about themselves, and their bribery money circumvented the government's responsibility to WTP. Not very comforting to the general public.

In the case of a national health care program, why is Socialism not good? Too many people, corporations, and industries make too much money from it the way is right now to allow it to change to serve WTP.

Whenever the topic of a National Health Care Program comes up, the rallying cry from these entities is, "No National Health Care. We are not a Socialistic country!" Well, that is just not true! In some instances, we have socialistic policies. WTP have deemed them good, and they are working well for us, including the police and fire department, paramedic and EMT services, public libraries, Medicare, Medicaid, social security, the minimum wage, and child labor laws, to name a few.

There is also a provision for this socialistic thinking in the Preamble to the constitution: ***Promote the General Welfare.*** Check out this article.

Source: https://civiced.rutgers.edu/documents/civics/middle-school-civics/the-american-experience/89-promote-the-general-welfare/file (New Jersey Center for Civic Education, n.d.)

What does "promote the general welfare" mean?

Prepared by: The New Jersey Center for Civic Education, Rutgers University, Piscataway, NJ Grade Level: 6-8

Objectives: Students will be able to:

- Explain what "promote the general welfare" means
- Give examples of governmental actions that promote the general welfare
- Engage in a simulated legislative hearing

What does "promote the general welfare" mean?

The Preamble to the United States Constitution lists as one of the purposes for creating our government: "...to promote the General welfare". Article I of the U.S. Constitution, which lays out the powers of the national government, reiterates this language in greater specificity: "to lay and collect Taxes, Duties, Imposts and Excises, to pay the Debts and provide for the common Defense and "General welfare."

What is the "General welfare"?

In listing the purposes for establishing the government of the United States of America, the Constitution makes clear that a main purpose is to make decisions for the common good—to improve our society for the benefit of all of its members. The general welfare, also sometimes referred to as the "public welfare" or the "public good" or the "common good", is the concern of the government for the health, peace, and safety of its citizens.

How has "promote the general welfare" been defined historically?

General national welfare pertains to purposes and policies states could not achieve on their own due to lack of coordination among the states. For example, centralizing power over tariffs in the national government eliminated the lack of coordination by the states regarding ports under the Articles of Confederation, allowing revenues to be raised from tariffs on imports.

Historically, promoting the general welfare has meant improving transportation, promoting agriculture and industry, protecting health and the environment, and seeking ways to solve social and economic problems. The idea that the government should be working for the "general welfare" or benefit of all has been repeatedly stated.

In 1914, before he became the 23rd president, Calvin Coolidge explained this idea concretely to the Massachusetts Senate: "We are all members of one body. The welfare of the weakest and the welfare of the most powerful are inseparably bound together. Industry cannot flourish if labor languishes. Transportation cannot prosper if manufactures decline. The general welfare cannot be provided for in any one act, but it is well to remember that the benefit of one is the benefit of all, and the neglect of one is the neglect of all."

More recently, Harvard historian Jill Lepore described the connection between providing for the general welfare and taxes: "Taxes are what we pay for civilized society, for modernity, and for prosperity. The wealthy pay more because they have benefitted more. Taxes, well laid and well spent, insure domestic tranquility, provide for the common defense, and promote the general welfare. Taxes protect property and the environment; taxes make business possible. Taxes pay for roads and schools and bridges and police and teachers. Taxes pay for doctors and nursing homes and medicine. During an emergency, like an earthquake or a hurricane, taxes pay for rescue workers, shelters, and services. For people whose lives are devastated by other kinds of disaster, like the disaster of poverty, taxes pay, even, for food."

"We are all members of One body," by Calvin Coolidge, says it all!

When the Oneness fact is acknowledged by a majority of people and acted upon, great things happen.

We are all evolving; hopefully, every citizen can evolve along with us. We all can live for The All or move away from this knowing; to focus upon only our own ego affairs.

Tragic historical events bring us all together, relieving us of the constant oppression from our ego. Reminding us of the Truth of our Reality, that we are all One.

After World War Two, there was a tremendous sense of relief and camaraderie. The relief was as deep as the pain inflicted by the war. That relief opened us all to the feeling of Oneness and that sense of fellowship. That period, following the war, saw the most significant expansion of the middle class ever.

Everyone was happy to get back to the American Dream. People began designing, building, manufacturing, and consuming. People were proud of where they lived. They took care of their homes and their public places. People gathered to enjoy themselves and each other when they weren't working.

It was a glorious time. It was easy to get a job that paid well. It was easy to buy a home. It was easy to go to college if you wanted to. People felt like they were living the American Dream.

So do we need another colossal calamity to renew our familiarity with that feeling of Oneness? Can't we acknowledge the lessons learned, know that we are all One, and act as if we are all One right now? That would simplify getting us back on track with an achievable American Dream.

Admittedly, capitalism has played a crucial role in facilitating the development of the American Dream. However, it is time to admit that it has also done some harm. Socialism has been selectively utilized, very adeptly, to "promote our general welfare." So, for a moment, let's stop praising one of these ideologies and demonizing the other and closely examine what each of them will do for us.

Here is an article comparing and contrasting the two of them.

Source: https://www.thoughtco.com/socialism-vs-capitalism-4768969 (Longley, R., 2022, 11 April)

Socialism vs. Capitalism: What Is the Difference?

By
Robert Longley

Updated on April 11, 2022

Socialism and capitalism are the two main economic systems used in developed countries today. The main difference between capitalism and socialism is the extent to which the government controls the economy.

Key Takeaways: Socialism vs. Capitalism

- Socialism is an economic and political system under which the means of production are publicly owned. Production and consumer prices are controlled by the government to best meet the needs of the people.
- Capitalism is an economic system under which the means of production are privately owned. Production and consumer prices are based on a free-market system of "supply and demand."
- Socialism is most often criticized for its provision of social services programs requiring high taxes that may decelerate economic growth.
- Capitalism is most often criticized for its tendency to allow income inequality and stratification of socio-economic classes.

Socialist governments strive to eliminate economic inequality by tightly controlling businesses and distributing wealth through programs that benefit the poor, such as free education and healthcare. Capitalism, on the other hand, holds that private enterprise utilizes economic resources more efficiently than the government and that

246

society benefits when the distribution of wealth is determined by a freely-operating market.

	Capitalism	Socialism
Ownership of Assets	Means of production owned by private individuals	Means of production owned by government or cooperatives
Income Equality	Income determined by free market forces	Income equally distributed according to need
Consumer Prices	Prices determined by supply and demand	Prices set by the government
Efficiency and Innovation	Free market competition encourages efficiency and innovation	Government-owned businesses have less incentive for efficiency and innovation
Healthcare	Healthcare provided by private sector	Healthcare provided free or subsidized by the government
Taxation	Limited taxes based on individual income	High taxes necessary to pay for public services

The United States is generally considered to be a capitalist country, while many Scandinavian and Western European countries are considered socialist democracies. In reality, however, most developed countries—including the U.S.—employ a mixture of socialist and capitalist programs.

Capitalism Definition

Capitalism is an economic system under which private individuals own and control businesses, property, and capital—the "means of production." The volume of goods and services produced is based on a system of "supply and demand," which encourages businesses to manufacture quality products as efficiently and inexpensively as possible.

In the purest form of capitalism—free market or laissez-faire capitalism—individuals are unrestrained in participating in the economy. They decide where to invest their money, as well as what to produce and sell at what prices. True laissez-faire capitalism operates without government controls. In reality, however, most capitalist countries employ some degree of government regulation of business and private investment.

Capitalist systems make little or no effort to prevent <u>income inequality</u>. Theoretically, financial inequality encourages competition and innovation, which drive economic growth. Under capitalism, the government dooc not omploy tho gonoral workforoo. Ac a rocult, unomploymont can increase during <u>economic downturns</u>. Under capitalism, individuals contribute to the economy based on the needs of the market and are rewarded by the economy based on their personal wealth.

Socialism Definition

Socialism describes a variety of economic systems under which the means of production are owned equally by everyone in society. In some socialist economies, the democratically elected government owns and controls major businesses and industries. In other socialist economies, production is controlled by worker cooperatives. In a few others, individual ownership of enterprise and property is allowed, but with high taxes and government control.

The mantra of socialism is, "From each according to his ability, to each according to his contribution." This means that each person in society gets a share of the economy's collective production—goods and wealth—based on how much they have contributed to generating it. Workers are paid their share of production after a percentage has been deducted to help pay for social programs that serve "the common good."

In contrast to capitalism, the main concern of socialism is the elimination of "rich" and "poor" socio-economic classes by ensuring an equal distribution of wealth among the people. To accomplish this, the socialist government controls the labor market, sometimes to the extent of being the primary employer. This allows the government to ensure full employment even during economic downturns.

The Socialism vs. Capitalism Debate

The key arguments in the socialism vs. capitalism debate focus on socio-economic equality and the extent to which the government controls wealth and production.

Ownership and Income Equality

Capitalists argue that private ownership of property (land, businesses, goods, and wealth) is essential to ensuring the natural right of people to control their own affairs. Capitalists believe that because private-sector enterprise uses resources more efficiently than government, society is better off when the free market decides who profits and who does not.

In addition, private ownership of property makes it possible for people to borrow and invest money, thus growing the economy.

Socialists, on the other hand, believe that property should be owned by everyone. They argue that capitalism's private ownership allows a relatively few wealthy people to acquire most of the property. The resulting income inequality leaves those less well off at the mercy of the rich. Socialists believe that since income inequality hurts the entire society, the government should reduce it through programs that benefit the poor such as free education and healthcare and higher taxes on the wealthy.

Consumer Prices

Under capitalism, consumer prices are determined by free market forces. Socialists argue that this can enable businesses that have become monopolies to exploit their power by charging excessively higher prices than warranted by their production costs.

In socialist economies, consumer prices are usually controlled by the government. Capitalists say this can lead to shortages and surpluses of essential products. Venezuela is often cited as an example. According to Human Rights Watch, "most Venezuelans go to bed hungry." Hyperinflation and deteriorating health conditions under the socialist economic policies of President Nicolás Maduro have driven an estimated 3 million people to leave the country as food became a political weapon.

Efficiency and Innovation

The profit incentive of capitalism's private ownership encourages businesses to be more efficient and innovative, enabling them to manufacture better products at lower costs. While businesses often fail under capitalism, these failures give rise to new, more efficient businesses through a process known as "creative destruction."

Socialists say that state ownership prevents business failures, prevents monopolies, and allows the government to control production to best meet the needs of the people. However, say capitalists, state ownership breeds inefficiency and indifference as labor and management have no personal profit incentive.

Healthcare and Taxation

Socialists argue that governments have a moral responsibility to provide essential social services. They believe that universally needed services like healthcare, as a natural right, should be provided free to everyone by the government. To this end, hospitals and clinics in socialist countries are often owned and controlled by the government.

Capitalists contend that state, rather than private control, leads to inefficiency and lengthy delays in providing healthcare services. In addition, the costs of providing healthcare and other social services force socialist governments to impose high progressive taxes while increasing government spending, both of which have a chilling effect on the economy.

Capitalist and Socialist Countries Today

Today, there are few if any developed countries that are 100% capitalist or socialist. Indeed, the economies of most countries combine elements of socialism and capitalism.

In Norway, Sweden, and Denmark—generally considered socialist—the government provides healthcare, education, and pensions. However, private ownership of property creates a degree of income inequality. An average of 65% of each nation's wealth is held by only 10% of the people—a characteristic of capitalism.

The economies of Cuba, China, Vietnam, Russia, and North Korea incorporate characteristics of both socialism and communism.

While countries such as Great Britain, France, and Ireland have strong socialist parties, and their governments provide many social support programs, most businesses are privately owned, making them essentially capitalist.

The United States, long considered the prototype of capitalism, isn't even ranked in the top 10 most capitalist countries, according to the conservative think tank Heritage Foundation. The U.S. drops in the Foundation's Index of Economic Freedom due to its level of government regulation of business and private investment.

Indeed, the Preamble of the U.S. Constitution sets one of the nation's goals to be "promote the general welfare." In order to accomplish this, the United States employs certain socialist-like social safety net programs, such as Social Security, Medicare, food stamps, and housing assistance.

Socialism

Contrary to popular belief, socialism did not evolve from <u>Marxism</u>. Societies that were to varying degrees "socialist" have existed or have been imagined since ancient times. Examples of actual socialist societies that predated or were uninfluenced by German philosopher and economic critic <u>Karl Marx</u> were Christian <u>monastic</u> enclaves during and after the <u>Roman Empire</u> and the 19th-century utopian social experiments proposed by Welsh philanthropist Robert Owen. Premodern or non-Marxist literature that envisioned ideal socialist societies include <u>The Republic</u> by <u>Plato</u>, Utopia by Sir Thomas More, and Social Destiny of Man by Charles Fourier.

Socialism vs. Communism

Unlike socialism, communism is both an ideology and a form of government. As an ideology, it predicts the establishment of a dictatorship controlled by the working-class proletariat established through violent revolution and the eventual disappearance of social and economic class and state. As a form of government, communism is equivalent in principle to the dictatorship of the proletariat and in practice to a dictatorship of communists. In contrast, socialism is not tied to any specific ideology. It presupposes the existence of the state and is compatible with democracy and allows for peaceful political change.

Capitalism

While no single person can be said to have invented capitalism, capitalist-like systems existed as far back as ancient times. The ideology of modern capitalism is usually attributed to Scottish political economist <u>Adam Smith</u> in his classic 1776 economic treatise The Wealth of Nations. The origins of capitalism as a functional economic system can be traced to 16th to 18th century England, where the early <u>Industrial Revolution</u> gave rise to mass enterprises, such as the textile industry, iron, and <u>steam power</u>. These industrial advancements led to a system in which accumulated profit was invested to increase productivity—the essence of capitalism.

Despite its modern status as the world's predominant economic system, capitalism has been criticized for several reasons throughout history. These include the unpredictable and unstable nature of capitalist growth, social harms, such as pollution and abusive treatment of workers, and forms of economic disparity, such as <u>income</u>

inequality. Some historians connect profit-driven economic models such as capitalism to the rise of oppressive institutions such as human enslavement, colonialism, and imperialism.

It sounds like communism is the one ideology we should guard against, for it's very oppressive. Violence and social stratification are part of the ideology.

Socialism promotes the general welfare; too much could prove troublesome, and we are now learning too much capitalism can oppress and disregard the general welfare.

The rhetoric that socialism is inefficient and stagnates our economy comes from the industries that make money, providing overpriced, essential social services to WTP.

If WTP, task our government with providing healthcare for all our members, the first thing that would happen is the price would go down because there would be no more insurance companies skimming off the top.

Government healthcare and insurance-driven healthcare are both run like a collective. Everyone pays for healthcare before they need it. When they need it, some of the money from the collective is used for the individual needing the care. The difference between the two is one line-item on the balance sheet. That line item is profit, and it goes to the insurance companies. If the insurance companies would be significantly better than a government-run system, then okay, I would capitulate. My experience is that insurance-driven healthcare is slow to let me book appointments, slow to approve treatments, and costs more money because they need to make a profit.

Out-of-pocket for WTP goes to zero.

Practitioners providing service would now compete, further driving down the price of healthcare. Have you ever received an estimate for a medical procedure before having that procedure? Can you imagine having someone work on your car or house without first receiving an estimate?

When WTP are back in charge of this government, there will be a lot of opportunities to lighten the load for WTP.

A National Health care plan is just one of them. If WTP so desire one...

Interesting to find out that the USA is not a purely capitalist country. In fact, due to the Preamble in the Constitution, the United States has some social safety net programs already in place. What lowers their score as a capitalist vs. socialist country is the number of government regulations of business and private investment.

There wouldn't be so many regulations if only the corporations would police themselves and cooperate as responsible contributing members of society. Then again, that is one of the usual downfalls of capitalism, rampant abuse by corporations negatively affecting WTP.

As human beings, we all have the same needs, wants, and desires. If we set up a system that made obtaining those needs for oneself easier, this would lift the constant oppression of having to take care of our basic needs; eating, sleeping, breathing, and shelter.

Why is this important? Let me introduce you to Maslow's Hierarchy of needs.

Source: https://www.theschooloflife.com/article/the-importance-of-maslows-pyramid-of-needs/ (The School of Life, n.d.)

The Importance of Maslow's Pyramid of Needs

One of the most legendary ideas in the history of psychology is located in an unassuming triangle divided into five sections referred to universally simply as 'Maslow's Pyramid of Needs'.

This profoundly influential pyramid first saw the world in an academic journal in the United States in 1943, where it was crudely drawn in black and white and surrounded by dense and jargon-rich text. It has since become a mainstay of psychological analyses, business presentations and online lectures – and grown ever more colourful and emphatic in the process.

The pyramid was the work of a thirty-five year old Jewish psychologist of Russian origins called Abraham Maslow, who had been looking, since the start of his professional career, for nothing less than the meaning of life. No longer part of the close-knit orthodox family of his youth, Maslow wanted to find out what could make life purposeful for people (himself included) in modern-day America, a country where the pursuit of money and fame seemed to have eclipsed any more interior or authentic aspirations. He saw psychology as the discipline that would enable him to answer the yearnings and questions that people had once taken to religion.

Maslow suddenly saw that human beings could be said to have essentially five different kinds of need: on the one hand, the psychological or what one could term, without any mysticism being meant by the word, the spiritual and on the other, the material. For Maslow, we all start with a set of utterly non-negotiable and basic physiological needs, for food, water, warmth and rest. In addition, we have urgent safety needs for bodily security and protection from attack. But then we start to enter the spiritual domain. We need belongingness and love. We need friends and lovers, we need esteem and respect. And lastly, and most grandly, we are driven by what Maslow called – in a now legendary term – an urge for *self-actualization*: a vast, touchingly nebulous and yet hugely apt concept involving what Maslow described as 'living according to one's full potential' and 'becoming who we really are.'

Part of the reason why the description of these needs, laid out in pyramid-form, has proved so persuasive is their capacity to capture, with elemental simplicity, a profound structural truth about human existence. Maslow was putting his finger, with unusual deftness and precision, on a set of answers to very large questions that tend to confuse and perplex us viciously, particularly when we are young, namely: What are we really after? What do we long for? And how do we arrange our priorities and give due regard for the different and competing claims we have on our attention? Maslow was reminding us with artistic concision of the shape of an ideal well-lived life, proposing at once that we cannot live by our spiritual callings alone, but also that it cannot be right to remain focused only on the material either. We need, to be whole, both the material and the spiritual realms to be attended to, the base lending support while the summit offers upward direction and definition.

Maslow was rebutting calls from two sorts of zealots: firstly, over-ardent spiritual types who might urge us to forget entirely about money, housing, a good insurance policy and enough to pay for lunch. But he was also fighting against extreme hard-nosed pragmatists who might imply that life was simply a brute process of putting food on the table and going to the office. Both camps had – for Maslow – misunderstood the complexity of the human animal. Unlike other creatures, we truly are multifaceted, called at once to unfurl our soul according to its inner destiny – and to make sure we can pay the bills at the end of the month.

Operating at the heyday of American capitalism, Maslow was interestingly ambivalent about business. He was awed by the material resources of large corporations around him but at the same time he lamented that almost all their economic activity was – unfairly and bizarrely – focused on honouring customers' needs at the bottom of his pyramid. America's largest companies were helping people to have a roof of their heads, feeding them, moving them around and ensuring they could talk to each other long-distance. But they seemed utterly uninterested in trying to fulfill the essential spiritual appetites defined on the higher slopes of his pyramid. Towards the end of his long life, Maslow expressed a hope that businesses could in time learn to make more of their profits from addressing not only our basic needs but also – and as importantly – our higher spiritual and psychological ones as well. That would be truly enlightened capitalism.

In the personal sphere, Maslow's pyramid remains a hugely useful object to turn to whenever we are trying to assess the direction of our lives. Often, as we reflect upon it, we start to notice that we really haven't arranged and balanced our needs as wisely and elegantly as we might. Some lives have got an implausibly wide base: all the energy seems directed towards material accumulation. At the same time, there are lives with the opposite problem, where we have not paid due head to our need to look after our fragile and vulnerable bodies.

Maslow was pointing us to the need for a greater balance between the many priorities we must juggle. His beautifully simple visual cue is, above anything else, a portrait of a life lived in harmony with the complexities of our nature. We should, at our less frantic moments, use it to reflect with newfound focus on what it is we might do next.

It makes sense that if a person can meet their physiological and biological needs (food, air, water, sleep, and warmth), they can focus on the next set of requirements… making them viable candidates to be self-sufficient members of society, and ultimately, isn't that what we want for all members of the human race? Are we not all One?

When a Soul incarnates into a human body, the adults responsible for creating this new physical body also have a responsibility to take care of its physiological and biological needs until they can do so for themselves.

WTP has charged the government with that same responsibility. To help us when we cannot do so for ourselves, enabling us to enact self-sustaining self-care procedures, making it possible to move toward the next level. This process of self-care and development, through all levels for every individual, becomes a normalized process that our government facilitates through education and funding.

Fostering the development of each individual to become happy, joyous, and free and a sustaining and continually contributing member of our society presents many opportunities to enjoy life, liberty, and the pursuit of happiness. To be clear, contributing does not necessarily mean producing and adding too. The essence of each individual is the Light and Love at their core, and when an individual has the ability and freedom to share that Light and Love with those around them. They are contributing.

As an extension of WTP, the government is obliged to aid anyone trapped in a dire situation, be it a hurricane, tornado, flood, loss of job, old age, or illness. Nobody should have to fend for themselves. We are much stronger and more resilient together.

What will you do if your Mom gets sick, loses her job, and can't work? Tell her good luck. We are all in this together. We don't know who will get sick or lose a job, and as long as it doesn't happen to us, are we okay with telling everyone else—Good luck.

When something does happen to us, and it will, we will want these social safety nets to be strong, readily available, and viable. Can we want that for everyone? Does that now make sense?

For people just starting out or people who have to start over, Maslow's hierarchy of needs deftly explains what is needed before one can elevate themselves from the base of the pyramid to a level of self-sufficiency—eventually, being able to participate in society once again.

It is vital to understand that, while in the physical world, in a physical body, the seeming feeling of separateness can sometimes become overwhelming. The isolation from society can become its own type of oppression. People can get confused, scared, lonely, and lash out. We have all seen it in our urban communities. Angry homeless people lashing out, yelling at themselves and provoking people that walk past them. And, of course, we have all heard about individuals isolated from people and society. Unable to help themselves. Angry at the world. They purchase a gun and vent their frustration on innocent people, using bullets as their mouthpiece.

Strong social safety nets will help everyone avoid having to walk this path because of neglect by our society. I do not wish this misery on anyone. And if we do nothing, we force far too many people to go down this path of isolation and exile, sometimes ending in violence, forcing society to endure the pain of these lost individuals due to our neglect.

We are all One, and when we start to behave as One, most of the social ills we now face will dissolve without a struggle and affect us no more.

What about people traversing the upper ends of the pyramid model? Theoretically, mastery of one level creates a vacuum that draws one to the next level. However, being inexorably drawn into new and unfamiliar situations can be scary. Some people prefer to remain in place, re-experiencing known scenarios. Many people get stuck at the esteem level, seeking esteem through recognition or achievement, focusing only on themselves and what they can do. In extreme cases, that focus, be it money, a hobby, collecting antiques, hoarding, or addictions, becomes the only significant feature of their life, excluding all else. Getting stuck at this level comes from confusing capitalism as a way to live one's life. A capitalistic mentality is an efficient way to produce and sell products. It is a very inefficient way to view one's life or life path. Or to try and understand the value of human life or the ultimate purpose of experiencing a human life.

Human life has immeasurable value regardless of what they produce. The purpose of human life is not to make or sell anything, even though that may occur during most people's lives. The general idea is to experience and traverse all these levels, eventually, throughout one's lifetime. Not as a goal to check off but as an opportunity; to explore when one is ready. No right or wrong way to go about this journey. Getting stuck is part of the journey. The willingness to be on this path, to accept all challenges with an open heart, and to be open to what may be, is all the preparation and direction you will need to get started. Please allow room to be delighted, making the journey worthy of savoring.

Having to support the needs of a physical body starts the journey. It draws one fully into the experience of separateness. Our Creator asked each and every one of us to experience this separation so that we could fully understand the immensity and blissful nature of being at One with The All. We all accepted this request, and that is why we are here.

In order to achieve this feeling of separateness, limitations were placed upon our knowing of the Truth of our ultimate Reality. Who are we really? A Soul incarnated into a physical body. Our Soul is who and what we are. We experience our Soul as something we have hidden under layers of physicality and ego doubt.

We have been seemingly and completely separated from our Soul. The ultimate journey is finding our way back to the Truth. Our Soul and the Creator are one, and we are a Soul incarnated into a human body. We are all truly Divine and human at the same time! We are all daughters and sons of the living, breathing Divine Oneness. And as such, we are drawn toward our Divinity. The success of our journey back to wholeness is guaranteed for each and every one of us. We merely have to open up to the possibility.

In this state of readiness, a journey will be offered, and our only job is to say yes to the opportunity, and our way home has begun. We are all in love with the drama of being human. Until we no longer desire it, and then Oneness steps in to show us the way. So there is no need for fear; we were all asked to come here for this experience. When it is over, we all get to go home.

This human body is the vehicle used to experience this journey; for the Creator and us. The limits placed on our knowledge of the Truth are challenging enough. The added oppression of being unable to secure basic needs for our human body suit makes the journey so much harder for all of us.

Are you interested in making your journey easier? Make the journey easier for others, and your efforts will make your way easier. This equation mostly becomes evident to those exploring the upper levels of our evolution, but it is available to all humans.

Maslow's original pyramid apex was Self Actualization: Fulfillment of personal potential through mastery, dignity, and independence. In his later years, he realized there was another level. Self-Transcendence: Where you desire to know the Truth more than you care about the drama of your human self. You wake up to the knowing, of your true relationship, to the Divine Oneness. You invite it in and encourage it to take over and guide your life.

Allowing you to co-create, for humanity, in benevolent ways that which only divinity could devise. You become the arms and legs, hands and feet, that carry out the desires of the Oneness. You get a front row seat as a Co-Creator; this is the way home.

The pyramid now becomes a circle. A circle that connects the top end all the way around to the base end, with everyone doing their part as best they can. The energy that sustains our universe will flow around this circle, helping, revitalizing, and guiding everyone from right where they are into flowing around and around this circle. And we will all, eventually, get to experience every level before we go home.

For those feeling the desire to explore the upper levels of our evolution, just know that a sincere desire is all that is necessary. The cosmos will conspire to deliver all that you ask for in terms of inviting in the benevolence of the Divine Oneness.

We all exist in a sea of Oneness, just like the fish that doesn't notice the water that allows it to live. We aren't always aware of that which we truly are. Just like the sun that always shines, the clouds make us think we have no sun. The clouds are just our limitations, that when cleared away, reveal the sun, shining down upon us, as it always has and always will.

There are many reasons for choosing to experience a human existence, and they are all for the betterment of the Soul. Sometimes, we may not understand a particular human being or their reason for being. And that is because we are looking and judging with human eyes. Souls are interested in experiencing everything... good and seemingly bad, for it is all good and all beneficial!

Thank you for sharing that deep dive into what is possible when we are open to it. Now back to our previous discussion.

Will a National Health Care social safety net of assistance be abused? Of course, there will always be abuse by a certain portion of the population, primarily because corporations and government model that abuse. The whole reason we are here, talking about this mess, is the abuse and neglect by corporations and the government. The only reason, ultimately, for the abuse is that the abusers do not understand their relationship to the whole. Marginalized people have no concept of reciprocating moral and honest behavior. When corporations are forced to operate ethically, that moral behavior will become normalized and spread to everyone. When the government does its job with an awareness of the "Golden Rule" in mind, trust and goodwill become the norm, and people will flourish.

People are the only reason our government has a job! Taking care of people, and helping them to become self-sustaining, is the most liberating journey an individual can experience, and one that has become the birthright of every United States citizen as a result of our governing documents.

Childhood, illness, loss of employment, and death are built into the human experience. Helping humans through these stages with dignity, so they may become self-sustaining and blossom into their next evolution of awareness, is why we have consented to form a Government. Who else is going to take care of us but us?

That is why this book came into being. To help everyone realize our prodigious potential and learn to develop a connection to the Oneness, which will show us the way to freedom for all citizens.

And that brings us to the last visionary change:

Education:

We are all in this together, and just like a barn-raising party, when we all work together, we can accomplish some tremendous things.

Now, to build a barn, some of our members have to understand and know how to build a barn. For future generations to build barns, that knowledge has to be passed down to each generation. Much the same way that facilitating the development of each citizen into a viable participating member of our society is vital to the continuation of this uniquely American experiment.

In hunter-gathering societies, citizens needed to hunt and gather, and most members were adept by age 12. Our society is more complex. Without proper education, some citizens will be left behind and unable to participate.

Currently, our K-12 educational system is lacking and unequal to the point of turning out many students who cannot participate and are prime candidates for the criminal justice system.

Advanced degree education has turned into a "for-profit" endeavor. They are cheapening the whole experience and leaving many students hungover with debt from student loans, unable to get good jobs, keeping them from becoming full participants in our society.

The changes needed in this area are many and varied. And once again, I cannot even begin to explain them all. I trust WTP will agree and endeavor to create a new sustainable educational system that develops real-life skills that can be passed down to their children and grandchildren.

Conclusions:

Every century or so, we need to clean up and dust off the Charters of Freedom and ensure they do what we have set them out to do. The Constitution is less than nine pages long. The Affordable Care Act is over 900 pages long. Can we really operate a government for a country of 329.5 million people from under nine pages of words? We have been doing it for over 230 years. Do we really need 900 pages of words to say, "When someone is sick, please, help them get better"?

Do we really think, we can skip educating our children and they will be able to continue governing themselves? You can't raise a barn if you don't know how to build a barn! We are fooling ourselves if we really think that computer and television screens will prepare our children to figure out how to navigate and enjoy life, liberty, and the pursuit of happiness.

Preparing our children is the single most important job we have as parents and as a nation of people. We have to teach them so many more things than they needed 200 years ago. Still, the most crucial skill is the ability to think critically and not be fooled by beliefs that no longer serve a useful purpose.

Our children have to be able to question outdated belief systems that will allow them to evolve to become more enlightened than we are as we developed and grew to be more enlightened than the Founders of this nation. It is a process! One that makes this experiment worth living. None of this would have been possible without removing the overt oppression resulting from the previous feudal governing system.

When our government does an excellent job of ensuring the protections written into our governing documents, it makes it possible for all of us to enjoy life, liberty, and the pursuit of happiness—making it possible to enjoy some of the unspoken benefits, which is, realizing the Truth of our Reality, discovering our innermost desires and expressing them fully. This leads us to the discovery of our Soul Mission. Making possible the connection, to Divine Oneness. Enabling us all to experience the full circle of human evolution and enlightenment.

After reviewing all of this material, I have noticed that throughout history, someone has always been taking advantage of someone else. Obviously, they haven't gotten the message that we are all One. When we act as if we are all One, incredible, beautiful synchronicities provide for us and lift us up. Right now, we are being asked to take a hero's stand and say to those making us suffer, "No More!"

We can do this. Vote out the corruption, make changes to put our country back on track, and revitalize our determination to protect life, liberty, and the pursuit of happiness for every citizen if we all pull together. In so doing, we will have accomplished something incredibly miraculous, unexpected, and remarkable.

We have seen past the deception. We have targeted the true enemy. We have a surefire way to defeat our enemy. The only barrier to victory is our willingness to open up to our True Nature, releasing our illusory-self propped up by the ego, and realizing the depth of our Unity. Then we can come together and vote as a single unified group, intent upon freeing WTP from the clutches of corporations and oligarchs. Our victory lap can begin on November 6th, 2024. I hope to see each and every one of you there.

And that sums up the message of this book.

The middle class is under siege because of the darkness and limitations from our collective ego.
Can we evolve past these limitations?
Are we interested in learning how?
A desire is all that is needed to start.
Guided action steps will take you all the way home.

And the United States will once again provide for life, liberty, the pursuit of happiness, and the evolution of the human species.

Here are all of the issues and changes that, if WTP so decided, would be essential to include:

Get the word out... WTP are joining together for change!

We have discovered the actual cause of our pain and are taking steps to help ourselves.

Our government has been overrun by corporate money, and they no longer serve us.

Republicans and Democrats are no longer the true enemies, but just a smoke screen issue to keep WTP divided and unable to launch a counteroffensive to strike a blow at the real enemy; corporations and oligarchs who are only interested in profits over WTP.

We need to replace a large percentage of our elected federal representatives to instigate real change. A watchdog group to monitor elected officials and candidates would be helpful.

We need volunteers sympathetic to our cause to step forward and be our voice in government.

We need 470 volunteers for elected office on the Federal level. The vote will happen in November 2024. We need to get organized fast or wait for the next election cycle in 2026.

Create a third party called *"We The People."*

We need Volunteers to get the word out, organize, plan protests, fundraise, and help facilitate this new change.

After we have a majority of representatives elected, we work on these issues: (Which may be changed and amended by WTP at any time. I am making a list to get us started.)

First things first, we need an impenetrable firewall between government and corporations through which no money can flow.

Second, the goals of corporations must match the goals of WTP, or the corporations lose their license to operate and are shut down, never to open their doors again.

Institute a plan for National Health Care for all citizens of the United States of America.

Create a curriculum and an understanding that we are all in this together.

Rewire our K-12 educational system to be equal, producing viable, enthusiastic young adults from all walks of life excited to begin their Soul journey. At the same time, managing their affairs as a human being in a multi-level system in which every individual is essential, and so are their contributions, even if it is just sharing their Light and Love.

Advanced Degree Education should be made available, at no cost, to all interested in specialized training that would facilitate the advancement of their Soul Mission and help enrich our society.

Adequate housing is a base need, and this needs to be alleviated immediately.

Expand the middle class for the good of the All.

Expand the tax base by allowing corporations and oligarchs to pay their fair share of our tax burden.

Close the tax evasion loop holes.

Close down or re-tool Government agencies that have outlived their usefulness.

Mandatory Charters of Freedom orientation class for all incoming Federally Elected Officials.
Mandatory Charters of Freedom continuing education classes for all returning Federally Elected Officials.

To be middle class, you need to have a job. There are plenty of jobs that need people, but these people first need to be trained to be proficient at that job. Create free training programs that help people get good-paying jobs and assist competent corporations with qualified workers.

Create jobs that fit the people. Invest in the people. Invest where the people live, work, and gather. Make our place a beautiful place, safe for all. Encouraging that which is deep within us all to emerge, blossom, and flower for all to see and appreciate. Making it okay to go within and be who you truly are. A human being, truly Divine, at peace, and one with The All. May the love and peace, of our benevolent Mother-Father-God always be with you All. As we all know, She is... Amen!

Epilogue

This book would not have been possible without the extraordinary help I received from Divine Creative Energy Source. It took me six months to write and six months to edit to a finished product with the service Word 2 Kindle. (The actual editor who worked on my book was amazing. Ingrid Delle Jacobson really kept me focused on what mattered the most.)

Whenever I sat down to write, I would close my eyes, breathe, and try to feel Divine Essence. The moment I could feel the Energy surging, I started writing, and the words flowed. Whenever I got stuck, I would breathe, feel the energy, ask a question and start writing again. Developing a dialogue with Spirit really made the project flow. I was never stuck for long. I am very grateful for the process, and the lessons learn during this project, even if I don't sell one book. It was a great ride!

A sincere and heartfelt thank you to Gina Lake and her husband Nirmala for the many outstanding programs they provide and their fantastic books. Your humble connection to the Divine is inspiring!

A link to their information: https://www.radicalhappiness.com/

She also has a YouTube channel: https://www.youtube.com/c/GinaLakeChannelingJesus

I would also like to send a "shout out" to Thom Hartmann for the beautiful insightful books he has written. He is so knowledgeable about the history of the United States. His books got me started down this path of Truth. And a huge thank you for your advice before I started writing my book; it was priceless. Thank you, Thom!

https://www.thomhartmann.com/

Also, a thank you goes out to Robert Reich, whose tireless efforts are starting to have an effect. Thank you, Robert!

https://robertreich.org/

And kudos to Dennis Leary, whose show, "Rescue Me," helped me and my wife, Elizabeth feel normal while we were on our journey with ALS.

Elizabeth also watched Hoda, Kathy Lee, and Jenna and Ellen every day. It really helped her stay connected. Thank you!

If you are interested in getting involved, I have a website and email.

Website URL: https://wethepeoplearenowone.com

Email address: Jointogether@wethepeoplearenowone.com

Are you interested in experiencing Oneness? One of the best ways to do that is to start a meditation practice. So many ways and places to learn. Below are two recommendations to get you started.

Sarah McLean is an inspiring teacher who can help you establish a practice you'll love. Find her and free meditations at: https://mclean-meditation.com/

You can also watch/listen to her teachings on YouTube: https://www.youtube.com/SarahMcLeanMeditation

Her book can help you too, entitled *Soul-Centered: Transform Your Life in 8 Weeks with Meditation.*

Another avenue to help you on this path to Oneness.

Holly McNeill has intuited and developed a new meditation program called P.E.R.L.O.V.E

Which is a practical and transformative set of mindfulness and meditation practices that guides you towards discovering your true nature, your inherent Oneness, your power, freedom, and joy.

For more information, visit Mindfulness Practices | P.E.R.L.O.V.E.

One last item to explore before we wrap it up. What is Oneness? I keep talking about Oneness, and I want to make sure everyone understands what Oneness is as we close out this book.

I want to thank everyone for opening up to the ideas I have presented, and I hope you have enjoyed the ride. I know I have enjoyed it immensely. Thank you!

Oneness: It Is All God

from Jesus Speaking: On Embodying Christ Consciousness

By Gina Lake

If you could see from the Divine's eyes, you would see yourself everywhere and see yourself in everything. And if you knew yourself as God, you would experience yourself as being everywhere and in everything. Every experience is an experience that God is having.

This is Oneness. Oneness doesn't mean that everything looks alike, but that everything is animated by the same force, what I've been calling the Divine or God. Your intimate experience of life is God's intimate experience of life.

Within creation, God is expressing in great diversity. Nothing is identical. Everything is unique. And yet, everything is made of the same "stuff." A good metaphor for this is clay: Infinitely many shapes can be formed of clay—a woman, a dog, a butterfly, a flower, an anteater—and yet, each is fundamentally clay. These things that look so different are fundamentally the same. They are different and they are the same. This is one of the great paradoxes of life: Everything is unique, but everything is the same at its core, in substance.

And so it is with you: You are formed from God, although you appear as different forms. You believe you are these forms, but your true nature is that of God, that of love. The most essential quality of your true nature is love, so you could say that everything is most fundamentally love. Love is the substance from which all creation is shaped. Love is the clay that life is made of.

God experiences itself through its creations. God is surprised and pleased with the variety of expressions that is possible. What fun! Each new expression of itself is a new experience for God. God is continually discovering what is possible and what it's like to be something it has never been before.

God loves creating and exploring life through its creations. God loves the adventure and loves the learning and evolution these experiences bring. This joy of being alive, of exploring, of learning can be felt within you. It is the joy of God, the joy of the Divine within you. Your joy is God's joy.

The creations, themselves, have a very different experience, since most are not aware of their fundamental divine nature. Eventually, this is discovered, but initially God is lost in creation in such a way that the creations believe they exist as separate entities rather than direct expressions of God. This sense of separation allows God to have a unique experience through every creation.

A videogame can be a useful metaphor for understanding this special relationship between God and creation. When you play a videogame, you pretend you are the character in the videogame. While you are absorbed in that game, you forget who you really are, although you still exist as the player of the game.

So it is with God: God intentionally becomes lost in its creations, while continuing to exist as God, in order to fully experience all the possibilities in being something or someone. Like an actor playing a part, the more fully you become the character, the richer the experience is.

God splits off in this way, but God can never really forget the truth. The truth is temporarily suspended for the purpose of exploration, but at some point, the truth is remembered or realized and returned to. This is what happens in the human journey: God, while remaining God, gets lost in the human experience. Lifetime after lifetime, God pretends to be a particular character, until one day, that character has explored the human condition fully enough and is ready for a different adventure.

The metaphor of the videogame is good for making one other point. The character in the videogame, although engaged in terrible challenges, is not shying away from those challenges, blaming others, complaining, or playing the victim. Instead, he or she meets each challenge courageously, doing whatever is necessary to overcome it. That courage and perseverance is in you too. That strength and drive to overcome all odds is within you too. That capacity to meet life's challenges rationally is within you too.

However, that's as far as we will take this metaphor, since violence is no way to deal with challenges. But to the extent that the character's actions represent acceptance of what life brings, courage, and perseverance, this metaphor is useful.

Throughout the experience of being the human character you are playing in this lifetime, the possibility exists to realize the love, peace, and strength at your core. Your true nature is always available to you, no matter what your circumstances are. Not only at the end of your earthly lifetimes is it possible to realize your true nature, but also to some extent throughout your life as this character—potentially in any and every moment.

The truth of your God-nature is not that hidden from you. When life is hard, you are meant to draw on the qualities of your true nature—and you often do. Without the challenges of life, there could be no growth, no discovery, no learning, no evolution. There are places in creation where God rests from all challenges and has little or no experience, but God loves a challenge, and so does the God in you if you are honest with yourself.

The real dragon to be overcome is the fear, discouragement, victimhood, and negativity of the human mind. Without those, a dragon is just something to be dealt with, not something horrible, scary, overwhelming, or that "shouldn't have happened." Without your human emotions, you would simply do what needs to be done and experience little suffering in the process.

Without resistance to life's challenges and the emotions that follow from that, you would enjoy the experiences of life or, at the very least, find them interesting. Every new experience is interesting to your soul, to God. Life is interesting! Why label something as "bad" and resist it or become upset over it? Resistance to an experience and the emotions that follow from that are what make an experience bad, not the experience itself.

The challenge you must overcome in this videogame called life is your own negative mind, which creates negative emotions. Once you overcome your negative emotions by mastering your mind, then any challenge you face in life will be manageable. The character in the videogame doesn't have the luxury of having emotions, and neither do you if you want to be happy.

You determine your own happiness, not circumstances, by what you say to yourself and how you respond to any circumstance. You are not a victim of anything that happens to you. There is no such thing as a victim. Victimization is the experience of believing you are a victim.

If you believe you are a victim, then you feel like a victim. Believing makes it so.

The biggest challenges in this life are of this nature: the machinations and stories of your own mind. Life, itself, is simpler than the mind makes it. The mind complicates life by making it all about "me," but life is not about you or any other individual. Life is not personal. It is what it is, and the way to get through it is to tap in to your innate God-given strengths: love, courage, compassion, gratitude, and peace. Find God within yourself, and your life will be transformed.

God is hiding behind the scenes, but God is not all that hidden. God is evidenced in every feeling of happiness, love, peace, joy, strength, and courage and in every wise, loving, and rational thought you have. God is right here, because there is nothing here but God. The character you are playing is God play-acting. The other characters are God play-acting. The scenery and setting were created by God for God. The actions you take are either God or God allowing the character to act according to its beliefs and illusions, which God put there.

This is all to say that there is nothing that isn't of God. God says yes to it all and enjoys it all. God fights with God and God makes love to God. God is doing it all and enjoying it all, including the drama and suffering, because God created it to be the way it is, and God is willing to have the experiences it is having through its creations.

When you have realized this sufficiently, you will also enjoy the ride you are on, and you will learn to travel the ups and downs more gracefully, with more love and less pain. The winners of this videogame called life are the ones who learn to be in life without suffering, who accept life as it is, and who love life as it is and as God does. Game over.

Thank you for being here. Thank you for your strength and courage and willingness to grow. I am with you always.

So who would like to experience this Oneness?

What do we do? How do we get to that place of Peace that comes with the knowing of Oneness?

It is really just a series of realizations that dawn on us as we go about the business of questioning anything that is not from Love. As we release our beliefs, habits, addictions, and concepts that no longer serve us we are able to glimpse the truth setting us free to realize, understand and know the Truth of our Reality; that we are Human and Divine at the same time. Focusing on our Divine side, going toward Peace and Love will bring about the Oneness experience we desire.

Let's stroll the path home and hear some more wisdom to keep us going.

Here is an essay from Gina Lake:

You Are Transmitters

Greetings! This is the one you have known as Jesus the Christ. No matter what your state of consciousness is, you are transmitting. You transmit your state to others, and they receive it. So, you are also receivers. In this way, everyone affects everyone else. You are connected for good or for bad with everyone you come in contact with—and beyond. You are connected with all of humanity in this way. A great web of human thought and feeling is shared between you all.

There are ways you can improve the quality of what you transmit and protect yourself from the more negative emanations of others. That would be the goal, because these are related. **If you are absorbing the negative emanations of others, it will be difficult for you to transmit more positive emanations, or vibrations. And the opposite is also true: If you are emanating negativity, it will be difficult for you to absorb positive emanations from others. Others may try to help you consciously or unconsciously, but you won't be able to make use of their help if your own emanations are strongly negative.**

People get attached to their negativity, as odd as that sounds. They are attached to not changing their state even when their state is negative. It is the ego that wants to hold on to its beliefs even when those beliefs cause pain to itself and others. To change those beliefs would be seen as a defeat to the ego, and it doesn't like to lose! Egos will wallow in negativity rather than see things differently or allow others to help them. They may say they want help, but their subconscious mind rejects or sabotages that help. So, to make a change, the subconscious mind needs to be worked with.

Nonphysical beings, such as myself, work with people's subconscious minds to heal beliefs and help people grow. But we can only do so much without more conscious participation. This is where prayer comes in, as I have often spoken about. **Prayer is a conscious appeal for help, and that sets nonphysical forces free to do their healing work more effectively. Be sure to ask for this help.** That call for help will be enough to overcome the ego's resistance to help. It is that simple really.

What isn't simple about this is acknowledging the need for help, which the ego often will not do. Or if it does, it says, "Yes, but..." to everything that is offered. It finds reasons for why that help won't work or excuses for being unwilling to do what is necessary to make a change in one's life. The ego is a tricky devil! It may seem to want to comply and seem very sincere—meanwhile, it has every excuse for why it can't do what it needs to do to be free and happy.

The ego plays the victim, and being a victim is a powerfully attractive identity for the ego. Egos like to be victims. Victimhood gets other people's attention and gives people an excuse to not live full lives, an excuse to not take risks, an excuse to not love, and an excuse to not grow or develop oneself. Being a victim is one of the ego's favorite identities. Professional helpers and others meet these self-styled victims all the time.

A soul may remain in the role of victim for many lifetimes before it breaks free from this identity, as others can only do so much to help such individuals. Usually, someone must realize that he or she is playing this role before becoming free of it.

Today, like never before, it is possible to heal and become free of limiting identities such as this. It is our intention to offer some tools for doing that. The first is prayer. The second is recognizing your responsibility in creating your own unhappiness. As long as you are blaming others or blaming events or blaming circumstances for your unhappiness, you will not be happy. You will go around and around in a loop: "I'm unhappy because of you" or "because of what happened" or "because of how things are" makes you unhappy and keeps the unhappiness going. Unless you see that such beliefs are the cause of your unhappiness, how are you to get out of this loop?

"I'm unhappy because of something I'm thinking" is the truth, and the truth will set you free. You must see the truth about your situation before you can be free of it. You see the truth by being willing to see the truth and then looking for the truth. **Nonphysical helpers will help**

you gain insight into your situation if you ask for their help and then listen inside yourself for that insight. So, the second tool is: Accept responsibility for your unhappiness or any other negativity and ask for insight into healing that. Then listen inside yourself for that insight, that "Ah-ha."

Taking responsibility for your unhappiness or for a negative feeling you have is not the same thing as blaming yourself for it. Blame belongs to the ego's world, not to God's. You are not to blame for the ignorance of your ego. The ego is not you. The ego is the mechanism that causes all suffering, and everyone has an ego.

See this truth and accept it, and you are well on your way to freedom from suffering. You are not at fault for your suffering. You simply have to understand the origin and nature of suffering to get beyond it, and there is something here that is capable of doing that. No one is without the inner wisdom and strength to do this, since those belong to your true nature.

The beauty of being willing to heal and grow is that this willingness brings you in touch with your true self. Suffering can be seen as a blessing once you recognize that suffering is what propels you toward the Truth, which it eventually does for everyone. Suffering is self-correcting: When you suffer, you want out of suffering, and you will find a way out—because there *is* a way out. How benevolent life is that *you* are the cause of your own suffering (not life) and that there is a way out! You don't have to suffer, no matter how it seems.

The third tool is being open to receiving help and positive influences from others. You don't have to do all the healing yourself. As soon as you open to receiving healing from others, healing arrives. The work you do on yourself of being willing to accept responsibility and being willing to heal is enough to open you to the positive emanations that are available to speed your healing, which are available to everyone. These positive emanations are only lost on those who are closed to them, but who could open to them at any time. Once you open to the positive energy available to you from both human beings and nonphysical beings, your healing and growth can accelerate.

Most people are caught in blame, unhappiness, victimhood, and victimizing. But once you have seen enough of the Truth, which we are teaching, you move beyond that state of consciousness to a more open one and begin to drink in the beautiful energies that are available to everyone who is able to partake in them.

You are swimming in positive energies! They are being showered upon earth from other dimensions and pouring out from certain individuals on earth. You may not be aware of this when you encounter these individuals. All you know is that you feel better. Some people just make you feel better! Why is that? It is more than that they are nice or friendly. They are literally healing others with what is beyond nice, with the love of the Creator. They are expressing their divine selves in such a way that they are healing others in everything they do and say. By just being, they are healing others.

This is what you all can be and will be. This is the enlightened state, which you will all experience before you graduate this earthly plane in this lifetime or another. **The more you want to experience this and be this in the world, the more quickly you can become this. The willingness, intention, and desire to serve the Divine in others in this way is key to becoming a servant of healing. If you focus on this willingness and intention, then these will strengthen in you, and your capacity to be that instrument of healing will strengthen.**

You are meant to do this. No one is not worthy of doing this. It is ultimately what you came into incarnation to do, especially those of you here today who are obviously ready to live more in alignment with Truth and be all that you can be in the world today. So many of you are healers, whether you do that professionally or not. You are healers and helpers to those you touch each day. Know that this is valuable and important work.

Your state of consciousness matters because you *are* broadcasters. Know that it is your choice whether you broadcast love or something else. It is your choice. It is in your control. **To the extent that you have mastery over your thoughts, you are in control of this.** So, gain mastery over your thoughts through meditation or other spiritual practices.

The only thing that can cause you to broadcast negativity and block the positive energy available to you is believing a negative thought, and only you can change that. Only you can do the work that is necessary to heal yourself and transcend your ego and live from your divine self.

This is *your* work, but you have lots and lots of nonphysical helpers who will give their all in supporting you in being the best human being you can be. **Go toward love and peace** and you cannot go wrong. Please call upon us. It is our great honor to serve you. Thank you for being here. We are with you always.

Asking for help will bring you everything you need to awaken out of the grip of your ego.

More from Gina Lake.

Help Is Available from Other Dimensions

I'm happy to be here with you today. I am with you all. I am with each and every one of you, by your side, because you have called me in. You have opened to me. You have made an intention to connect with me. So, I am here for each and every one of you, right now and whenever you call upon me.

It may seem an impossible task for a being to be present in so many places at once, but I assure you that it is not at all impossible for me or others like myself to be present with all of you wherever you are whenever you call upon me. So, please know that I am here. I am here, right now, and always.

Some of you have a strong connection to me in your Heart. Others are quite ambivalent about this individual known as Jesus, and I would like to address that a little bit today, because it seems important that you understand that I am not the Jesus that so many of you imagine or believe me to be based on the beliefs you have been given in your childhood and beyond.

The ideas and beliefs most people have about me today are distorted and not at all representative of who I was, what I taught, or what I would teach today. What I taught then and what I teach today is not very different, but people were very different then.

It bears noting that humankind was much less evolved two thousand years ago. Their intellect was much less evolved and so was their conscience, which is something that evolves in a species and in a soul over many lifetimes. So, when humanity was very young, it didn't have very much of a conscience, generally speaking. Of course, there were individuals who were very evolved back then, as I was, who understood Truth, lived Truth, and expressed Truth, but they were few and far between, much less so than today.

You are greatly blessed now because there are so many who are awakened, who are walking among you and available to you. This greatly accelerates your evolution and the possibility for a truer understanding and for eliminating the distortions and misunderstandings many of you were given.

Two thousand years ago, there wasn't much Truth around. I came to break the orthodoxy and to question it and the hierarchy, which was so prevalent. It was not for me to create hierarchy, orthodoxy, or dogma. I came to push those aside and be a voice for the Truth.

Some could hear this truth, while others misunderstood it. Most, I would say, misunderstood what they were hearing. Once I was no longer on earth, there was little opportunity for me to correct the misunderstandings and distortions, so they were inevitable. This couldn't help but happen, and I knew that. We knew that—those of us who designed this incarnation of mine. We knew what would befall the teachings, and yet, that wasn't reason enough to not give the teachings.

The option was to leave humanity in the darkness, so we had to try to share the Truth with the people. Even if it would be distorted, there would be those who could see the Truth, know the Truth, and pass it on. It was always for those relatively few people that we shared the Truth, for those few who could understand the Truth and pass it on.

So, here you are, two thousand years later, and the Truth has been passed on, not just by me, of course, but by so many other enlightened Masters. Although we have been able to do little about the distortions, those who are living who know the Truth have tried to clear them up. They do the best they can, which is all anyone can do.

Those who believe these distortions will likely remain entrenched in their beliefs. But it is not to them that we speak today. It was not to them that we gave our teachings two thousand years ago. It is to people like yourselves who are open, ready, and willing to see the Truth.

What I mean by Truth is simply seeing reality as it is, without the distortions created by the egoic mind, by the primitive aspect of yourselves that distorts the Truth and casts the illusion—this very compelling and believable illusion that humanity is caught in.

We are here to dispel that illusion. We dispel it by pointing to the Truth. The Truth two thousand years ago is the same truth today. And the greatest truth is something I've spoken about before. The greatest truth is that love is behind all life. No matter what it looks like to you, it is love that is behind creation, guiding creation and holding it, keeping it going and nurturing it.

You and all of creation are deeply, deeply loved and deeply supported. You are never left alone. You are connected to so many who are carefully guiding your life. They speak to you through your intuition. And they stir your courage, they stir your patience, and they stir your kindness. They activate these innate qualities. They make it possible for you to be the best human being you can be.

You are always being guided to be the best human being you can be. And you all know what that means. To be the best human being is to be a loving and peaceful human being. You know that in your Hearts, because your Heart knows the Truth. The Truth is something you all want.

What you all want is love. That is encoded in you—to go toward love. But you misunderstand how to get love. Your ego misunderstands how to get love. It doesn't even believe in love. That is the distortion, the great lie, which holds the illusion in place. The lie is that love is not behind creation, that life must be feared, that life and God are unkind and cruel, and that it is a dog-eat-dog world.

Then, if those are your beliefs, that becomes your experience. These are not true beliefs, but they can certainly seem true. So, it is for you to discover that love is the truth. You discover this by choosing love instead of hatred and then experiencing the result. The result is always good. Love, giving, is always good, when it is done in a balanced way, because you must give to yourself as well, not indiscriminately.

Giving is quite an art. Sometimes not giving is the most loving thing to do: withholding something that would not be good for someone. That is what also happens in life. Sometimes life withholds something you want because it is better for your growth to experience not having that. Life is always kind and very wise this way. It gives you what you need, not always what you want. But it does give you what you need, and that is the truth.

Life is designed for you, for your growth, for your evolution, for your learning to love. It is designed to point you toward love and away from negativity: When you go in the direction of negativity, it hurts. When you go in the direction of love, it feels good. That is the great, good guidance system you have been given. It is an inner guidance system you can rely on. Follow your joy. Do not go in the direction of suffering.

Look at what causes you to suffer. The Truth will never cause you to suffer, only lies, the lies your mind tells you and the lies other minds tell you—things like: "I'm not good enough," "Life isn't good enough," "I don't have enough."

When you believe these lies, you suffer. And that is the right experience, because you are not meant to believe a lie. Go in the direction of joy and love. There is no fulfillment in living for yourself, your small self. There is only fulfillment in love and unity. That is the Truth.

The truth is also that you are a divine being. You are a spiritual being. You have a spirit that is eternal. You are not going anywhere but toward greater and greater goodness, love, happiness, and joy. You will not go backwards into more pain. Life is that benevolent that you only have these difficult lifetimes until you are finished with them. Then you go on to serve love, to be in love. That is the nature of life, and that is the experience you will have throughout eternity once you get through these more difficult lifetimes on this plane of existence.

There have always been beings who have come to earth to tell those who live in such dense dimensions the Truth. There is pain here, but there is a way out of pain, and there is help to relieve the pain, not just words but also a transmission of energy. This transmission is our gift to you, but you must open to it.

Please understand, and I will underline this one more time, that I am not the Jesus of your imagination. I am here now to serve you, love you, and support you. Every good and imagined idea that you may have about Jesus as love, you can keep. And every other idea that doesn't lead to love, that might take you away from love or create separation between you and others, is not of love and therefore doesn't belong to my teachings.

You are here to become free and to learn to live in peace and love. That is the goal of life. When you have learned that sufficiently, you will no longer come back to this difficult level of existence. Many of you are ready to move on, ready to experience love as an ongoing experience. You do not have to suffer even within this realm, but you surely will not suffer beyond this realm.

That is where you are all headed, and so you might as well get on with it now. Get on with making love the cornerstone of your life, the guiding light. Follow your love, follow your joy, do what is loving, do what is joyful. Create more love, create more joy. That is what you are here to do.

My words and transmissions are all about changing your consciousness so that you can move in the world with greater love, greater peace, and a sense of unity with All That Is. That is what I want for you. And if that is what you want for yourself and others, then fully give yourself to the transmission now. Thank you for being here. Thank you for your openness. Thank you for your love. I am with you now and always.

Everything is unfolding perfectly, and if you feel ready to experience Light and Love every day, all you need to do is ask, and help will be provided. Release anything that is not Love, and the Oneness will permeate your life, emanating through you and out to others. Transmitting this Light and Love will transform you and the whole world, Unifying all people one at a time in their own time.

Oh, to live in a world where the children are taught about their Divine nature and the purpose for coming to this earth plane and encouraged to see through the falseness of their ego, allowing them to discover the Divinity that resides within and engage with life from this place of Enlightenment. What a different world we would create.

No longer do we need to scare our youth with tales of Hell to get them in line. When one lives from a place of Divinity, they are naturally good because that is what they are on the inside. Once they discover their Divinity, they feel an innate desire to develop that aspect of their being and share the Love emanating from their Heart.

To gift this new way of life to our children, adults must step up to the challenge and release themselves from their ego, allowing their Creator to transform them into an Enlightened state of being.

Evolving into an enlightened state will eventually happen to everyone, and you can get started down this path today if you so desire.

Having enlightened individuals expressing the Love emanating from their Hearts in our government-elected offices would change everything.

Enlightenment is the result of the amount of Light one is exposed to and the willingness of the individual to embody and share that Light.

The earth is currently being inundated with more Light than ever before to facilitate an awakening that will usher in the wisdom to help us past our egos and the crippling effect it has had on us All.

Blessings of Light and Love to All.

References

American Civil Liberties Union. (2023). The Bill of Rights: A Brief History. [Online] Available at: https://www.aclu.org/other/bill-rights-brief-history

Anderson, J. (2019, 22 May). America Spends Much More on Prisoners Than Students — Here's Why. [Online] Available at: https://finance.yahoo.com/news/america-spends-much-more-prisoners-090300648.html

Aranda, E. (2017, 17 March). The Three C's that Make the Golden Rule. [Online] Available at: https://www.claremontlincoln.edu/engage/claremont-core/three-cs-golden-rule/

Armitage, D. (n.d.). The Declaration of Independence in Global Perspective. [Online] Available at: http://ap.gilderlehrman.org/history-by-era/road-revolution/essays/declaration-independence-global-perspective. The Gilder Lehrman Institute of American History.

Berkeley Law. (2008). Witch Trials in Early Modern Europe and New England. [Online] Available at: https://www.law.berkeley.edu/research/the-robbins-collection/exhibitions/witch-trials-in-early-modern-europe-and-new-england/

CAP (Center for American Progress). (2012, 17 May). The American Middle Class, Income Inequality, and the Strength of Our Economy. [Online] Available at: https://www.americanprogress.org/article/the-american-middle-class-income-inequality-and-the-strength-of-our-economy/

Carpenter, J. (2013). Thomas Jefferson and the Ideology of Democratic Schooling. [Online] Available at: https://democracyeducationjournal.org/cgi/viewcontent.cgi?article=1084&context=home

Center for Civic Education. (n.d.). Pursuit of Happiness. [Online] Available at: https://www.civiced.org/9-11-and-the-constitution-terms-to-know

Churchwell, S. (2021, Winter). A Brief History of the American Dream. [Online] Available at: https://www.bushcenter.org/catalyst/state-of-the-american-dream/churchwell-history-of-the-american-dream

Cohen, A. (2009, 10 August). A Century-Old Principle: Keep Corporate Money Out of Elections. [Online] Available at: https://www.nytimes.com/2009/08/11/opinion/11tue4.html

ConstitutionUS. (2023, 24 January). Life, Liberty, and the Pursuit of Happiness. [Online] Available at: https://constitutionus.com/constitution/rights/what-are-unalienable-rights/

Cook, E. (n.d.). How Money Became the Measure of Everything. [Online] Available at: https://getpocket.com/explore/item/how-money-became-the-measure-of-everything?utm_source=pocket-newtab

Educating for American Democracy. (2021, 2 March). America's Constitutional Democracy Requires Better Civic and History Education. [Online] Available at: https://www.educatingforamericandemocracy.org/wp-content/uploads/2021/02/Educating-for-American-Democracy-Report-Excellence-in-History-and-Civics-for-All-Learners.pdf

Emory University. Emory News Center. (2018, 3 July). What the Declaration of Independence really means by 'pursuit of happiness. [Online] Available at: https://news.emory.edu/stories/2014/06/er_pursuit_of_happiness/campus.html

Ettlinger, M. (2012, 1 August). The Middle Class and Economic Growth. [Online] Available at: https://www.americanprogress.org/article/the-middle-class-and-economic-growth/

Family Guardian Fellowship. (n.d.). Thomas Jefferson on Politics & Government. [Online] Available at: https://famguardian.org/Subjects/Politics/ThomasJefferson/jeff0650.htm

Flores, E. (2016, 10 November). This Is What the Claremont Core Taught Me. [Online] Available at: https://www.claremontlincoln.edu/engage/claremont-core/claremont-core-taught-me/

Fox, A. (2020, 18 June). Nearly 2,000 Black Americans Were Lynched During Reconstruction. [Online] Available at: https://www.smithsonianmag.com/smart-news/nearly-2000-black-americans-were-lynched-during-reconstruction-180975120/

Hanson, T. (2018, 17 December). How the Iroquois Great Law of Peace Shaped U.S. Democracy. [Online] Available at: https://www.pbs.org/native-america/blogs/native-voices/how-the-iroquois-great-law-of-peace-shaped-us-democracy/

Jefferson Monticello. (n.d.). The Role of Education. [Online] Available at: https://www.monticello.org/the-art-of-citizenship/the-role-of-education/

Jewitt, T.O. (2008, 30 January). Thomas Jefferson and the Purposes of Education. [Online] Available at: https://www.tandfonline.com/doi/abs/10.1080/00131729709335239?journalCode=utef20

Kahlenberg, R.D. and Janey, C. (2016, 10 November). Putting Democracy Back into Public Education. [Online] Available at: https://tcf.org/content/report/putting-democracy-back-public-education/. The Century Foundation.

Kennedy, L. (2017, 29 March). Corporate Capture Threatens Democratic Government. [Online] Available at: https://www.americanprogress.org/article/corporate-capture-threatens-democratic-government/

Lake, G. (2013). Ten Teachings for One World: Wisdom from Mother Mary. [Online] Available at: https://www.amazon.com/Ten-Teachings-One-World-Wisdom/dp/1492173452

Lake, G. (2016). *In the World but not of it: New teachings from Jesus on Embodying the Divine.* CreateSpace Independent Publishing Platform.

Lake, G. (n.d.). Oneness: It Is All God. [Online] Available at: https://radicalhappiness.com/jesus-speaking-series

Lawyers for Good Government. (n.d.). 7 Principles of Good Government. [Online] Available at: https://www.lawyersforgoodgovernment.org/mission

Longley, R. (2022, 11 April). Socialism vs. Capitalism: What Is the Difference? [Online] Available at: https://www.thoughtco.com/socialism-vs-capitalism-4768969

McLendon, R. (2012, 4 November). Red deer. [Online] Available at: https://www.biologicaldiversity.org/news/center/articles/2012/mother-nature-network-11-04-2012.html

Merriam-Webster. (n.d.). Civility. [Online] Available at: https://www.merriam-webster.com/dictionary/civility

Millet, P. (2014, 5 March). The Worst Form of Government. [Online] Available at: https://blogs.fcdo.gov.uk/petermillett/2014/03/05/the-worst-form-of-government/ Foreign, Commonwealth and Development Office.

National Archives. (2023, 31 January). The U.S. Bill of Rights. [Online] Available at: https://www.archives.gov/founding-docs/bill-of-rights-transcript

National Archives. (n.d.). Declaration of Independence: A Transcription. [Online] Available at: https://www.archives.gov/founding-docs/declaration-transcript

National Archives. (n.d.). The Constitution of the United States. [Online] Available at: https://www.archives.gov/founding-docs/constitution-transcript

National Archives. (n.d.). Thomas Jefferson to the Republicans of Washington County, Maryland. [Online] Available at: https://founders.archives.gov/documents/Jefferson/03-01-02-0088#:~:text=To%20the%20Republicans%20of%20Washington%20County%2C%20Maryland,-The%20affectionate%20sentiments&text=that%20the%20great%20%26%20leading%20measure,be%20doubted%20by%20candid%20minds.

National Center for Constitutional Studies. (n.d.). Natural Law: The Ultimate Source of Constitutional Law. [Online] Available at: https://nccs.net/blogs/our-ageless-constitution/natural-law-the-ultimate-source-of-constitutional-law?_pos=2&_psq=natural+law&_ss=e&_v=1.0

National Constitution Center. (n.d.). What is the U.S. Constitution? [Online] Available at: https://constitutioncenter.org/education/constitution-faqs

New Jersey Center for Civic Education. (n.d.). What does "promote the general welfare" mean? [Online] Available at: https://civiced.rutgers.edu/documents/civics/middle-school-civics/the-american-experience/89-promote-the-general-welfare/file

Olson-Raymer, G. (n.d.). The Original Inhabitants - What They Lost and What They Retained. [Online] Available at: http://gorhistory.com/hist110/na.html

Open Secrets. (2023, 16 February). Top Spenders. [Online] Available at: https://www.opensecrets.org/federal-lobbying/top-spenders

Patrick, J.J. (2016). Majority Rule and Minority Rights. [Online] Available at: https://www.worldcat.org/title/understanding-democracy-a-hip-pocket-guide/oclc/64510833

Pearson, C. (2010, 12 June). The Kingdom of God is Within You. [Online] Available at: https://www.tm.org/blog/enlightenment/kingdom-of-god-is-within-you/

Reich, R. (2022, 13 December). How the Corporate Takeover of American Politics Began? [Online] Available at: https://www.youtube.com/watch?v=bbbgfnpJN9w

Scarboro Missions. (n.d.). Understanding the Golden Rule. [Online] Available at: https://www.scarboromissions.ca/golden-rule/understanding-the-golden-rule

Singer, A. (2014, 15 December). Why Many Inner City Schools Function Like Prisons. [Online] Available at: https://www.huffpost.com/entry/why-many-inner-city-schoo_b_5993626

SparkNotes. (n.d.). Theodore Roosevelt 26th President – 1901-1909: Domestic Policies. [Online] Available at: https://www.sparknotes.com/biography/troosevelt/section10/

Tankersley, T. (2012, 18 May). The 100% Economy: Why the U.S. Needs a Strong Middle Class to Thrive. [Online] Available at: https://www.theatlantic.com/business/archive/2012/05/the-100-economy-why-the-us-needs-a-strong-middle-class-to-thrive/257385/

The Institute for Civility in Government. (n.d.).What is Civility? [Online] Available at: https://www.instituteforcivility.org/who-we-are/what-is-civility/

The School of Life. (n.d.). The Importance of Maslow's Pyramid of Needs. [Online] Available at: https://www.theschooloflife.com/article/the-importance-of-maslows-pyramid-of-needs/

USHistory.org. (2023). Foundations of American Government. [Online] Available at: https://www.ushistory.org/gov/2.asp

USHistory.org. (n.d.). The Economic Bill of Rights. [Online] Available at: https://www.ushistory.org/documents/economic_bill_of_rights.htm

Washington, G., and Toner, J. M. (eds.) (1888). Washington's rules of civility and decent behavior in company and conversation: A paper found among the early writings of George Washington. Copied from the original with literal exactness, and edited with notes. [Online] Available at: https://www.loc.gov/item/09030979/

Wikipedia. (n.d.). Ebenezer Scrooge. [Online] Available at: https://en.wikipedia.org/wiki/Ebenezer_Scrooge

Wikipedia. (n.d.). Public discourse ethics. [Online] Available at: https://en.wikipedia.org/wiki/Discourse_ethics

Permission to use material from Gina Lake

Hello Gina,

Michael Allison here.
Hope you are doing well!

I am writing a book. Just completed the first draft, working on the edits.
Writing you to ask for permission to use some of your material. First
one is a message from Jesus. Titled, Perfect Imperfection.
Second one is from Mother Mary.
It is the tenth teaching, The Power of Love.
I am definitely receiving help and guidance writing this book. Not as
direct as I would like. It seems as if this book is my school to teach me
how to be better receiver of information.
Anyway, these passages were given to me and they fit perfectly. May I
please use them?
There is really no way to paraphrase them, they are just so perfect!

Either way!
Thank you very much!!

With Light and Love,

Michael

On Saturday, January 28, 2023 at 06:05:51 AM PST, wrote:

Yes, you have my permission to use them as long as you give credit. So
glad you are excited about this project. Wonderful! Lots of love...

Warmly,
Gina Lake
https://RadicalHappiness.com/

On Sat, Jan 28, 2023 at 9:22 AM Michael B. Allison

Thank you so much!

While I was writing the email asking for permission, I stumbled across another email of yours about experiencing oneness and it also fits perfect. Should I finish the book first and then send over request for permission with all articles chosen?
Have a wonderful weekend!
With Light and Love,

Michael

Gina Lake
To: Michael B. Allison
Sat, Jan 28 at 8:35 AM

You have permission to use anything as long as you give credit. ❤

Warmly,
Gina Lake
https://RadicalHappiness.com/

Interested in getting involved?

Website URL: https://wethepeoplearenowone.com

Email address: Jointogether@wethepeoplearenowone.com

Made in the USA
Middletown, DE
18 September 2023